The Other Peace Process

In Praise of *The Other Peace Process*

"A seasoned dialogue-partner with Muslims and Christians, Rabbi Kronish shares his experience building relations with Palestinian Arabs in Israel, East Jerusalem, and the Occupied Territories. This memoir of peace-building is also a program others can follow to supplement the high-profile politics of peace-making. The program centers on a four-step process of transformative dialogue, interreligious education, discussion of core issues and joint action. I know the process works, because Rabbi Kronish has been modelling it for years in my own interfaith friendship with him. This book will spread peace further among Jews and Muslims, Arabs and Israelis, Palestinian and Jewish Israelis."
—Imam Feisal Rauf, Founder and Chairman of the Cordoba Initiative, author and interreligious activist

"I can't imagine a more necessary reminder coming at this moment than Rabbi Ron Kronish's new book, *The Other Peace Process*. When legal, diplomatic and political interventions around the Israeli-Palestinian conflict are stalled, Rabbi Kronish offers up examples where real people engage in interreligious dialogue, education and shared action to make change. From his own well-lived life, Kronish offers hope that though the work of justice and peace is a long process, it is worth it and will, in the end, succeed."
—Rev. Dr. Katharine Henderson, President, Auburn Seminary

"When it comes to peace between Israel and Palestine and to relations among Jews, Muslim, and Christians, no one is more qualified than Dr. Ron Kronish to give us direction and—most important—to give us hope. Dr. Kronish has devoted his life to the proposition that leaders of the Abrahamic traditions can strengthen each other, inspire one another, and promote the values of love, justice, and peace that are common to each of our faiths. For more than 40 years, he has done the hard work of bringing Jews, Muslims, and Christians together, and encouraging us all to proclaim that we will not permit fanaticism to grow or prejudice to harden. His message, now more than ever, must be heeded: In Israel/Palestine, he tells us, and around the world, the children of Abraham must reclaim their common heritage and find a common path."
—Rabbi Eric H. Yoffie, President Emeritus, Union for Reform Judaism, writer and speaker

"Rabbi Ron Kronish was inspired by his father, the rabbi of the Reform temple in Miami Beach, to become a "compassionate Zionist"—proud of his Jewish identity, with strong emotional ties to the land where Judaism was born and yet also deeply respectful and empathetic towards Christians and Muslims, the other spiritual descendants of Abraham and their emotional ties to the land. As someone who views all members of the family of the great patriarch Abraham as my family, I have in turn been inspired by Rabbi Ron and

have come to share his hope and prayers for a future filled with peace, prosperity and security for all who feel spiritually connected with the Holy City of Jerusalem and especially those who live there and hear the sound of the shofar from the Western Wall, the church bells from the Holy Sepulcher and the muezzin's call to prayer from Al Aqsa mosque."
—S.A. Ibrahim, businessman and interreligious activist

"In this book, Rabbi Ronald Kronish of Jerusalem combines his extensive theoretical background in the areas of peace-building and interreligious dialogue with more than twenty-five years of actual experience in these fields to provide original insights into the accomplishments as well as challenges confronting Palestinian Arabs and Israeli Jews in the ongoing struggle for peace and coexistence. Kronish captivatingly describes his own life journey and offers anecdotes garnered from a lifetime of coexistence work to supplement and illuminate the theoretical and practical directions he offers in this book. The tapestry of *The Other Peace Process* should be read by all who are engaged in the efforts to forge peace in Israel and Palestine."
—Rabbi David Ellenson, Director of the Schusterman Center for Israel Studies, Brandeis Univ.; Former President, Hebrew Union College-Jewish Institute of Religion

"Rabbi Ron Kronish has been a heroic figure in the ongoing search for the peace of Jerusalem. Unlike so many others, he has understood the high urgency of reckoning with explicitly religious elements of Middle East conflicts. As his books and essays testify, he has set a high standard for this centrally intellectual task, but he has also been a leader at the grass-roots level of authentic interreligious encounter. Ron Kronish is a prophet of peace."
—James Carroll, author of Constantine's Sword and many other books

"At a time when messages of hope are more sorely needed than ever, Rabbi Ron Kronish brings us *The Other Peace Process*. There is no better guide to this subject than Rabbi Ron Kronish, the founder of the Interreligious Coordinating Council of Israel, and the acknowledged dean of all interfaith work in Israel. Rabbi Kronish has decades of experience in both grassroots and leadership dialogue in Israel and Palestine and around the world. His inspired and inspiring work vividly illustrates the potential of interreligious dialogue as a dimension of sustainable peacebuilding, and his theoretical observations will be studied by practitioners for years to come."
—Rabbi Amy Eilberg, author of *From Enemy to Friend: Jewish Wisdom and the Pursuit of Peace*, and interreligious activist

"Ron Kronish is a rabbi, educator and prolific writer. He is one of the leading personalities in the field of interreligious dialogue in Israel. His initiative to establish the Interreligious Coordinating Council in Israel (ICCI) at the beginning of the 1990s, which was revolutionary at that time, and his comprehensive activities to advance interreligious dialogue, have become an established foundation for mutual understanding among religious groups both within Israel and abroad. Thanks to his engaging personality and determination to bring about change in this field, Ron Kronish has succeeded in this book to leave a lasting imprint for future generations."

—Kadi Dr. Iyad Zahalka, Judge, Shari'a Court, Jerusalem, and lecturer at universities in Israel

"Ron Kronish's leadership of interreligious cooperation for peace in the Holy Land is critically important. Again and again, he has demonstrated that sincere believers—Jews, Christians and Muslims—can use their faith to build a moral alliance for peace. His work makes clear that peace is possible."

—William F. Vendley, Secretary-General, Religions for Peace International

The Other Peace Process

Interreligious Dialogue, a View from Jerusalem

Ronald Kronish

Hamilton Books

Lanham • Boulder • New York • Toronto • Plymouth, UK

Copyright © 2017 by Hamilton Books
4501 Forbes Boulevard, Suite 200, Lanham, Maryland 20706
Hamilton Books Acquisitions Department (301) 459-3366

Unit A, Whitacre Mews, 26-34 Stannary Street,
London SE11 4AB, United Kingdom

Library of Congress Control Number: 2017940050
ISBN: 978-0-7618-6933-7 (pbk : alk. paper)—ISBN: 978-0-7618-6934-4 (electronic)

∞™ The paper used in this publication meets the minimum requirements of American
National Standard for Information Sciences Permanence of Paper for Printed Library
Materials, ANSI/NISO Z39.48-1992.

Contents

Preface

Writing this book has been a labor of love for several years. The process of putting my thoughts down on paper (more correctly, into a computer), along with the reading and research that I have done for this book, has been a great learning opportunity for me. It has given me the chance to reflect deeply on my career of a quarter of a century in the field of interreligious dialogue, education, and action in Israel and internationally, as well as the time to read many books and articles which inform my thinking about the topic and my writing on this subject. In addition, I interviewed many scholars and practitioners in Israel, which was a special opportunity to get to know people better and to learn their approach to the issues discussed.

This book is the first book ever written by someone who lives and works in Israel to describe and analyze the work of interreligious dialogue as a form of peacebuilding in Israel and Palestine. While there have been a few essays written on this and parts of some books, this is the first book to deal fully with this topic.

Much of the book is based on lectures and speeches that I have given at conferences and in communities in Israel and abroad over many years, as well as articles that I have published in various journals and on my blogs for the *Times of Israel* and the *Huffington Post*. In addition, I share with the reader many amazing anecdotes and invigorating experiences that have inspired and challenged me over the years, including those that give me hope for the future and others that continue to create obstacles to progress to all of us who labor in the vineyards of interreligious dialogue and action in Israel and elsewhere.

I have been fortunate to have had an exciting and enlightening career in interreligious dialogue over the past 26 years. One of my main goals in this book is to share all that I have learned from experience, and from research,

with students and faculty in universities around the world and anyone concerned with the interrelated fields of Peacemaking and Peacebuilding, Interreligious Dialogue in Theory and Practice, Arab-Jewish Coexistence Education in Israel, Religions and Peace, Religions and Conflict Resolution or
Transformation or Management or Mitigation, The Israeli-Palestinian Conflict, Israeli Society, Palestinian Society, Israel-Vatican Relations, Jewish-
Christian Relations, Jewish-Muslim Relations, and Reconciliation. These are
the areas and the issues with which I have been intimately involved in my
professional work during the past quarter century, and in my personal life in
Israel during the past 38 years.

In addition, this book is intended not only for students and teachers in all
of the above-mentioned disciplines, but also for the general reader who cares
about the future of Israel and Palestine, about the prospects for peace, and
about the role that interreligious dialogue can serve in bringing people to live
in peaceful relations with each other, as persons and as peoples. In this sense,
it is a book with a message as well as a method. When asked to brand my
work by a web consultant many years ago, I came up with this catch phrase:
Peaceful Coexistence is our goal. Dialogue, Education and Activism are our
methods.

I begin the book with an autobiographical introduction which explains to
the reader how I got involved in this field, and how I came to write this book.
It has been a long personal journey from being a mainstream Jew who lived
only among Jews and had nothing to do with non-Jews in my personal or
professional life, to someone who became deeply involved in encountering
the non-Jewish 'Other' on a regular basis and one whose identity has been
greatly enriched and expanded through this encounter.

In chapter one of the book, I describe the context in which I have been
involved in interreligious dialogue as a form of peacebuilding in Israel and
Palestine, and I present the theoretical background for my work in peacebuilding as a supplement to the political process of peacemaking. For me, the
social-political-security context is critical for anyone engaged in dialogue of
any kind. It is one thing to be involved in dialogue in America or Switzerland
or England, and it is quite another thing to be involved in dialogue in the
context of the ongoing, unresolved, not-likely-to-be-resolved-soon Israeli-
Palestinian conflict, with the ups and downs of the so-called political "peace
process", and the recurring violent outbreaks of what I have called "the war
process". As I explain in this first chapter, doing dialogue in the midst of an
ongoing conflict, with periodic flare-ups of violence, has been extremely
difficult and challenging. Yet, it has not been without some accomplishments
and achievements.

In the second chapter of the book, I share with the reader my insights
about Palestinian Muslims and Christians in Israel, based on formal and
informal dialogues with them over many years. I have been fortunate in that I

have come to learn a great deal about the complex components of the identity of Palestinian Muslims and Christians who are citizens of Israel as well as those who live in the West Bank (which some people call "Judea and Samaria" and others call the "Occupied Territories" and others call the "Disputed Territories."). I have encountered Palestinian Muslims and Christians both professionally through dialogue groups and personally through life experiences for over 25 years. Many of them have visited in my home, and I have been guests in their homes and communities. This has been an amazing journey, one that few people in Israel have experienced. In addition, I reflect upon the implications of these encounters for the future of Jewish-Muslim dialogue and Jewish-Christian dialogue in Israel and the region.

I have also been deeply involved and engaged in Jewish-Catholic relations and Israel-Vatican relations during my many years of participation and leadership in these interrelated issues. I was privileged to witness the signing of the historic "Fundamental Agreement between the State of Israel and the Holy See" in the offices of Israel's Foreign Ministry on December 30, 1993, three and a half months after the signing of the equally historic Oslo Accords on the White House Lawn on September 13, 1993. Throughout the 1990s, I was very involved in Jewish-Catholic dialogue at many levels, and attended several important seminars and conferences with leading Catholic theologians and educators, both in Israel, (where I planned and implemented some of these conferences) and in Europe, especially at the Vatican. In so doing, I became a trusted partner in dialogue among leading Catholics who were deeply involved in the dialogue with the Jewish people. As a result, I learned that the establishment of diplomatic relations between the state of Israel and the Holy See in 1993 was directly connected to the peace process which began with the Oslo Accords that year. I discuss these and related developments in chapter three of this book, especially how all this is connected to the overall theme of this book, interreligious dialogue as a form of peacebuilding.

In chapter four, I outline the achievements and successes, as well as the problems and obstacles, facing educators and activists who attempt to educate for mutual understanding and peaceful coexistence via interreligious and intercultural dialogue within Israel and the region. I describe some of the cutting-edge programs, as well as sharing meaningful stories from my many years of organizing dialogue programs. In addition, I share reflections and anecdotes from my extensive experience in facilitating intensive dialogue programs for a wide variety of target populations in Israel and Palestine. I do this with reference to some of the recent literature about conflict resolution and peacebuilding strategies.

The final chapter of the book focuses on lessons learned and on concluding thoughts and recommendations for the future. I share with you, my readers, the main lessons that I have learned about interreligious dialogue in

Israel. I focus on both achievements and accomplishments, as well as on challenges and obstacles for the future. In so doing, I describe my most significant experiences in dialogue—the ones that have inspired me and others over the years—through some amazing anecdotes which have guided my thinking and practice, especially in recent years. In addition, I offer some thoughts for the future about the main challenges facing interreligious dialogue, both in Israel and Palestine and internationally.

Acknowledgments

I am grateful for the assistance of many people who have shared this journey with me.

I want to acknowledge all those people who influenced me deeply in my professional work who are no longer alive. They guided me in my thinking and my actions in many ways over many years: Owsley Brown II, Professor David Cobin, Br. Jack Driscoll, William I. Frost, Judge Mayer Gabay, Nathan Hacker, Ambassador Shmuel Hadas, Mayor Teddy Kollek, Abdessalam Najjar, Dr. Mithkal Natour, Ari Rath, Dr. Bernard Resnikoff, Daniel Rossing, Jack Rudin, Archbishop Pietro Sambi, Rabbi Michael A. Signer, Alan B. Slifka, Sir Sigmund Sternberg, Naomi Teasdale, Sr. Rose Thering, Rabbi Eugene Weiner, Dr. Geoffrey Wigoder.

I would like to thank my editor, Susan Kennedy, for her excellent editing and her helpful comments and suggestions during the process of preparing this book for publication. I have had the privilege of sitting in the same library with her during the past few years, at the Van Leer Jerusalem Institute, where I am a library fellow. At the same time, I want to express my gratitude to Professor Gabi Motzkin, former director of this institute, as well as to Bayla Pasikov, the librarian, and to other library fellows with whom I have discussed my book, including Professor Jay Rothman, Professor Yehuda Gellman, and Rabbi Naftali Rothenberg. Our conversations were always collegial and helpful. In fact, some of them led me to my publisher, Hamilton Books.

I would like to thank Holly Buchanan, acquisitions editor at Hamilton Books, for her interest in this book and for her effective and efficient shepherding of the book through the whole process of preparation and publication.

I would like to thank many colleagues with whom I worked closely in Israel for their advice and support throughout the years. They have helped me both in my organizational work and in the creation and development of new programs: Dr. Hakan Bengtsson, Dr. Geert Cohen-Stuart, Sr. Maureen Cusick, Professor Mohammed Dajani, Rev. Sidney DeWaal, Rabbi Tamar Elad-Applebaum, Rev. Samuel Fanous, Sr. Prof. Maureena Fritz, Dr. Gadi Gvaryahu, Rakheli Hever, Mayor Issa Jaber, Sr. Rita Kamemeyer, Rabbi Michael Klein-Katz, Yehezkel Landau, Ambassador Aharon Lopez, Rabbi Joel Levy, Sr. Kay MacDonald, Sheikh Ghassan Manasra, Fr. Russ McDougall, Fr. Mike McGarry, Rabbi Michael Melchior, Dr. Yitzhak Mendelsohn, Avigail Moshe, Sr. Trudy Nabuurs, Canon Fr. Hosam Naoum, Fr. David Neuhaus, Rabbi David Rosen, Rabbi Marc Rosenstein, Archbishop Aris Shirvanian, Fr. Thomas Stransky, Rawan Suleimann, Clarence Wagner, Rabbi Levi Weiman-Kelman, Bishop Munib Younan and Kadi Iyad Zahalka. Their friendship and collegiality have meant a great deal to me in my professional and personal life.

I would like to thank all of the student interns, who worked with me over the years, most of whom are by now serious professionals in the field of interreligious relations, academia, the rabbinate or other related fields: Abby Alfred, Nasser Alqaddi, Joanna Arch, Rabbi Justus Baird, Rabbi Sarah Mason, Rabbi Brandon Bernstein, Rachel Blumberg, Lior Davidi, Brian Freedman, Morgan Furlong, David Goodman, Rebecca Keys, Ilana Lubka, Andrew Luissi, Chagit Lyssy, Adrienne Mannov, Rabbi Bethie Miller, Rabbi Heather Ellen Miller, Heather Renetzky, Rebecca Russo, Omar Smiley, Thilo Schoene, Rabbi Adam Stock-Spilker, Nomi Teutsch, Rabbi Melissa Weintraub, Breanne White, Merrill Zack, Hauke Ziessler. One of the most enjoyable parts of my career as director of an interreligious organization was to mentor young people who wanted to learn and grow during their internship experience.

I would like to thank all those people and organizations with whom I have worked closely in genuine partnership over many years: Religions for Peace, especially Secretary-General Dr. William Vendley and Associate Secretary-General Kyoicho Sugino; Auburn Seminary, especially President Rev. Katharine Henderson and Rabbi Justus Baird; the International Council of Christians and Jews; the St. Ethelburga's Centre for Peace and Reconciliation in London, especially its former director Simon Keyes; FAITH, the Foundation for Interfaith Trust and Harmony, especially its president Rabbi Mark Winer; the Corrymeela Community in Northern Ireland, especially Susan McEwen; the Konrad Adenauer Foundation, including all the directors of their Jerusalem office for the past 25 years, especially Michael Mertes; the Focolare Community, based in Italy, with chapters around the world, including in Israel and Palestine, especially Margaret Karram, Corres Cwak, and Sonia Zelazzo; the Community of Sant'Egidio, based in Rome, especially Secretary-General Alberto Quattrucci, who invited me to many of their annual Meetings of Peoples and Religions; the Rissho Kosei-kai Foundation in Japan; "Interfaith Kosovo", especially Petrit Selemi, the former Acting Foreign Minister of Kosovo; the Pontifical Commission for Religious Relations with the Jews of the Vatican, especially its long time secretary, Fr. Norbert Hoffman (who always reminded me that I was the first rabbi whom he met when he began in this position), Cardinal Edward Idris Cassidy, and Cardinal Walter Kasper; the Pontifical Commission for Interreligious Dialogue especially Archbishop Michael Fitzgerald; the M.A. program on Coexistence and Conflict at Brandeis University, led by Professor Alain Lempereur; the Center on Religion, Culture and Conflict at Drew University, led by Professor Jonathan Golden; the Three Cultures Foundation of Seville, especially Germinal Gil de Gracia; the Cordoba Initiative, especially its founder and chairperson, Imam Feisal Rauf; various embassies and ambassadors to Israel especially UK, the Netherlands, Germany, and the USA, especially Ambassadors Dan Kurtzer and Dan Shapiro.

I would also like to express gratitude to some special colleagues abroad with whom I was in dialogue for many years about issues of interreligious relations and peace: Adalberta and Armando Bernadini, Sr. Professor Mary Boys, Prof. Marshall Breger, James Carroll, Alan Divack, Rabbi Amy Eilberg, Rabbi David Ellenson, Eugene Fischer, Professor Mari Fitzduff, Rabbi Richard Jacobs, S.A. Ibrahim, Rabbi Howard Jaffe, Luna Kaufman, Rabbi Roly Matalon, Professor Joe Montville, Carol and Jim Nettleton, Fr. Professor John Pawlikowski, Rev. Peter Pettit, Bonni and Steve Schiff, Alan Silberstein, Rabbi Josh Stanton, Rabbi David Strauss, Prof. Burton Visotzky, Sybil and Steve Wolin, Rabbi Eric Yoffie.

I would also like to thank the many individual and family foundation donors, as well as governments and foundations, who have supported my work financially for a long time. While I did not always love fundraising, I was often gratified and even flattered that so many people and institutions put their trust in me for so many years. The list is too long to thank all of you here, but you know who you are (and I expect that you will be among the first people to read this book).

I would also like to thank the many rabbis/colleagues who supported my work in interreligious dialogue in Israel both spiritually and financially, from their rabbi's discretionary funds. I have been blessed by your faith in me and by your friendship.

Last but not least is my family. Actually, they are first and foremost. I am always grateful to my father, Rabbi Leon Kronish, who instilled in me my faith in the future, and to my mother, Lillian Kronish, who read every word that I wrote while she was alive and was my greatest fan and at the same time my severest and most loving critic.

My three wonderful daughters—Sari, Dahlia and Ariella—read many of the drafts of the chapters of this book, and offered helpful comments and suggestions. More than that, their whole lives have enriched me greatly in every way, every day. I really wrote this book for them and their children.

In addition, I will always be eternally grateful to my wife of the last 48 years, my life partner, Amy. She has been my source of strength and support for everything that I have done in my life, including this book. I am forever grateful for her abiding love and partnership.

Introduction

My Personal Journey

Let me begin with a few words about myself and my family. I am a Reform rabbi who grew up in the United States and made *aliyah* (lit. "going up", the word refers to Jewish immigration to Israel) with my wife Amy and then two daughters in June 1979, 38 years ago, which means that I have spent more than half of my life in Israel. We now have three wonderful daughters, three terrific sons-in-law, and five fabulous grandchildren.

CHILDHOOD YEARS

I grew up in Miami Beach, Florida, in the late forties, the fifties and the early sixties of the twentieth century, in a fervently Zionist Jewish home. As a result, I imbibed Zionism from my youth, mostly from my father, Rabbi Leon Kronish, of blessed memory. He was the Founding Senior Rabbi at Temple Beth Sholom (House of Peace) from 1944-1996[1], where he preached and taught by example the central meaning of the synagogue and the Jewish state to Jews in America for four decades. He was also one of the leaders of the Reform Jewish movement[2] in the United States from the 1960s until 1984, and was particularly active in Israel-related activities in the years following the Six Day War in June 1967, for the Reform Jewish movement, the Miami Jewish Federation, Israel Bonds, the American Jewish Congress, and the Histadrut (Israel's Labor Union) in America.

Growing up in Miami Beach during this period was a little bit like growing up in a pioneering town, from a Jewish point of view. My father and mother moved there in 1944 from New York City, the main center of Jewish life in the United States, where they had both grown up. It was a big move at that time, before jet airplane travel. The cities of Miami and Miami Beach were backwater towns. In fact, during World War II, much of Miami Beach was inhabited by military personnel, connected to the war effort.

There were very few Jews in Miami Beach then.[3] It was a brand-new community, and the synagogue which my father nurtured and developed began in a store front. By the mid-1950s it had transformed itself into one of the most thriving and dynamic synagogue centers in the United States. My father's leadership—especially vis-a-vis Israel—became legendary in South Florida, and later on throughout the United States and in Israel. In addition to being a dedicated congregational rabbi, he became one of the leaders of Reform Judaism in those decades, especially with regard to Reform Judaism's increasing commitment to Zionism and Israel. Following the Six Day War in summer 1967—which he repeatedly referred to as "the Six Days that shook the world"—he became the chairman of Reform Judaism's Joint Commission on Israel for several years, and in so doing, brought his dedication to Israel to center stage in the Reform Jewish movement.

In addition, he was one of the pioneers of Israel Bonds. Until his debilitating stroke in 1984, he raised millions of dollars for the state of Israel, and hosted many of Israel's leaders at Bonds dinners in Miami Beach, and at his synagogue. As a teenager, I heard Abba Eban, Yigal Allon, Golda Meir, David Ben Gurion and many other legendary leaders of the young pioneering Labor-oriented state of Israel, and was swept away by their charisma and by the Zionist message of redemption at that time.

In fact, I was totally swept away by the mainstream Zionist narrative—by the story of the almost miraculous rebirth of the Jewish People in its ancient homeland—and I was not the least bit aware of any other narrative. Like most Jews of the period (and most Jews until this day), I only learned and understood one narrative, the Jewish Zionist mainstream one, and did not become aware of other narratives—especially the mainstream Palestinian narrative—until I became involved in interreligious and intercultural dialogue between Jews and Palestinians in the early 1990s, more than 10 years after I moved to Israel in the summer of 1979.

I also remember reading Rabbi Abraham Joshua Heschel's book *Israel: Echo of Eternity*[4] at that time, as well as many other books by Heschel during my rabbinical school years and afterwards. Heschel spoke of the Six Day War in wondrous terms. For him, as for many other Jewish thinkers and leaders at the time, it was a deeply spiritual—almost miraculous—moment for the Jewish People, and I felt that I was a part of it.

In an essay that I wrote about my father in a book about him which was published the year he died (1996), I wrote:

Often, when I am asked why I decided to live in Israel, I answer that I took Ben Gurion's speeches[5] and my father's sermons too seriously! My parents took my sister (Maxine Kronish Snyder, of blessed memory) and me to Israel for the first time in 1964, the summer after I finished high school. I fell in love with Israel on that first visit because my father's love for Israel was infectious and overwhelming.[6]

Later in that same essay, I explained why the state of Israel was so important to my father, even though he never lived there:

My father has been a great teacher of the concept that both Israel and the Diaspora are vital for the continuity of Judaism and the Jewish People. Not one or the other, but both are crucial and inextricably intertwined—this has been his greatest message. It is certainly a message that I learned from him and cherish deeply until this very day. And, it is the sort of concept that I believe that we still need to strengthen and develop, as we work towards the future of the local community and the State of Israel with a growing realization of the fact of our interlocking destiny as a people, which binds us together in common concern, caring and commitment.[7]

LIVING THROUGH THE SIXTIES

In addition to my personal upbringing at home, I am also very much a product of the turbulent social and political movements of the 1960s in the U.S.A. Not only did I live through and participate in the civil rights' movement and anti-Vietnam War demonstrations as a student at Brandeis University (1964-68) and as a rabbinical student at the Hebrew Union College-Jewish Institute of Religion in New York (1968-73), but I was profoundly moved and inspired by the victory of Israel over a group of Arab countries which sought to annihilate the young Jewish state (the state of Israel was 19 years old at the time; I was 21). Just 22 years after World War II, the existence of the state of Israel was being threatened in what would surely have been perceived as another Holocaust or a continuation of the one that began in Europe in the late 1930s. It is amazing to me how easily this is forgotten. Jews everywhere in the world live with this consciousness and visitors to Israel begin to understand this better after paying a visit to *Yad Vashem*, Israel's national Holocaust museum.

In my first year at Brandeis University (1964-65) I remember attending an anti-war rally in the then famous Ford Hall on campus, where influential professors like Herbert Marcuse[8] appeared in a kind of epiphany and told us young, naive, impressionable students that it was our role and responsibility to go out and change the world! Not only did we believe him, but we actually did as we were told! The student movement against the war in Vietnam made such an impact that eventually the American government could no longer ignore us, and actually ended this useless and terribly destructive war[9]. The Vietnam War was so much a part of our consciousness as students in the Sixties that we organized a special pre-commencement ceremony the day before our graduation in 1968. This "Vietnam Commencement" helped us tell the story of those turbulent years when we challenged the U.S. government over the morality and wisdom of waging war, and ultimately prevailed.

As a student, I also looked up to the leader of the Civil Rights Movement, Rev. Dr. Martin Luther King Jr., and to Rabbi Abraham Joshua Heschel who marched with King at Selma and led a group called Clergy and Laymen Concerned about Vietnam.[10] I vividly remember that when Rev. King was assassinated in early April 1968 (my senior year in college), I helped organize a memorable interreligious memorial service for him on chapels' field in the heart of the Brandeis campus. One of my classmates, Jon Landau, recently spoke about this in an interview for Brandeis Magazine.[11]

FIRST VISITS TO ISRAEL

During my college years, I spent a semester in Israel on the Hyatt program (a special program sponsored by Brandeis) in the Fall of 1966, during which I deepened my knowledge of the Hebrew language, Jewish history—especially modern Jewish history and contemporary Israeli history—and lived in Jerusalem for six months in a quaint little hotel (called a "pension") in the heart of West Jerusalem, a few blocks from the current residence of the President of Israel. Actually, it was probably then that I first actually fell in love with Jerusalem, its sights and smells, its history and historiographies, its religious ambiance and ambivalence, and its Jewish rhythms and reflections.

During this semester I lived in Jerusalem, which was divided between Israel and Jordan from 1948 until 1967. The Armistice Line, known as "the Green Line", divided the city between East and West.

I remember clearly that there were a few spots where you could see into Jordanian Jerusalem—from Mount Zion, the roof of the Notre Dame Cultural Center, and a particular street in the Jewish part of the neighborhood of Abu Tor, just south of the Old City. I remember the walls all around the Old City, and the palpable fear people felt towards the Jordanians who had a sizable army.

In my courses I learned about the history of Zionism in a systematic and substantive way for the first time in my life. I learned from some of the best professors at the Hebrew University of Jerusalem, and I became deeply involved intellectually and personally in these subjects. Years later, I would teach about Zionism and Jewish identity in the School for Overseas Students at Tel Aviv University and at the Institutes for Jewish Zionist Education.

In addition, I toured the length and breadth of Israel, and learned about its founding and history, as well as its achievements and its challenges. Israel was a small close-knit, growing society in 1966, led by the Labor Zionist parties which had flourished before the state of Israel and were still in charge. The kibbutz movement ethos—a pioneering, egalitarian, caring collective existence which espoused coexistence with its Arab neighbors—was still very much the social and cultural ethos of the young socialist country. Almost all of Israel's leaders at that time had lived on a kibbutz or still lived on a kibbutz.

Actually, I had been in Israel once before. I spent my first extensive period there in summer 1964, after finishing high school. I too had been enchanted by the ideal of the kibbutz.[12] During this period I read a famous essay by Martin Buber called "The Kibbutz—the Experiment that did not Fail." Since that time, the kibbutz movement has become less and less influential in Israeli society, especially since the rise of the Likud and other right-wing capitalist political parties since 1977. Also, the "privatization" of the kibbutz has led to a situation in which most are now just bedroom communities.

At that time, I worked as a volunteer at Kibbutz Kfar Menachem, one hour south of Tel Aviv (in those days). It was an inspiring experience. I loved kibbutz life. I didn't carry a wallet all summer. I worked hard and learned to appreciate the meaning and value of physical labor (for the first time in my life). And, I absorbed the deeply Jewish socialist spirit of this left-wing *HaShomer HaTza'ir*[13] kibbutz, which I imbibed mostly from the late Yehuda Ben Chorin, my father's childhood friend from Brooklyn, New York (who was formerly "Julie Freeman"). For many years I dreamed of living on a kibbutz, where I believed that egalitarianism was both a Jewish and human ideal fulfilled.

After this summer at a kibbutz, I enrolled at Brandeis University where I majored in psychology and minored in Jewish Studies. I studied Humanistic Psychology under the famous American Jewish professor, Abraham Maslow,[14] and other professors of psychology, such as James Klee, who integrated ideas from Eastern religions, especially Buddhism, with ideas from contemporary psychology. I also studied Medieval and Modern Jewish Thought with Professors Nahum Glatzer, Alexander Altman and Ben Halpern—some of the leading teachers of Jewish Studies at that time—who were all at pains to show how Jewish Studies could be relevant to contemporary Jewish life. It was during this time that I read Buber[15] and Heschel[16] who were influential in the development of my own Jewish thought and my Jewish way of life.

In the spring of 1968, I faced a pivotal decision which revolved around my personal identity and my ambivalence about becoming a Jewish professional. For a long time, I thought that I would continue my professional studies in psychology. But as I looked into graduate programs in the field, I discovered that the general direction was more statistical and scientific and not humanistic. In addition, I learned that I could get a "divinity deferment" (an exemption from the draft) if I went to rabbinic school. As a result, I—and many of my fellow students at the time—sought out "the Divine" in rabbinical institutions whose faculty and training methods were very far from the divine!

I suffered through my first two years of rabbinical training at the Hebrew Union College-Jewish Institute of Religion (HUC-JIR) in New York from 1968-1970 while the Vietnam War raged. Most of the teachers were nothing like those that I had enjoyed at Brandeis or during my semester in Israel on the Hyatt program. The few exceptions were Professor Eugene Borowitz, who taught Jewish theology, with whom I continued to read Buber, Heschel and others, and Professor Abraham Aaroni, with whom I studied Modern Hebrew Literature about which I was passionate during that period. I'm sorry to say that most of the other teachers were a complete waste of time, and had no influence on my thinking or my life, except for one professor who will remain nameless who taught "Human Relations", which was the closest thing to psychology at the school at that time. We students said that he was a great teacher, since he taught human relations by negative example! We learned from him how not to be behave towards other human beings.

During those first two years of rabbinical school, I wanted to drop out every day. The classes were not just awful, but the whole administration had absolutely no idea how to relate to us as Jewish activists who were involved in the real world of the anti-war movement, the civil rights movement, the Jewish student movement and the *havurah*[17] (literally, fellowship) movement and other social concerns. They were clueless and we activists wasted a lot of time trying to change the administration, which proved hopeless at the time. I am happy to say that under the presidencies of Rabbi Sheldon Zimmerman and Rabbi David Ellenson, both colleagues and friends, rabbinical training at this institution has improved greatly in recent decades.

What saved me at that time was my decision—the best one of my life—to marry Amy, whom I met during my senior year in college (when she was an impressionable freshman!). After a whirlwind courtship in 1967-68—and a summer together in Israel, after I graduated college—we were married in March 1969, during my second semester of my first year in rabbinical school, in the magnificent sanctuary of Temple Rodeph Shalom on the Upper West Side in New York City. My father officiated at the ceremony, which was without question one of the greatest days of my life. Moreover, without Amy, I would never have made it through those first two very problematic years of rabbinical school (nor would I have made it to the end of rabbinical training in June 1973!). She helped me understand theology by living it, not just thinking about it, as she does to this very day. In addition, she and I decided to spend our second year of marriage, in Jerusalem, where we would both study at the School for Overseas Students[18] at the Hebrew University in Jerusalem, then on the beautiful Givat Ram campus, a decision that would alter the course of our lives forever.

So off we went to Jerusalem in the summer of 1970, just three years after the Six Day War. It was a time of great euphoria in Jewish history. I was already beginning to feel that Israel was the place where I could live out my Jewish identity in the most comprehensive way possible, but I still wasn't sure. Little did I know that my year in Israel in 1970-71 would lead to the decision to make Israel our home.

That year I had the great privilege to study Bible with Professor Moshe Greenberg and Nechama Leibowitz, two of the greatest teachers of Bible in Jerusalem at that time. For me, this was an uplifting, relevant, intellectual and spiritual experience. One of the highlights of my year was learning all night with Professor Greenberg at a *Tikkun Leil Shavuot*[19] in his home, and then walking with him and with other rabbinical students to the Western Wall at sunrise for the morning worship service. I also studied Hasidism with Professor Yossi Dan, and Second Temple Jewish History with Professor Shmuel Safrai. In addition, I studied Hebrew language and literature at the excellent *ulpan* (center for Hebrew language learning), so that by the end of the year I was able to read Hebrew fluently. In short, I learned more about Judaism and Israel in one year in Israel than I did in all four of my years in rabbinical school in New York. And I became deeply immersed in the Hebrew language and its literature, which I was able to read with great fluency by the end of that year.

It was during that year that my wife and I decided that Israel would become our home. We felt a great sense of belonging to the land and to the country, to its people and to its culture. We felt that Jewish history was being worked out in the state of Israel, and we wanted to be part of it. However, it took me another 8 years to finish all my graduate studies.

FINISHING MY EDUCATION IN THE USA

We went back to New York City for two more years of studies at HUC-JIR in New York. During these years, I stopped trying to change the rabbinical school, but worked on changing myself and my community. I continued my studies and majored in Modern Hebrew Literature. My Hebrew level was so high that the rabbinical school had very little to offer me and agreed to let me learn at other academic institutions in New York. I studied the works of the Nobel prize-winning author Shai Agnon with Professor Shmuel Leiter at New York University and with Professor Isaac Barzilay at Columbia University, both of which were great experiences for me.

In addition, I learned a great deal of Modern Hebrew Literature with Professor Aaroni, and wrote my master's thesis on "Problems of the Uprooted in the Stories of Micha Berdichevsky."[20] This monograph very much reflected my own personal struggles with my Jewish identity at that time. In fact, I wrote my first article for a Jewish contemporary periodical on this subject during the summer of 1973,[21] since this topic was very much on my mind at that time.

During my last 2 years of rabbinical school in New York, I was also part of the New York *havurah*, a group of young Jewish rabbinical students and activists who sought to learn, pray and engage in social justice and peace activism, all at the same time. I learned informally with some fabulous teachers (much more serious than most of my teachers in rabbinical school), and I was engaged in peace work with like-minded people. In addition, I created and hosted in our apartment in Manhattan a pluralistic group of rabbinical students from Hebrew Union College, the Jewish Theological Seminary and Yeshiva University before the existence of organizations that do this professionally. We studied texts together and had discussions on contemporary issues, which unfortunately could not be held in the poorly administered rabbinical schools of that generation.

In the spring of 1973, a few months before I was about to be ordained a rabbi, I had to make another fateful decision, i.e. whether to go straight to Israel to accept a job with the Reform Jewish movement, to work with college students on a kibbutz (it was very tempting!), or to accept a job as a Hillel staff person at the University of Michigan in Ann Arbor (I had often considered going into campus work, where I would have spent my professional life working with Jewish students and faculty from all denominations, since I was always a pluralist rabbi rather than a "Reform" rabbi), or whether to continue my studies by enrolling for a doctorate in Education at Harvard. After visiting the Harvard Graduate School of Education in April 1973 and enthused by this once-in-a-lifetime opportunity to study at Harvard, my decision was made, even though it would delay our *aliyah* to Israel for six more years.

Compared to rabbinical school, my studies at Harvard were heavenly. I was accepted into a fascinating interdisciplinary program known as "Learning Environments" with professors from the departments of Philosophy, History, Curriculum Development, Psychology, Sociology and Anthropology, and a wonderfully diverse group of students. I relished my studies and discussions with Professor (and Rabbi) Israel Scheffler in Philosophy of Education, Professor Donald Oliver in Social Studies Curriculum Development, Professor Lawrence Kohlberg in Moral Development, Professor Carol Gilligan in Psychology of Education, Professor Sarah Lightfoot Lawrence in Sociology of Education, Jay Featherstone in History of Education, and many more fabulous scholars and teachers. For me, it was an intellectual Garden of

Eden and I loved every minute of it. I got to know my professors well—and they got to know me—and I was a Teaching Fellow in a number of courses, which I enjoyed thoroughly.

In those days, I was tempted to pursue an academic career, but, as you will see later in my unfolding journey, my activist side and my practical educational impulses overruled an academic career for me at that time. Later, I was able to combine academic teaching at Tel Aviv University with practical educational work for a number of years. I have often wished that I could have combined an academic life alongside my practical life, but I did not manage to do this (except for a short time in my early years in Israel). I was able to do this partially by writing a lot, mostly essays, op-eds and, in recent years, blog posts.

It was during my years at the Harvard Graduate School of Education that I became an educator in my philosophy and my practice which shaped the rest of my life. I would say that since then, I have always seen the world— and especially my professional work—through the lenses of an educator. I wrote my doctoral thesis on the influence of the American pragmatist philosopher of Education John Dewey upon Jewish Education in America,[22] which established me as one of the foremost scholars of Dewey and of Jewish Education in the 1970s. In those years, I spoke at conferences and wrote articles on this subject in many journals and became a progressive educator in thought and in deed. (In later years, I taught courses on Dewey and Education in the School of Education at Tel Aviv University.)

THE MOVE TO LIVE IN ISRAEL

Three weeks after I received my doctorate in Education from Harvard, in June 1979, we were on the El Al plane to Israel to make Jerusalem, the capital of Israel, our home (we have lived there now for 38 years). In contemporary Hebrew, we refer to this emigration as *aliyah*. It is the same word that is used when a Jew is called up to say a blessing when the Torah is read in the synagogue. In this case, it refers to the idea that going to live in the land of Israel for a Jew represents an "elevation" in his or her Jewish identity. Indeed, that is exactly how we felt at the time, and still feel today.

We lived in the French Hill neighborhood, on the east side of Jerusalem, near the Mount Scopus campus of the Hebrew University. In our early years there we did not refer to this neighborhood as part of "East Jerusalem" and we were hardly conscious that this was land that was captured from the Palestinians in the Six Day War of June 1967. Today we call this a neighborhood of Jerusalem, but the Palestinians still call it a "settlement."

In those years, there was no *intifada* (Palestinian uprising, literally "shaking off" of the occupation) and we thought naively that we were living with

what Moshe Dayan[23] called a "benign occupation" with regard to the Palestinians in the West Bank and Gaza Strip. During that period, the Israeli
government thought that Palestinians in these disputed territories were entitled to civil rights (hence the establishment of the so-called "Civil Administration" as part of the "benign occupation"), but not to national rights. At that
time, it was illegal to recognize the existence of the P.L.O. (Palestine Liberation Organization) or to speak with any of its leaders. For those who don't
remember, from 1967 until December 1987 (the outbreak of the First Intifada), Israelis could travel the length and breadth of the West Bank and Gaza
Strip without violence or threat of terror.

When my wife and I—and our two young daughters—actually made the
move and came to live in Israel in June 1979, it was a time of relative quiet,
six years after "the earthquake" of the Yom Kippur War of 1973 when Israel
was attacked by surprise by the Egyptian and Syrian armies but recovered to
win the war, albeit with severe losses. We were deeply moved—as we still
are—by the unique historic opportunity and obligation to live in the Jewish
state of Israel, the state of the Jewish People, where we have been able to
raise our children as full-fledged and proud Jews in the language and culture
of the people of Israel.

I have never regretted this decision, although at times—especially during
periods of intense conflict between Israelis and Palestinians—it has been
quite a challenge. Israel has been my home for more than 38 years and I
identify with its achievements and accomplishments as well as with its problems and challenges. I have served in the Israel Defense Forces, mostly as a
lecturer in the Education Branch, and I am well aware of the security needs
of Israel even if I spent much of my later professional life in peacebuilding
activities between Israeli Jews and Palestinian citizens of Israel as well as
Palestinian non-citizens of Israel who live in East Jerusalem or the West
Bank.

During my first years as a citizen of Israel—from 1979-1986—I was
involved in Jewish education in my professional life. I spent my first two
years in Israel on a post-doctoral fellowship at the Hebrew University of
Jerusalem. I served as a lecturer and research fellow at the Melton Centre for
Jewish Education at the Hebrew University's Mount Scopus campus, where I
was the managing editor of a book[24] and taught some courses. At the same
time, I worked at the Institutes for Jewish Zionist Education, later known as
Melitz (a Hebrew acronym for the institutes), based in Jerusalem, where I
was on the senior staff with a brilliant and diverse group of people. This was
a pluralistic Jewish institution (rare in those days) which engaged in informal
Jewish Zionist education with high school students and their teachers
throughout Israel. I was in charge of evaluation and staff training, and as I
reflect back, I remember how much I loved the work which not only brought
me face to face with dilemmas in contemporary Jewish life in Israel, but

helped me understand the challenges facing Zionism and Israeli society, especially vis-a-vis Jews in their formative teenage years.

During this period, I came to understand the critical issues facing Jews of all persuasions in grappling with the meaning and message of being Jewish in the Jewish state of Israel. In my work with religious and secular high school youth and their teachers, I discovered much identity confusion,[25] especially among the so-called "secular" Jewish youth of Israel, who rejected religion but did not find a solid practical alternative in "cultural" Jewishness. It seemed that many of them had lost their way as Jews, even though some of them were actually beginning to look for new meaningful expressions of Judaism.

As I set these reflections down, I am mindful of how much the issue of Jewish identity was an internal affair, for me and most of my colleagues. Somehow, we—like most of Jewish society in Israel—had blinders on, such that we did not consider the way we related to the non-Jewish minority within the state of Israel or the way we treated Palestinians in the Occupied Territories as one of the central issues of our identity. It was perceived by us as a political and security issue and not a "Jewish" issue.

At that time the Jewish mainstream in Israel, of which I was a part, did not understand how central to our identity as Jews the issue of how we related to Palestinian Arabs—within Israel and within the territories that we control—would become in the years and decades ahead. It was only much later in my personal and professional life—after I founded the Interreligious Coordinating Council in Israel in 1991—that I came to develop a much fuller understanding of my Jewish identity that included rights and responsibilities as a Jew to the minorities living in my midst and to the Palestinians living under our control in the Territories (the West Bank and Gaza) and in the Jewish state or the nation-state of the Jewish people, as some people prefer to refer to it.

A SABBATICAL BACK IN THE USA

In January 1984, my father, Rabbi Leon Kronish, suffered a severe stroke. This had a strong impact on my adult life. In the years following the stoke, I commuted from Jerusalem to Miami Beach several times a year, which took a lot out of me, physically and emotionally. In 1986, I was offered a job for one year in the USA, to be the director of the Office of the Chairman of the Board of Governors of the Jewish Agency for Israel, a very fancy title for a major organization in contemporary Jewish life. After much introspection, I accepted the job and moved with my family (by then with three daughters), to be close to my American family for that year. My sister, Maxine (of blessed memory—she passed away from cancer in July 2004), and her family lived one hour away in Silver Spring and my father and mother were a two-hour plane ride away, in Miami Beach.

During this sabbatical year in the USA (1986-87), I came to know the leadership of North American Jewry at that time. I worked for a famous American philanthropist named Charles ("Chuck") Hoffberger, who was chairman of the Board of Governors of the Jewish Agency for Israel, and developed a close professional and personal relationship with him and with members of his family. During the year and a half that I spent as director of his office in Baltimore, I was instrumental in helping him and others in creating some fundamental changes in the philosophy and operations of the Jewish Agency. For example, it was in this year that we literally introduced the concept of the "Streams", i.e. the religious denominations of Reform and Conservative Judaism, and helped to provide them with funding as well as to incorporate them into the workings of the Jewish Agency and the World Zionist Organization, in which they remain central actors today. Since that time, millions of dollars have flowed to the Reform and Conservative movements in Israel to help them grow and develop into significant Jewish players on the Israeli scene, even if the number of members in each movement is still rather small.

In addition, I met and got to know many of the professional and lay leaders personally and became familiar with the ways in which they related to Israel. Mostly, they were interested in helping with absorption of immigrants, with Jewish Zionist education in Israel (and the Diaspora), with the social needs of Jews in Israel, and with settlement in all parts of the land of Israel.[26] The Settlement Department of the World Zionist Organization financed much of the settlement enterprise in the Occupied Territories, which funded hundreds of illegal (according to international law) settlements on Palestinian lands then and today. Most of the Diaspora philanthropists for the Jewish Agency were not fully aware of what was going on until a series of exposés were written for the *Baltimore Jewish Times* in 1986, by Charles Hoffman, much of which appeared in his comprehensive book three years later.

The idea of relating to the Arab minority in Israel or to the Palestinians in the Territories was hardly on their radar screen, except for a few iconoclastic leaders and communities, such as the federation in San Francisco, led by Rabbi Brian Lurie (a friend and colleague for several decades, Lurie became the president of the New Israel Fund, a non-profit organization which promotes democracy and pluralism in Israeli society), and later the Jewish Federation of New York, led by John Ruskay (with whom I collaborated in the New York Havurah during my student days), which funded small projects for Arab Israelis and for Arab-Jewish coexistence, including a project that I planned and implemented with Israeli Arab Muslim religious leadership for two years, in cooperation with Rabbi Marc Rosenstein and his organization,

Makom BaGalil, a Place in the Galilee. I discovered during this year and a half that "Jewish survival" and "Jewish identity" did not include relating to "others". Mainstream Diaspora Jews—and their counterparts in Israel—had become more and more particularistic and less and less humanistic or universalistic in the decades since the Holocaust and the Six Day War.[27] While I had been aware of this trend towards "tribalism" or particularism before this, it became even clearer to me during my time in the USA, working with many of the leaders of the American Jewish establishment.

During my sabbatical year in the USA, I was able to devote some of my time to writing and editing. With the help of a wonderful editor, Rabbi Nina Beth Cardin, in Baltimore, I edited a Festschrift, a book of essays in honor of my father's 70th birthday, called *Towards the Twenty-First Century: Judaism and the Jewish People in Israel and America*, which included essays by many famous American and Israeli Jews, such as Elie Wiesel, Shlomo Avineri, and others, all of whom knew my father and me personally. The book[28] was published in cooperation with CLAL, the National Jewish Center for Learning and Leadership,[29] headed by the charismatic modern Orthodox rabbi Irving ("Yitz") Greenberg, with whom I have cooperated professionally over the years.[30]

In my essay entitled *Bridging the Gap. Israel and the Diaspora: Problems and Possibilities*[31] in that book, I spelled out some of my views towards Israel at that time. I felt then, as I do now, that the destinies of Jews in and outside of Israel (what we call the "Diaspora") are inextricably intertwined. What happens in Israel is a Jewish concern for all Jews everywhere, and the crises affecting Jews outside of Israel are of concern to the Jewish state, or the state of the Jews (more on this below).

This is why I believe that Jews outside of Israel need to care about the nature of the values of Jewish society within the state of Israel now, as they have in the past. In every society in which Jews live, the issue of "Israel" (usually referring to the political positions of the Israeli government on critical issues such as the peace process, religion and state, etc) is a Jewish issue. Diaspora Jews should not be apathetic to this, even though many of them, if not most, are so assimilated that they do not care very much about Israel, or if they do care to some extent, they have very little knowledge or awareness of what is really going on in Israel except for a relatively small group of elitist Jewish "leaders" who are actually very knowledgeable and involved. In addition, the leadership of the American Jewish community, which is overwhelmingly liberal, has trouble identifying with a state of Israel which is becoming less and less liberal, so that there is now a clash of values between the American Jewish mainstream and the Israeli one.

Since we clearly nevertheless share interlocking destinies and identities, if Diaspora Jews feel, for example, that Israel as a Jewish society founded on the precepts of social justice of the biblical prophets of Israel, has to act more fairly to the Palestinian minority within the state of Israel or to the Palestinian majority in the West Bank, which is controlled by Israel (despite the supposed division of control as agreed upon as part of the Oslo Accords),[32] they ought to speak their mind to the leaders and the people of Israel. Actually, this is happening more in recent years through the good work of excellent progressive organizations such as J Street[33] and the New Israel Fund.[34]

RETURNING TO ISRAEL, BEGINNING OF INVOLVEMENT IN INTERRELIGIOUS AFFAIRS

After my sabbatical year in the USA, I came back to Israel and worked for an American Jewish communal organization for four years (1988-92), directing their Israel office. It was then that I became more and more of a political observer and commentator on contemporary Israel. During those years, I scoured the Israeli press each week, and every Monday morning I would write a four-page bulletin which was called "Insight Israel". This was widely read all over the United States, and I became well known as someone who had good sources and important insights concerning contemporary developments in Israeli politics, society and culture. As a result, during those years I was regularly interviewed by Israeli correspondents of the *New York Times, the Washington Post, the Wall Street Journal* and others, and wrote several op-eds for the *Jerusalem Post.*[35]

It was also during this period (1988-1992) that I was introduced to the issue of interreligious relations in Israel by Dr. Bernie Resnikoff, of blessed memory, who became a mentor and friend for many years. Indeed, it was then that I first began to meet non-Jews in Israel. As I reflect on this, I am mindful that until this time, most of my professional and personal relations were with fellow Jews within Jewish society in Israel. Since Jews and Arabs live mostly separate lives in separate communities all over the country, it was no accident that my life had not brought me into contact with the non-Jewish citizens of the state in which I live. The reality is that most Jews in Israel have scant opportunity or need in their lives to interact with Palestinian Arabs who are citizens of the same state, so that it is totally "normal" for Jews to live among, and only know, Jews in Israel.

As a result, a new professional opportunity afforded me the experience of encountering Muslims, Christians and Druse religious leaders, educators, women, youth and young adults throughout Israel—and in East Jerusalem and the West Bank, over the next 25 years. I was approached by Dr. Resnikoff and Rabbi David Rosen and others at that time to found a new interreligious organization, since the existing organization (the Israel Interfaith Association) was in dire straits and many of the veteran members were abandoning it and looking for something new. Not only did this radically change my professional life—although I remained essentially an educator through all these years—but it changed my Jewish identity profoundly. Through my work in interreligious dialogue, education and activism, the way we as Jews relate to the minority in our midst became one of the central components of my Jewish identity. In recent years, I have written more and more about this on my blogs,[36] where I argued that this subject must become a central Jewish value for us as Jews, especially as Jews who live in the sovereign state of Israel. In addition, I came to know the main issues of Palestinian identity—of Christians as well as Muslims (and even to some extent the Druse)—in great detail.[37]

The Interreligious Coordinating Council in Israel (ICCI) was founded by me and a group of Jews and Christians on January 16, 1991. The date is easy to remember since it was the night before the "Gulf War", during which Iraq (led by Saddam Hussein) sent tens of missiles into Israel for several weeks, paralyzing Israeli society for that period. About 25 people, with gas masks in hand, gathered in the basement of the Ratisbonne Seminary in central Jerusalem for our founding meeting. It was the beginning of a 25-year period of service as director of this non-profit organization, which was to become the leading organization for interreligious dialogue, education and action in Israel for more than two decades, with an excellent national and international reputation for integrity and excellence in the field.

It is probably no coincidence that this organization for dialogue between Jewish Israelis and Palestinian Arabs (both Muslim and Christian) was founded in 1991, at the beginning of the 1990s peace process in Israel.[38] From the beginning, I saw the organization as part of the networks of those organizations in civil society in Israel and Palestine which were seeking to promote peacebuilding programs which brought Palestinians—within Israel and in the Territories—and Jews to encounter one another for the sake of peaceful coexistence.[39]

During the 25 years that I served as the director of the Interreligious Coordinating Council in Israel (ICCI)—which is also the Israel chapter of Religions for Peace[40] and was one of the Israel chapters of the International Council of Christians and Jews[41]—I became one of Israel's few experts in this field. As a result, local representatives of the foreign press, as well as local journalists, would often seek me out for quotes and background information about developments in interreligious relations and peacebuilding programs in Israel. In my capacity as the professional leader of this institution for more than two decades, I was privileged to have been invited to speak at and participate in international conferences all over the world, from North America to Europe to the Far East. These experiences brought me into contact with Jews, Christians and Muslims (and others) who genuinely believe in and practice the art of interreligious and intercultural dialogue, and who actively work for peace in their countries, regions and internationally.

In addition, I have been invited to several conferences and seminars at the Vatican where I met Pope John Paul II, and I met Pope Benedict when he came on a pilgrimage to Israel. For a while, I was one of the few Jews in Israel (and the world) who was intimately familiar with the details of the revolutionary changes that the Catholic Church had implemented since Vatican II in the 1960s towards Jews and Judaism. Had I not gotten involved in Jewish-Christian dialogue, I—like most mainstream Jews in Israel and everywhere else—would have known little or nothing about this amazing transformation of the largest Christian denomination in the world vis-a-vis the Jewish people.

I spent much time in the 1990's and in the first years of the new millennium in engagement with local and international Catholic leadership. In chapter 3, I will discuss this involvement in some detail. As part of my activism in this field, I got to know all of the ambassadors of the Vatican to Israel from 1993 onwards.

In particular, my friendship with the Vatican nuncio (ambassador) to Israel at that time, Msgr. Pietro Sambi, led to my being asked to organize a series of briefings for the foreign and local press during the month leading up to this historic visit of Pope John Paul II to Israel in March 2000 (I discuss this visit in depth and its implications for interreligious dialogue and peacebuilding in chapter 3). The briefings that I organized in cooperation with the Israel Government Press Organization turned out to be very important for members of the foreign and local press, who knew very little about the revolutionary changes within the Catholic Church in relation to Judaism and the Jewish people since Vatican II in the 1960s.

At one of the press briefings, an Israeli couple who make documentary films (Elaine and Eli Talel) came up to me and said: "We (and most Jews) have absolutely no idea of what you are talking about. We are not aware of these changes of the Catholic Church regarding Jews and Judaism in recent decades, and we feel that most Jews are ignorant about these developments. Why don't we make a documentary film to explain this to Jews in Israel and around the world?" This led to the production of an award-winning film entitled, *I am Joseph Your Brother*,[42] which was produced by ICCI in cooperation with the U.S. Council of Catholic Bishops in 2001 for broadcast on ABC-TV throughout the United States.

My involvement with this historic visit of Pope John Paul II to the Holy Land in March 2000 left an indelible impression on me. I was greatly moved by all the poignant speeches and gestures that he made during this visit. Reflecting back, I can say that it changed my life and inspired me to be more active in dialogue for many years to come, especially during the difficult years that would follow. Without doubt, the Jewish-Catholic reconciliation-through-dialogue process that has occurred since World War II and since Vatican II, and in the decades since then—has motivated me and many others to expand this dialogue to be more inclusive of leaders and followers of other religions, especially Islam. While the settings and the sensitivities of the dialogue will vary from religion to religion, the essential principle of dialogue as a powerful force for reconciliation between religious communities which have been deeply estranged for decades (not to mention engaged in active conflict) remains central to my religious and educational outlook and to the person I have become.[43]

ESTABLISHING A LOCAL CULTURE OF DIALOGUE

As time went on, I spent more and more time with local Christians and Muslims, rather than with their counterparts abroad (although I continued to do this as well). I made a conscious decision to develop local Jewish-Christian dialogue, and then later local Jewish-Muslim dialogue, as well as local Jewish-Christian-Muslim trialogue. All of the dialogue and trialogue work that I did during more than 25 years was done in the context of peacebuilding processes that were supplementing the political/diplomatic peace processes from 1993 until 2015. For me, dialogue was not a goal but rather a means to an end. After many years, I came up with a slogan that characterized my work in interreligious dialogue in Israel and Palestine: peaceful coexistence is our goal; dialogue, education and action are our methods.[44]

For many years, I co-facilitated an indigenous Jewish Israeli - Christian Palestinian dialogue group with my friend and colleague Bishop Munib Younan, the Palestinian bishop for the Lutheran Church in Israel, Palestine and Jordan.[45] Over time, we came to call ourselves "The Jonah Group", as a reminder that we were not to flee from our responsibilities. I brought local Israeli Jewish educators and rabbis from all the denominations to the table, and Bishop Younan brought Lutherans, Catholics, Armenians and Anglicans, all of whom were local Christian Palestinian clergy or educators. We did this for more than a decade, mostly quietly and behind the scenes. We studied the Bible together, shared experiences about the *matzav* (situation), comforted each other, and sought ways to work together. This was a very conscious attempt to contextualize our dialogue, to make it less "foreign" and to connect it with the realities of the ongoing conflict.

I can say that this local Christian Palestinian - Jewish Israeli dialogue, which went on for many years, influenced my life profoundly. Many of the members of the group have not only remained friends, but have also worked together in common cause over the years. Not only did we engage in study and fellowship, but we have offered each other what I call "gestures of reconciliation." In addition, for many years, I would invite him to share his views with visiting Jewish or interreligious groups interested in hearing a clear and peaceful Palestinian Christian perspective on the situation. He was

always forthright and candid about how peace would be beneficial to both
Palestinian Arabs and Israeli Jews

GETTING MORE DEEPLY INVOLVED IN INTERRELIGIOUS DIALOGUE

During this period, which included the very difficult years of the Second
Intifada, from 2000 -2003 or even 2004, I persisted in the dialogue process,
primarily inside Israel and Palestine, but also abroad, despite the violence
and obstacles. In January 2002, I was invited by Rabbi Ronald Sobel, who
was then the Senior Rabbi of Temple Emanuel in New York City, to speak at
an annual clergy conference, along with my colleague Bishop Younan, and
also an Israeli Muslim Arab educator, Dr. Muhammed Hourani, with whom I
had worked for many years.

The three of us travelled together for nine days and spoke in New York,
Chicago and other cities about our views on how interreligious dialogue can
contribute to peacebuilding (the theme of this book). I remember well that
whenever we appeared together, Bishop Younan in his introductory remarks
said that the root cause of the Israeli-Palestinian conflict was "the occupation", and on every occasion I responded that there are two primary causes to
the ongoing unresolved conflict: the occupation by Israel of the West Bank
and Gaza and the refusal of rejectionists on the Palestinian side to recognize
Israel and demonstrate willingness to live in a state side by side with the state
of Israel.

A few weeks later, after we had returned to Jerusalem, on March 7, 2002,
I hosted 50 rabbis at the ICCI Education Center in the prestigious German
Colony in Jerusalem for a panel discussion with the same Christian and
Muslim colleagues on "The Contribution of Interreligious Dialogue to Peacebuilding in Israel and the Middle East." After the opening remarks by each of
us, one of the rabbis asked the bishop about the root cause of the conflict. He
replied: "There are two root causes to the conflict..." It was then that I
realized that our dialogues in the USA had made a significant impact on him
as well as on me.

After the session, I joined a number of other rabbis and their spouses for
lunch at the nearby Café Cafit. During the lunch a terrorist tried to enter the
café. A vigilant waiter tackled and disarmed him, thus saving our lives. The
next morning we went back to thank the waiter, named Shlomi, and were
interviewed by Israeli television. By the end of the day the whole world knew
about this incident. (During the following summer, a rabbi who was visiting
me from Los Angeles told me that she had heard that I had tackled the
terrorist! I informed her that she got the story wrong!)

A few days later, in an emotional and heart-warming ceremony, my rabbinic colleagues and I offered a special blessing of gratitude to God at Shabbat morning services held in the beautiful Blaustein Hall at the educational and cultural center of the World Union for Progressive Judaism in Jerusalem. I will never forget this occasion. It was a moment of great catharsis and meaning for me and my family, imbuing me the spiritual energy to return to my peace-building activities.

Notwithstanding this traumatic experience, I have tried to be a voice for interreligious and intercultural peaceful coexistence here in Israel and Palestine. Since Israeli society has been moving to the political right in recent years, I find that my voice is increasingly a lonely one. Moreover, in my lectures to visiting groups in Israel and around the world, I am often asked if Israel will ever live in peace, and my answer is "Yes!" At a recent lecture, a journalist followed up my answer with the wry comment: "So how long do you plan to live?!"

To summarize what I have been saying up to now, I want to make clear that I have embarked on a long personal and professional journey. I began my career as a Jewish educator and activist, first in the U.S.A. and then in Israel. At the beginning of my journey, I was very much a mainstream Jewish educator, concerned mostly with internal Jewish issues of Jewish Identity, without much reference to "others." As my career developed, and especially when I founded the Interreligious Coordinating Council in Israel in 1991, my professional and personal life took a radical turn. The activist in me resurfaced when I began to meet and work with non-Jews in Israel and Palestine—first Christians and then Muslims.

Through my professional work, it became increasingly clear to me that the main issue that we have to deal with now and for the future—for the survival of the Jewish state of Israel—is to figure out how we can learn to live with the Palestinian Arabs in our midst, both those who live as citizens within the state of Israel, and those who live in the West Bank and Gaza, many of whom still suffer under military occupation and whose fate needs to be resolved through peace negotiations. Now that we have sovereignty and power, it is incumbent upon us to come up with a reasonable philosophy and practice which will help us learn to live in peaceful coexistence with our non-Jewish neighbors who are also our fellow citizens. I would go so far as to say that this is the major challenge of Zionist Jewish Identity in Israel today.

I also want to make it clear that I am very much a Zionist, even though I am in the minority liberal/progressive/humanist camp which used to be the majority in Israel many years ago, when I first moved here. I believe that the Jewish people should have a state in part of their ancient homeland of the land of Israel. This state should exist side by side with a peaceful Palestinian state, in part of this land. I also believe, as I explain more fully below, that Israel is the place where I can most comprehensively live out my own Jewish identity, but that I can no longer pretend to do this in a vacuum, without recognizing and dealing with the historical trauma and rights of the Palestinian minority within the state, or without reaching an agreement in which the Palestinian people can establish their own independence and identity, in freedom and security.

In order to clarify, I need to go back a bit and explain a few things about this movement called "Zionism", which I call the national liberation movement of the Jewish people. In my meetings with Christian and Muslim groups—and even some Jewish groups—over many years, I have felt that the essence of Zionism has been greatly distorted and misunderstood, sometimes out of ignorance, and sometimes out of malice. Accordingly, I feel that at the outset of this book, it is important for me to set the record straight.

MY HUMANISTIC/PROGRESSIVE LIBERAL ZIONIST APPROACH

Since the infamous "Zionism is Racism" resolution in the U.N.[46] and since the horrific and continuous anti-Zionist and anti-Israel propaganda of the Arab countries and of some European countries after the outbreak of the First Intifada in 1987, the term "Zionism" is greatly misunderstood and purposely distorted in much of the Western world, especially in much of mainstream Protestant churches, as well as in some right-wing Jewish circles.

First of all, it is important to note that Zionism is not simply a response to the Holocaust during World War II. Rather, its origins are to be found in Europe some 60-70 years before the Holocaust, during the rise of nationalism at the end of the 19th century.

Zionism is one of the major streams of modern Jewish thought (and action) which arose out of the historical experience of the emancipation of the Jews of Europe in the 18th and 19th centuries. It was—and still is—one of the central Jewish responses to modernity and it offered the Jews of the world a compelling option for Jewish survival in the modern and contemporary world.

In 1896 the father of modern Zionism, Theodore Herzl, wrote a famous book called *The Jewish State,* which diagnosed "the Jewish problem" as it was called at the end of the 19th century as one of anti-Semitism. According to his prophetic reading of the situation, there was no real possibility for Jews to survive in Europe after centuries of pogroms, blood libels and rampant anti-Semitism, culminating in the infamous Dreyfus affair in France. In his view—and the view of many other classical Zionist thinkers of the latter part of the 19th century—there was simply no future for Jews in Europe since hatred of the Jews was so endemic to European (Christian) society. The only solution was to leave Europe and return "home".

And where was home? Clearly, it was the ancient homeland of the Jewish people, the Land of Israel, with which this people had been connected throughout its history. Herzl's theory, known as "political Zionism," proposed that instead of anti-Semitism and rootlessness in Europe, the Jews should establish a sovereign state, which would be a "state of the Jews", i.e. a state in which this people would "live and breathe free."[47] In this state, the Jews would be a "people like all other peoples." This state would therefore be first and foremost a refuge for oppressed Jews anywhere in the world who suffer from anti-Semitism, a haven for Jews so that their suffering as a humiliated and despondent people would be no more.

This notion of Israel as a refuge for oppressed Jews everywhere still lies at the center of the self-consciousness of the modern state of Israel. It was therefore self-evident to all governments of Israel that when Jews were oppressed, whether in the Former Soviet Union or in Ethiopia, they ought to be rescued and brought home to Israel. The same of course was the case for the "remnants" of the Holocaust, as well as the hundreds of thousands of Jews who were expelled from Arab countries in the late 1940s and early 1950s.

It is important for me to add that what underlies this idea of Zionism— and all other theories of Zionism—is the concept that Jews are a people. In my briefings to Christian and interreligious groups who come to Israel, it has become clear to me how little this is understood. The Zionist movement—in all of its streams from the beginning until today—understands the Jews as a national movement which originated in biblical days and has survived a difficult history. To be a Jew, according to all versions of Zionism is to be a member of the Jewish people. This is its revolutionary message to the Jewish world, one that most Jews have accepted in theory, but not always in practice. One can express one's Jewishness nationalistically, culturally or religiously, but at the base of one's Jewish identity is the notion of belonging to an ancient people which has always maintained an attachment to its ancient homeland, the land of Israel.

Theodore Herzl was not the only Zionist thinker at the end of the 19th century to propose radical new ideas for the Jewish people. Asher Ginsberg, who took the name *Ahad Ha'am* (lit. "One of the people"), and his followers argued strongly with Herzl in the early years of the Zionist movement in Europe. In contrast to Herzl, Ahad Ha'am felt that the main problem facing the Jews—certainly those in Western Europe, as opposed to those in Eastern Europe—was assimilation, not anti-Semitism. In the West, Jews were neither persecuted nor oppressed. Indeed, in Germany, France and Britain, they were being welcomed as full citizens for the first time in Jewish history. Many subsequently abandoned the Jewish religion for the ideas of the Enlightenment, which encompassed science, democracy, rationality, and progress.

Ahad Ha'am argued that the only place where Jews would live out a full Jewish national culture (not necessarily a religious one) would be in their own homeland. In Israel, they would revive the Jewish language of Hebrew and with it Hebrew literature, art, music and dance, all major elements of a thriving national culture. Only in Israel would Jews study the Bible as their national history. Only in Israel would they feel a natural connection to the land and to every place in it as part of their own national cultural and religious heritage.

In contrast to Herzl, Ahad Ha'am argued that the goal of returning to Israel was not "normalization." Rather, Israel must be a unique Jewish society, living up to the ideals of the biblical prophets of Israel by setting up an ethical and just society which cares for the minorities in its midst.

Whether one subscribed to the political Zionism of Herzl or to the cultural Zionism of Ahad Ha'am, there was a definite sense that there was no future for the Jewish people outside of its homeland, the Land of Israel.

In addition, there was a minority point of view in the early years of the Zionist movement at the end of the 19th century and the beginning of the 20th century called "religious Zionism" whose proponents argued that genuine Judaism is an authentic combination of religion and nationality. Indeed, they said that the Jews are both a religion and a people, and have always combined both sides of their identity. Attempts of assimilated Jews of one stripe or another to separate the Jewish nation from the Jewish religion were deemed inauthentic.

Religious Zionism has grown and developed in Israel since the founding of the state in 1948 and especially in the past 48 years, since the Six Day War of 1967. Not only do Orthodox Jews espouse "religious Zionism" today, but so do Reform, Conservative and Reconstructionist Jews, who have all joined the Zionist Movement since 1967 and who all have major institutions in Israel to this day. In other words, there has been a general trend to combine the religious and national parts of our identity as Jews among all Jewish religious groups (except for the ultra-Orthodox groups, which are another story, or the ultra-secular, who hardly exist anymore) in contemporary Israel. In addition, there has been a dangerous growth of ultra-nationalism, which leaves no room for other opinions or identities, and is becoming more and more violent and xenophobic.

ZIONISM AND JEWISH IDENTITY IN ISRAEL TODAY

Israel has changed greatly since the state was founded in 1948. New waves of *aliyah* have helped Israel grow from a population of 600,000 to more than 8 million people today, 75% of whom are Jewish.[48] Over time, the idealism and socialism of the pioneering decades in the pre-state era and in the early years of the state, have dissipated greatly. Contemporary Western culture— for good and for bad—has inhibited the ability of non-religious Jewish culture to compete in the free market of ideas and trends, especially for the younger generation, although there has been a small renascence of Jewish pluralist culture in Israel in recent years. And, decades of war and intifada have pushed the mainstream Jewish population to the right, religiously and politically, with the feeling that the world is still out to get us via terrorism and wars that threaten to destroy the Jewish state (not to mention the possibility of a nuclear Iran which, in the narrative of current Israeli leadership, promises to wipe Israel off the map of the nations of the world!).

In other words, the right has taken over the center in Israeli political and cultural life. Despite our great military and technological power, we still live with the memory of the Holocaust and the belief that major elements in the world are bent on our destruction. Apparently, we are not yet entirely free, even though we live in a land of freedom, in our own national home. We are also not free as long as we continue to deny another people their freedom.

With the negative developments of recent decades, one wonders if the idea of a humanistic liberal Zionism is still tenable. My answer, of course, is yes. Let me explain.

Israel's founding document is our Declaration of Independence, published on May 14, 1948. It is an inspirational statement of the ideals on which this state and society are based. I quote below just a few paragraphs to give the reader an idea of the kind of state our founding fathers envisioned for Israel:

> THE STATE OF ISRAEL will be open for Jewish immigration and for the Ingathering of the Exiles; it will foster the development of the country for the benefit of all its inhabitants; it will be based on freedom, justice and peace as envisaged by the prophets of Israel; it will ensure complete equality of social and political rights to all its inhabitants irrespective of religion, race or sex; it will guarantee freedom of religion, conscience, language, education and culture; it will safeguard the Holy Places of all religions; and it will be faithful to the principles of the Charter of the United Nations.
>
> THE STATE OF ISRAEL is prepared to cooperate with the agencies and representatives of the United Nations in implementing the resolution of the General Assembly of the 29th November, 1947, and will take steps to bring about the economic union of the whole of Eretz-Israel.
>
> WE APPEAL to the United Nations to assist the Jewish people in the building-up of its State and to receive the State of Israel into the comity of nations.
>
> WE APPEAL - in the very midst of the onslaught launched against us now for months - to the Arab inhabitants of the State of Israel to preserve peace and participate in the upbuilding of the State on the basis of full and equal citizenship and due representation in all its provisional and permanent institutions.
>
> WE EXTEND our hand to all neighboring states and their peoples in an offer of peace and good neighborliness, and appeal to them to establish bonds of cooperation and mutual help with the sovereign Jewish people settled in its

own land. The State of Israel is prepared to do its share in a common effort for the advancement of the entire Middle East.

In many ways, all that is called for is a return to the values enshrined in our Declaration of Independence! Indeed, an organization of which I am a member, Rabbis for Human Rights, has written a commentary on the Declaration of Independence to remind all Israeli citizens of the state's basic values.[49]

But life is not so simple. We cannot simply return to 1948. Too many wars and too much violence have occurred since then. And, with them, the development of two very different national narratives—the Israeli Jewish one and the Palestinian Arab one. Sometimes I think that the only things they have in common are the dates.

For a long time, both sides denied the existence of the other. Until the Oslo accords in 1993, both sides did not officially recognize the existence of the other. The state of Israel refused to recognize the existence of a collective entity now known as the Palestinian people; and the Palestinians refused to recognize the state of Israel, referring to it as "the Zionist entity."

Since the Oslo Accords, we now recognize the Palestinians and they recognize us, at least in principle! The Jewish state recognizes the rights of the Palestinian people to self-determination, i.e. a state, even if right-wing Israeli governments have gradually distanced themselves from this principle in recent years. Moreover, the Palestinian Authority recognizes the state of Israel and its right to secure and recognized borders. In this sense, the Oslo Accords signed on the White House lawn in Washington D.C. on September 13, 1993, represent a sea-change in the whole Israeli-Palestinian conflict.

Yet, despite the signing of these accords, peace still eludes us. Over the past decade and more, we have been witness to terror and counter-terror, a second Lebanon war, and three mini-wars with the Hamas regime in Gaza. Naturally, people on both sides have begun to despair of the possibility of peace in our region. Instead of normalization, we have separation. Instead of negotiations, we have walls and fences. My response to this—and the answer shared by many of my colleagues in Israel—is that we must not lose faith and give up! Even if we cannot solve all the political problems at once, we must persevere via dialogue, education and action, wherever possible. This is one of the major themes of this book.

In the next chapter, I set interreligious dialogue in Israel and Palestine firmly within the context of the peace process which has occupied so much of our consciousness in recent decades.

NOTES

1. He retired from the active rabbinate in 1984, after a severe stroke, but maintained the title of Founding Senior Rabbi all of his life. He passed away in March 1996.
2. The Reform Jewish movement used to be called the UAHC, the Union of American Hebrew Congregations; since 2003 it has been called the URJ, the Union for Reform Judaism.
3. Deborah Dash Moore: *To the Golden Cities,* p. 25. Miami Beach enjoyed a fast growth rate, reaching 46,000 people by 1950, up from 28,000 before World War II. See also Henry A. Green: *Gesher VaKesher: Bridges and Bonds. The Life of Leon Kronish*, especially chapter 3, pp. 53-91 on "Miami Beach: America's Negev".
4. Rabbi Abraham Joshua Heschel: *Israel: Echo of Eternity.* Originally published in 1969. Republished by MacMillan in 2013.
5. David Ben Gurion was Israel's first Prime Minister and Minister of Defense; he was an inspiring leader and visionary of almost biblical proportions.
6. Henry A. Green, *Ibid,* p. 217.
7. *Ibid.*, p. 217.
8. Herbert Marcuse, a leading political science professor at Brandeis and an expert on Hegel and Marx, was a charismatic personality who was active in the anti-war movement in the USA in the sixties.
9. The Vietnam War dragged on until 1975 but its main impact on American society was in the late 1960s and early 1970s.
10. Clergy and Laymen Concerned about Vietnam (CALCAV) was officially founded on October 28, 1965 at the Church Center for the United Nations by Rev. Richard Neuhaus (Lutheran pastor), Rabbi Abraham Joshua Heschel (Jewish scholar and professor) and Fr. Daniel Berrigan SJ (prominent Catholic voice against the war). Martin Luther King Jr. became national co-chair, widening the reach of this new national organization. Neither pacifist nor radical, CALCAV drew upon the biblical roots of peacemaking as well as the strong tradition of democratic dissent. After the war ended, it changed its name to Clergy and Laity Concerned (CALC) and worked on a number of national and international peace and justice issues. From the website of the King Center: http://www.thekingcenter.org/.
11. "The Brandeis Questionnaire", Jon Landau '68, *Brandeis Magazine*, summer 2013.
12. Martin Buber, "The Kibbutz—the Experiment that did not Fail", in Martin Buber (translated by R F C Hull), Paths in Utopia , Routledge & Kegan Paul, 1949.
13. *HaShomer HaTza'ir* is the first Zionist Youth Movement established within the Jewish People. It was formed in Europe in 1913 by a group of Jewish young men who envisioned a new path for their contemporaries and their people. From the outset, this movement was set on realizing its dreams of a new life in the land of Israel. See website: https://www.hashomer-hatzair.org/pages/english.aspx
14. See Abraham H. Maslow: *Toward a Psychology of Being.* Van Nostrand Reinhold Company. New York. 1968.
15. Books and essays by Buber that influenced my thinking at this time, and still today, include: *I and Thou, Israel and the World—Essays in a Time of Crisis*, and *Pointing the Way.*
16. Books by Heschel that were and are very influential in my thinking include *Israel: Echo of Eternity, The Sabbath* and his famous essay "No Religion is an Island."
17. The *havurah* movement was a cultural/religious phenomenon of the sixties and seventies in the USA whereby groups of students and young adults formed Jewish associations, largely outside of synagogues, to pray together and to engage in social action. As time progressed, many synagogues adopted the idea, and set up small groups to do the same within synagogues. See Jonathan Sarna on *"havurah* Judaism" www.myjewishlearning.com, reprinted from his book on American Judaism, Yale University Press. Over time, a small national havurah committee was created and holds annual retreats to this day. See www.havurah.org.
18. It is now called the Rothberg International School, named after Sam Rothberg, a major donor to the Hebrew University for many years (and a close friend of my father's through their volunteer work for Israel Bonds for many decades), a man I knew personally and respected greatly.

19. The idea of staying up all night to study Torah on the Jewish holiday of Shavuot, which celebrates the revelation at Sinai and the giving of the Torah to the Jewish people, is called *Tikkun Leil Shavuot*. Following the holiday meal, many people proceed to synagogue for *Ma'ariv* [the evening service], followed by an all-night (or into-the-night, as many last only until midnight) Torah study session based on the kabbalists' [mystics'] practice. [This specifically refers to the 16th century mystics of Safed, Israel, under the leadership of Isaac Luria.] From www.myjewishlearning.com, written by Leslie Koppelman Ross. Excerpted from *Celebrate! The Complete Jewish Holiday Handbook*.

20. Micah Joseph Berdichevsky (1865 - 1921), author of works in Hebrew, German, and Yiddish. His impassioned writings, perhaps more than those of any other Jewish author, bear poignant witness to the "rent in the heart" of 19th-century Jews torn between tradition and assimilation. He was also the author of enduring reconstructions of Jewish legends and folklore. From the website of Encyclopedia Britannica www.britannica.com. My unpublished thesis on "The Problems of the Uprooted in the Stories of Micah Yosef Berdichevsky," was submitted in June 1973, as partial fulfillment of the requirements for the Master of Arts in Hebrew Literature and Ordination.

21. Ronald Kronish. "The Conflicts of Jewish Youth" in *Congress Bi-Weekly*, June 15, 1973, pp. 10-12.

22. Ronald Kronish, *The Influence of John Dewey upon Jewish Education in America*. Doctoral dissertation, the Harvard Graduate School of Education, 1979.

23. Moshe Dayan was a famous Israeli general and politician who served as Minister of Defense in several Israeli governments. He was the Defense Minister at the time of the Six Day War in June 1967. In addition, he later became a crusader for peace. He played a key role in four wars and helped negotiate the Israel-Egypt peace treaty. See www.jewishvirtuallibrary.org.

24. Barry Chazan, editor, Ronald Kronish. Managing editor, *Studies in Jewish Education I: Theory and Research*, The Hebrew University Magnes Press, 1983.

25. During this period, I wrote some articles about Jewish Identity in Israel, such as *Varieties of Jewish Expression in Israel*, in *The Jewish Frontier*, Spring 1988; *Understanding One Another: Jewish Identity in Israel and America*, in *Jewish Education News*, published by CAJE, winter/spring 1988 pp. 1, 10-11; *Educating for Jewish-Zionist Identity in Israel* in *The Melton Journal*, published by the Jewish Theological Seminary of America, spring-Summer 1983, later reprinted in *Forum*, 54/55.

26. Charles Hoffman. *The Smoke Screen. Israel, Philanthropy and American Jews*. Eshel Books, 1989.

27. For a full explanation about this loss of humanism among contemporary Jews, see Avraham Burg, *The Holocaust is Over; We Must Rise From its Ashes* , Palgrave Macmillan, New York, 2008. In recent years, Burg has been one of the few outspoken voices in Israeli society calling for a return to a balance between particularism and humanism.

28. Ronald Kronish, ed., *Towards the Twenty-first Century: Judaism and the Jewish People in Israel and America, Essays in Honor of Rabbi Leon Kronish on the Occasion of His Seventieth Birthday*, Ktav Publishing House, 1988.

29. Founded in 1974, Clal-The National Jewish Center for Learning and Leadership is a leadership training institute, think tank and resource center.

30. For example, when he published *For the Sake of Heaven and Earth: The New Encounter Between Judaism and Christianity* (2004) about his views concerning contemporary Christianity as a modern Orthodox rabbi, I co-hosted a book launch for him with the Pardes Institute in Jerusalem.

31. Ronald Kronish, "Bridging the Gap. Israel and the Diaspora: Problems and Possibilities" in *Towards the Twenty-first Century: Judaism and the Jewish People in Israel and America*, Ibid, pp. 137-149.

32. The Oslo Accords divide the West Bank into areas A, B and C. Area A is supposedly under sole Palestinian control, but the Israeli army operates freely throughout area A, as it deems necessary for security purposes. Area B is under shared control (Israel controls security and the PA controls civil issues). Area C, under the security control of Israel, is the largest sector.

33. Founded in 2008, J Street is the political home for pro-Israel, pro-peace Americans who want Israel to be secure, democratic and the national home of the Jewish people. Working in American politics and the Jewish community, it advocates policies that advance shared US and Israeli interests as well as Jewish and democratic values, leading to a two-state solution to the Israeli-Palestinian conflict.

34. The New Israel Fund (NIF) helps Israel live up to its founders' vision of a state that ensures complete equality of social and political rights to all its inhabitants. Its aim is to advance liberal democracy, including freedom of speech and minority rights, and to fight inequality, injustice, and extremism that diminish Israel.

35. See op-eds in the Jerusalem Post and in the Hebrew press, by Ronald Kronish from 1988-1992: *The Reasons Behind the Rhetoric*, in *The Jerusalem Post*, Feb. 9, 1992; *Cautious But Real Pursuit of Peace*, in *The Jerusalem Post*, Dec. 3, 1991; *Cautious Optimism Among Soviet Jews*, in *The Jerusalem Post*, Oct. 8, 1991; *Understanding the Differences*, in *The Jerusalem Post*, June 26, 1990; *Going Beyond Philanthropy*, in *The Jerusalem Post*, Oct. 28, 1990; *The Jewish 'intra-fada': One Year Later*, in *The Jerusalem Post*, Jan. 23, 1990; *Common Destiny*, in *The Jerusalem Post*, Feb. 20, 1990; *All the Problems Can be Solved*, in *The Jerusalem Post*, Feb. 5, 1989, p. 4; *On the Road to Becoming Israeli*, in *Davar*, July 21, 1989 (in Hebrew); *Getting Absorption on the Right Track*, in *The Jerusalem Post*, Aug. 1, 1989.

36. See blogs by Ronald Kronish on the websites of *The Huffington Post* and *The Times of Israel* from 2013 - 2015. www.huffingtonpost.com and www.blogs.timesofisrael.com.

37. See chapter three, in which I discuss what I have encountered and learned about Palestinian identity in Israel and the Occupied Territories.

38. See chapter one for a full description of the peace process from 1991-2015.

39. During my tenure of 26 years with ICCI, the organization belonged to two important networks. First, it was part of the Network of Organizations for Arab-Jewish Coexistence, co-sponsored by the Abraham Fund and the Forum for Civic Accord; and later, it was a member of the Peace NGO's Forum, a network of Jewish Israeli and Palestinian Arab organizations on both sides of the "Green Line" (the 1967 border), which remains active to this day (as of June, 2015).

40. Since its founding in 1970, *Religions for Peace* has been guided by the vision of a world in which religious communities cooperate effectively for peace, by taking concrete common action. *Religions for Peace* is the world's largest and most representative multi-religious coalition advancing common action for peace. From the Religions for Peace website: www.religionsforpeace.org.

41. The International Council of Christians and Jews (ICCJ) serves as the umbrella organization of 40 national Jewish-Christian dialogue organizations world-wide. The ICCJ member organizations over the past five decades have been successfully engaged in the historic renewal of Jewish-Christian relations. From the ICCJ website: www.iccj.org.

42. In addition to the production of the documentary film, which was co-directed by Amy Kronish and Eli Talel, a comprehensive study guide was written by Amy Kronish and Elaine Talel, in cooperation with the Institute of Christian and Jewish Studies, in Baltimore, Maryland. The film and subsequent guide have been used by many professors of Jewish-Christian dialogue in their courses.

43. A leading Catholic ecumenical and interreligious organization based in New York, the Graymoor Ecumenical and Interreligious Institute, commissioned me to write a series of three major articles which they published in *Ecumenical Trends* in 2004 and 2005:

- *Forty Years Since The Second Vatican Council:Central Challenges Facing Jewish-Christian Dialogue Today: A Jewish Point of View*, vol. 34, no. 6, June 2005.
- *The Role of Interreligious Dialogue in Peace-building in Israel*, vol. 33, no. 8, Sept 2004.
- *The Historic Visit of the Pope to Israel in March 2000: Jewish Israeli Memories and Hopes*, vol. 33, no. 2, February 2004.

44. I describe the messages and the methods of my dialogue work in chapter four.

45. The exact name of the church is the Evangelical Lutheran Church in Jordan & the Holy Land (ELCJHL). There are five congregations in Jerusalem, Ramallah and the Bethlehem area and one in Amman, Jordan. See www.elcjhl.org.

46. This United Nations resolution was passed in 1975 and revoked in 1991.

47. In the words of our national anthem, *HaTikvah,* Hope.

48. On Israel Independence Day 2015, Israel's population stood at a record 8,345,000. The Jewish population makes up 6,251,000 (74.9%); 1,730,000 (20.7%) are Arabs; those identified as "others" (non-Arab Christians, Baha'i, etc) amount to 364,000 people (4.4%). When the state was established, there were only 806,000 residents and the total population reached its first and second million in 1949 and 1958 respectively. https://www.jewishvirtuallibrary.org. These numbers include Jews who live in the West Bank and East Jerusalem, but does not include Palestinians who live there without citizenship.

49. *Tractate Independence* was published in an experimental edition by Rabbis for Human Rights in 2008. This document is used in courses on Judaism and human rights taught by educators from Rabbis for Human Rights at universities and other settings in Israel.

Chapter One

The Context—
Peacemaking and Peacebuilding

INTRODUCTION

Interreligious dialogue is dependent on the context of the community or country or region in which it takes place. Accordingly, dialogue in countries like the USA or England, or most Western countries, is part of "community relations" since there is not an ongoing national conflict taking place in those countries between two nation states. In contrast, the clash between Israel and Palestine is very different since we are still in the midst of an ongoing, unresolved conflict. The so-called Israeli-Palestinian "peace process" has in fact been stalled for many years and the conflict is no closer to being resolved now than over the past two decades. This has created a feeling of political despair on both sides of the conflict, which has negatively influenced the mood of the people and decreased their motivation to engagement in dialogue of any kind.

This chapter provides the context in which I have engaged in dialogue in Israel and Palestine during the past twenty-five years. It is divided into three main sections:

1. The recent history of the so-called "peace process"—since negotiations between Palestinian and Israeli diplomats in Madrid in the early 1990s until 2017, with clear implications for people like myself who have been involved in interreligious and intercultural dialogue as part of peacebuilding processes in the region.
2. Clarifying the differences between "peacemaking" and "peacebuilding", with a focus on the goals, objectives and methods of each, and of the interlocking relationships between them.

3. Background information on the political/security context concerning the situation of Arab-Jewish coexistence within the state of Israel. It is important to note that my work in interreligious dialogue and education during the past 25 years has focused largely on Israeli Jews and Palestinian Arabs who hold Israeli citizenship. This is very different from working with Palestinians who live in East Jerusalem or the West Bank or Gaza, who are not citizens of Israel and who do not share the same hopes of integration as citizens of Israel. This chapter therefore also provides the background to my second chapter of this book, which discusses Palestinian identity in detail, both within Israel and within the Territories (or the "Occupied Territories" or the "Disputed Territories" or "Judea and Samaria").

A RECENT HISTORY OF THE PEACE PROCESS — FROM MADRID TO THE CURRENT DAY

The International Peace Conference in Madrid, 1991

The peace process between the state of Israel and the Palestinians began in 1991, with the International Peace Conference in Madrid. The Prime Minister of Israel at that time, Yitzhak Shamir of the right-wing Likud party, under pressure from the U.S. government led by President George Bush senior and Secretary of State James Baker, formally agreed to give the process a go, even though he was not fully committed to it and probably thought that it would go nowhere. As an intransigent leader, he generally preferred stalling than to making real progress towards peace.

After a ceremonial opening, the Madrid Conference adjourned into separate bilateral negotiations between Israel and the Syrian, Lebanese, and joint Jordanian-Palestinian delegations. Negotiations quickly broke down on each front, but a start had been made.

The Oslo Accords, September, 1993

The real dramatic change took place in 1993, with the Oslo Accords. For ten months during that year, secret negotiations took place in and around Oslo, therefore the name of these agreements. This was before "wiki-leaks" and the pervasive presence of the internet and social media; one could actually keep a diplomatic secret back in those days! In June, 1992 head of the Israel Labor party Yitzhak Rabin had been elected Prime Minister, running on an "Israel waits for Rabin", ticket i.e. only he could make peace from a position of strength. But little did the Israeli public know about what was to occur in the Rabin administration during the next few years. In fact, Rabin did not begin his second premiership with a peace process with the Palestinians in mind, but was convinced by Shimon Peres (then Foreign Minister) and Yossi Beilin (deputy Foreign Minister) to pursue the back channel off-the-record secret track which became known as the Oslo Accords. [1]

The Oslo Accords in 1993 changed the nature of the Israeli-Palestinian conflict permanently. This is a fact, whether one agrees or disagrees with the goals of this process. In fact, I would say that the Oslo Accords changed the course of history in the Middle East. When they were promulgated, they offered great hope to the people in the region for the possibility of *peaceful* coexistence, which had been inconceivable prior to this dramatic breakthrough.

The first principle of the Oslo Accords can be called *mutual recognition*. For the first time in the history of the Palestinian-Israeli conflict, the Palestinians and the Israeli leadership agreed to recognize each other's existence in an official and public manner. Prior to this, it was against the law in Israel to even talk to a member of the PLO, and the PLO referred to Israel as "The Zionist entity" rather than the state of Israel. This all changed suddenly when on September 13, 1993, Prime Minister Rabin and PLO leader Arafat signed the "Declaration of Principles", which followed upon the ten months of back channel dialogue in and around Oslo.

The role of the Norwegians was critical. They hosted 5 rounds of off-the-record dialogue between representatives of Israel and the PLO from January 1993 through May of that year. These dialogues took place under the guise of academic conferences. The Israeli side was led by Prof. Yair Hirschfeld of Haifa University and Dr. Ron Pundak, who was an academic at the Truman Institute for Peace of the Hebrew University in Jerusalem at that time and later became the director of the Peres Peace Center in Tel Aviv, as well as the founder of the Peace NGOs forum (of which I was a member for many years and through which I got to know and appreciate Pundak's persistent pursuit of peace.) On the Palestinian side, they were led by Ahmad Qurei (Abu Alaa), who was one of the leaders of the PLO, and Hassan Asfour, who reported back to Mahmud Abbas (Abu Mazen).

The Norwegian husband and wife team of Terje and Jull Larsen stressed the need to create an informal atmosphere during the talks and used a variety of means to achieve that end, including having the two sides share meals. [2] In this way, the talks were similar to what I call "dialogue" and less like formal negotiations. The couple was also active in ensuring that the talks were discrete and that the atmosphere was conducive to serious discussion. The sense of trust they fostered allowed the two sides to reach an historic statement of principles.

There were a few other main principles of the Oslo Accords that are worth remembering, for our discussion here. The second main principle—which sounded completely revolutionary at the time—was that the conflict would be resolved *by negotiation and not by war*. In his famous speech at the signing of the agreement on the White House lawn on September 13, 1993—a day on which I and many Israelis cried for joy—Prime Minister Rabin said:

> We have come to try and put an end to the hostilities, so that our children, our children's children, will no longer experience the painful cost of war, violence and terror. We have come to secure their lives and to ease the sorrow and the painful memories of the past to hope and pray for peace.
>
> Let me say to you, the Palestinians: We are destined to live together on the same soil, in the same land. We, the soldiers who have returned from battle stained with blood, we who have seen our relatives and friends killed before our eyes, we who have attended their funerals and cannot look into the eyes of their parents, we who have come from a land where parents bury their children, we who have fought against you, the Palestinians.
>
> We say to you today in a loud and a clear voice: Enough of blood and tears. Enough. We have no desire for revenge. We harbor no hatred towards you. We, like you, are people who want to build a home, to plant a tree, to love, to live side by side with you in dignity, in empathy, as human beings, as free men. We are today giving peace a chance, and saying again to you: Enough. Let us pray that a day will come when we all will say: Farewell to the arms.[3]

I well remember the euphoria in Israel after the signing of this peace accord—the Declaration of Principles—on the White House lawn. In fact, I wrote an article in September of that year for a Jewish newspaper in the USA in which I talked about this euphoria[4]. However, this great hope for peace and the end of war between Israelis and Palestinians was not to become a reality. So many rejectionists—on both the Israeli side and the Palestinian side of the conflict—have preferred war and violence to peace for all these years since the signing of the Oslo Accords. What a pity.

The third main principle of the Israeli-PLO Declaration of Principles is *territorial compromise*. It was understood then—as it should be now—that neither side to the conflict can have everything that they want and that each side will have to make painful compromises for the sake of peace. The first article of the agreements, which discussed the aim of the negotiations to follow (during the next five years!), referred back to UN Security Council Resolutions 242 and 338 which explicitly called for territorial compromise.[5]

The fourth main principle was the hope to achieve *historic reconciliation* through the *political peace process*. In other words, not only does the Declaration call for an end to "decades of conflict and for each side to recognize the mutual and political rights, and to strive to live in peaceful coexistence and mutual dignity and security" and for both parties to "achieve a just, lasting and comprehensive peace settlement" but it calls on them to reach an "historic reconciliation through the agreed political process."[6]

I was not aware that the Declaration of Principles called for reconciliation until I went to the source. After reading this historic document, it became clear to me how far-reaching and optimistic it really was, and at the same time how distant it was from the psycho-social reality of both peoples on the ground, who apparently were not really ready for such far-reaching changes so quickly. This was a peace of the elites, as one of the main negotiators referred to it after the fact. In a detailed memoir about the negotiations with the Palestinians that led to the Oslo Accords, Uri Savir, a former director-general of Israel's Ministry of Foreign Affairs who was intensely involved in these talks wrote: "The greatest weakness of the three-year negotiation effort was that its messages did not filter down enough to the people."[7]

In addition, I would argue that whether one likes the Oslo Accords or not, or whether one agrees with them or not, the main principles of this declaration remain the underlying foundations of the political peace process of the last 25 years. In my view, there is no question that these accords represented an amazing historic breakthrough, certainly at the time, and I would hope also for now and for the future.

Agreement with the Vatican, 1993

Three months after the Oslo Accords, another historic agreement was signed. According to the papal nuncio at that time, Msgr. Pietro Sambi, who served as ambassador to Israel for eight years and whom I worked with closely during all of these years, "The Fundamental Agreement between the State of Israel and the Holy See"[8] could only have taken place as a result of the political process initiated by the Oslo Accords.[9] He explained that the Holy See could not establish relations with any one of them until there was recognition between the three peoples of the region—Israel, the Palestinians and Jordan.

The fact that the Vatican decided officially to recognize the state of Israel on December 30, 1993, is no small matter. For many years, Jews who were active in official and in unofficial dialogue (including myself), prodded the Vatican to take this step, but it took the Oslo Accords to make it happen! It was another important milestone in the political peace process of the 1990s, one that is usually overlooked by many people who write about the historical developments of this decade and who all too often ignore the role of religion and religious institutions in the political peace process.

Peace with Jordan, October, 1994

On October 26, 1994, the state of Israel which was still headed by Prime Minister Rabin who was seriously committed to the process, signed another peace agreement, this time with its neighbor to the east, the Hashemite Kingdom of Jordan, in the presence of President Bill Clinton, who had orchestrated the signing of the Oslo Accords a year earlier in Washington DC. This time, the agreement was signed in the region, at the Arava crossing point, in the south of Israel and Jordan. This important peace treaty followed a public declaration in Washington DC on July 24, 1994, in which both sides agreed to end the state of belligerency between their two countries.[10]

Achieving peace with Jordan—a country with a very long border with Israel and with a history of violent conflict going back to the 1948 War—was another important step on the road to peace. It was evidence of very strong political momentum at that time, under the Clinton administration, which was keenly interested in solving the Israeli-Palestinian conflict. Indeed, as we will see later, President Clinton spent a great amount of time during his two terms as President of the United States of America in trying to achieve a comprehensive peace agreement between Israel and the Palestinians.

The first four years of the new decade witnessed amazing progress in the political peace process. Not only was there the Declaration of Principles and a treaty with the Vatican, and one with Jordan, but there was the positive example of the historic peace agreement with Egypt, dating back to 1979[11] (based on the Carter-Begin-Sadat Camp David negotiations from September 5-18, 1978). This peace agreement has lasted until this day, even if it is a rather "cold peace" considering that normal relations exist only diplomatically but not for most of the people of both countries.

However, during this period of diplomatic progress, the rejectionists on both sides were very busy all the time. Palestinian groups opposed to the peace process committed many terrorist atrocities, and right-wing Jewish Israelis, who opposed any compromises with the Palestinians and were totally opposed to the peace process, were very active in verbally violent demonstrations filled with much incitement against Prime Minister Rabin and his government. Nevertheless—despite the ongoing violence and counter-attacks and an ugly atmosphere of rejectionist opposition on both sides, the process was moving forward because the leaders at that time—Prime Minister Rabin and Chairman Arafat, who had developed close working relationships in what became known as "the peace of the brave"—were committed to it, and because President Clinton was investing so much time and resources to make it happen.

The Assassination of Prime Minister Rabin, November 1995

The atmosphere of opposition to the peace process could be found on both sides of the conflict, but it was particularly dangerous and inflammatory on the Jewish side. Right-wing groups led a fierce public campaign against this peace process. This included leaders of the center-right Likud party, especially Benjamin Netanyahu, who was virulently opposed to the Oslo Accords, and took an active part in many of the anti-Rabin government demonstrations. The level of incitement was so high and widespread with right-wing elements in Israel that this led to the assassination of Prime Minister Rabin at a peace rally on November 4, 1995 by a Jewish extremist by the name of Yigal Amir, who imbibed many of his anti-peace ideas from his rabbis as well as from ultra nationalist sources.

Many observers say that the assassination of the Israeli prime minister, who took the boldest steps in the history of modern Israel towards resolving the Israeli-Palestinian conflict, was effectively the end of the Oslo Peace Process. I don't agree, but I do feel that it severely damaged the process. The fact is, as we shall see below, that the political peace process continued for the next several years, until summer 2000, under Israeli governments that were led by center-left leaders (Shimon Peres, Ehud Barak) as well as center right ones, Benjamin Netanyahu in his first term as Prime Minister in 1996-1999. Netanyahu defeated Peres in the elections of May 1996, and was defeated by Barak, three years later, in May 1999. In other words, throughout the nineties, when there was political momentum for peace, the leaders continued to persevere in the process—at least formally and largely to please their American and European counterparts—and essentially overruled the rejectionists on both sides, despite the ongoing violence and public opposition by vocal minorities.

The Wye River Memorandum, October, 1998

The next major milestone in the political peace process of the 1990s was the Wye River Memorandum [12] of October 23, 1998, signed by none other than Benjamin Netanyahu, who was the Prime Minister of Israel at the time, and by Yasser Arafat, who was still Chairman of the Palestine Liberation Organization, both of whom were obliging President Clinton by grudgingly cooperating in the official peace process led by the American government. Not too much happened that was new in this agreement, except for a rearrangement of control of areas in and around Hebron, but the important point to stress here is that the peace process was moving forward, and that President Clinton even managed to get Benjamin Netanyahu to agree to the process, even though he had been one of the most bitter enemies opposing the Oslo Accords earlier in the same decade. Netanyahu not only continued the process, but viewed Arafat as the official representative of the Palestinian people, with whom he needed to negotiate a peace treaty. Indeed, he actually lifted a pen and signed a diplomatic accord with the Palestinians, something which most of his followers would not have predicted, and something which he could have done in his later terms in office (March 2009-2017,) if he had only mustered the will to do so.

Camp David II—its failure and the beginning of the demise of the peace process

President Bill Clinton had spent much of his foreign policy time during his two terms in office from 1992-2000 trying relentlessly to resolve the Israeli-Palestinian conflict. By the time he reached his last year in office, he was still intent on finishing the job and so he summoned the leaders of Israel and

Palestine to the official retreat center of the White House in the hills of Maryland for what has become known as "Camp David II".[13] This was a desperate last chance move by him, one that he thought could work, especially given the change of leadership in Israel.

In May, 1999, Netanyahu lost the Israeli elections, in a landslide, to the Labor Party, led by Ehud Barak, who followed in the tradition of Yitzhak Rabin; he was a widely respected military man and he was presumably now ready to devote himself to making peace. The election was very much a referendum on the peace process, and the election of Barak meant that the Israeli public was in favor of continuing the process, especially since they elected another leader with a strong security background, which meant that Barak would not take any risks which would endanger Israel's security situation. When Clinton summoned Barak to come to Camp David II for talks with the Palestinian leadership in July 2000 (the talks went on from July 11-24, 2000), Barak was eager to go since he saw this as a real opportunity to conclude an historic deal with the Palestinians and he thought that Arafat was a serious partner. After all, it had been nearly seven years since the signing of the Oslo Accords—which had laid out a five-year time period for resolving all the outstanding major issues of the conflict, and it was time finally to get the job done. Moreover, there was a sitting American president who was passionately committed to making this a reality.

Moreover, Barak was known to be a very smart and self-confident individual (who played the piano and made watches!) and he apparently thought that he and his team of advisors had real answers to all the core issues of the conflict, including borders, Jerusalem, refugees, etc. Much work had been done by government officials and many think tanks during the previous seven years; Barak, the Israeli public and the Israeli media were confident of a positive outcome. One front-page headline in an Israeli newspaper boldly announced: "End of Conflict in Sight!"

As a result, many people, including myself, felt at that time that we had been climbing the mountain of the peace process throughout the nineties and that we were now at the peak of the mountain, and were ready to ascend to finish the climb. With a fresh new leader at the helm, who seemed well motivated and sincerely committed to the task, it seemed that a final status peace agreement between the state of Israel and the Palestinian Authority was in the offing, despite the persistent negativity and violence of the rejectionist camps on both the Israeli and Palestinian sides of the divide. Both sides hoped—apparently naively—that the leaderships were going to Camp David with the sincere intention of emerging with a historical agreement to the mutual benefit of both the people of Israel and the Palestinian people.

But it turned out that I and many other hopeful people in Israel were wrong. Despite the unceasing efforts of President Clinton and his staff, the Camp David talks failed to bridge the gaps between the two sides. I remember vividly a scene—broadcast widely on television and on the internet—in which President Clinton was seen pushing both Arafat and Barak back into a doorway and saying to them something along of lines of "let's give it one more try". And try, they did, for a few more days, but in the end, an agreement tragically was not reached. After this, the blame game began in all earnest. Each side, of course, blamed the other side for the failure of the talks. It was like a divorce. Each side felt that all truth and history was on their side, and that the inability to reach an agreement was clearly the fault of the other leader (and his team). According to the Palestinian narrative, the whole thing was a set-up since the most that Israel was willing to do was to divide the West Bank into "cantons". According to the mainstream Israeli narrative, Arafat came to Camp David without any real desire to reach an agreement, and rejected Israel's generous offer out of hand.

This blame game has persisted until this day. There is very little self-criticism on the part of the leadership of either side. Both sides seem to love posturing and blaming the other, rather than getting anything done. Both leaderships seem to have completely forgotten that territorial compromise—or just plain compromise—is the essential ingredient for reaching an agreement.

To sum up the decade of the nineties, I can say that it was the decade of the political peace process between Israel and the Palestinians. It began with an international conference which set the stage, but its main steps forward were developed during the back channel talks for 10 months in Norway, which created enough trust among Palestinian and Israeli negotiators at that time, that they were able to issue the historic Declaration of Principles on September 13, 1993. This declaration changed the situation on the ground fundamentally in Israel and Palestine, at that time and probably forever. Furthermore, despite the frequent changes in leadership on the Israeli side, and along with the phlegmatic leadership of Yasser Arafat during this whole decade on the Palestinian side, there was momentum in the peace process throughout the nineties, until the summer of 2000. This all ended with the failure of the Camp David Summit in July of that year, which brought the peace process to a grinding halt, and laid the foundations for the Second Intifada (uprising) and the ongoing cyclical violence of the next period.

The War Process replaces the Peace Process

As one can see from the appendix at the end of this chapter, it has all been downhill since the failure of the Camp David Summit of July 2000. This is why I have decided to call this period the "war process", since all attempts to restart the political peace process by various American presidents and the international community have led nowhere. Instead, we have witnessed one war with Lebanon and three mini-wars with Gaza, and ongoing cyclical terror by Palestinians and counter-terror by Israelis.

The Second Intifada and the building of the Security Fence/ Separation Wall

It all began with the completely unnecessary visit by Ariel Sharon—at that time a member of Knesset from the Likud party—to the Temple Mount / Haram al-Sharif on September 28, 2000, about two months after the failure of the Camp David talks. According to reports, Sharon called his old friend from the army, Prime Minister Barak, and asked if he could take a stroll on the Temple Mount. The rest is history.

On that very day, the Second Intifada (Arabic for "shaking off" the occupation) began. The First Intifada had begun in the late 1980s and continued through September 1991 (the Madrid Conference) or until September 1993 (the Oslo Accords), depending on one's point of view. In contrast to the first, which was characterized by slingshots and stabbings of soldiers and settlers in the West Bank and Gaza, the second was characterized by suicide bombings and the killing of Israeli civilians, usually in the name of the God of Radical Islam. In response, Israel took extreme "counter-terrorism" measures in the areas of the West Bank and Gaza. This uprising was much more violent, and much more serious, and it went on for several years, until at least 2004, or maybe even until 2005 (depending on whom you ask), causing severe existential despair and depression on both sides of the conflict, and probably also extensive post-traumatic stress, which affects the lack of progress toward peace until this very day.

The blame game continued. The official Israeli narrative accused Arafat and his henchmen of planning the uprising well before Sharon's visit to the Temple Mount. The Palestinian leadership continued to blame everything on the Israeli "Occupation", which it saw as the root of all evil, and naively repeated *ad nauseum* that if only the occupation would end, then everything would be fine, which they knew was not true. The Palestinian leadership continued to have their own serious problems with Islamic radical groups, especially Hamas, which rejected the peace process and negated any compromise with the state of Israel.

In the middle of this second uprising, there was a change of leadership; Ehud Barak lost the elections to Ariel Sharon's "centrist" Kadima party. During the first year of his term in office, Sharon ordered a military invasion known as "Defensive Shield", after an intensive month of suicide bombings in March 2000. (I was almost blown up in one of them, at Café Cafit in the German Colony of Jerusalem, but together with four other rabbis and two of their wives, we were saved by a miracle.) In the second year of his term, Sharon faced increasing pressure by the people and by other politicians to do something drastic to prevent suicide bombers from easily entering Israel from the West Bank to inflict terrible tragedies upon innocent civilians day after day. He consulted with experts in the Israel Defense Forces and they came up with a radical idea which they were convinced would work. Their idea was to build a "security fence" separating Israel from the West Bank and some parts of East Jerusalem, which would keep suicide bombers from crossing into Israel.

I first went on a tour of the route of the fence sometime in 2002 with a group of rabbis from the U.S.A, who were visiting Israel on a study tour. The person in the army responsible for designing and building this "fence" told us that it was going to be 96% fence and 4% wall, and that when peace came, it would be taken down! Many years later, in 2013, I went on another study tour with the same person, who was now retired, who still insisted that this security fence/wall was a temporary security measure and would be taken down when there is a peace agreement.

By now the security fence, or the separation wall, as the Palestinians prefer to call it, has become permanent. From my perspective, it also became the symbol of the new era. As opposed to peace and normal relations between two political entities, which were the goals of the peace process in the nineties, separation was considered the best that could be done for the time being. It became the new model for "coexistence". The idea was that the Palestinians should live in their towns and villages in a separate existence, not only from the state of Israel, but also from the hundreds of thousands of Jewish settlers who were living in the Territories, i.e. the West Bank and Gaza. As long as they would behave themselves by not committing terrorist acts against Israel, and by not shooting *kassam* missiles from Gaza against innocent Israeli civilians, then Israel would not do any harm to Palestinian communities. This was the security logic of the Fence/Wall. It was more of an armistice than actual peace.

Peace was abandoned as a goal because neither side thought an agreement could be reached. During Ariel Sharon's term as prime minister, Arafat and the Palestinian leadership were still branded as the arch enemies of Israel, and therefore there was no point in negotiating with them, since they were considered to not be serious about reaching an agreement. On the Palestinian side, there was also the same feeling. According to their leadership, there was no point in negotiating with the Israeli leadership, who only continued to crush their uprising and who had no plans to end the occupation of their lands, which they saw as "state terrorism" and as a form of continual oppression which made negotiations futile.

Accordingly, as a result of this Second Intifada, both sides became increasingly intransigent. The level of mutual fear and mistrust grew exponentially in those years, such that there was no real willingness to make the painful compromises that would have been necessary to have serious negotiations for peace. As a result, the government of Israel, under the leadership of Ariel Sharon, did not see any point in trying to negotiate with the Palestinian leadership at that time; rather, he and his colleagues came up with a new idea, which they thought could break the deadlock between the two sides.

Israeli Unilateral Disengagement from Gaza, 2005

In 2003, the Israeli leadership came up with what seemed at first a creative and bold new idea: unilateral withdrawal of all 8000 settlers, as well as all Israeli soldiers, from the Gaza Strip, and the withdrawal from four settlements in the northern West Bank. Sharon and his colleagues, especially Ehud Olmert (who succeeded him after he had a stroke in January 2006) conceived and implemented this move. This radical idea garnered the support of most of the Israeli public, with the exception of a vocal religious and nationalist minority of Jews in Israel who resisted it until the day it actually happened. Many of the extreme religious Zionist settlers actually believed until the end that God would not let this happen!

After many months of public debate and intensive preparations, the disengagement actually took place between August 15-September 11, 2005. Most people in Israel were happy to leave Gaza since it was a huge headache for many years, with such a large and growing Palestinian population which made the life of the small number of settlers in the strip very difficult, not to mention the huge expense of protecting them with large numbers of soldiers. Some groups opposed it vociferously and wore orange clothes or ribbons to show their opposition for many months. Other groups, especially the left-wing Meretz party, objected to the unilateral disengagement not because they wanted the military occupation to continue, but because they felt that only a mutually agreed upon withdrawal, negotiated in good faith with the Palestinian leadership, could prevent future disaster. As a result, a great division was created within Israeli society for many months. The unilateral withdrawal was followed by the takeover of Gaza by the extreme Hamas movement, which was fundamentally opposed to peace negotiations with what they referred to as the Zionist entity.

The official position of Sharon and his government was that if this experiment went well, they would withdraw from more and more of the West Bank. This was meant to be an incentive to the Palestinian leadership to ensure that the Gaza Strip would not become a terrorist-controlled entity. Later, reports in the media suggested that Sharon and his peers knew very well that Gaza would be taken over by radical Islamic groups and that no further disengagement from Palestinian areas would be possible.

Whether one accepts this theory or not, the fact is that the unilateral withdrawal from Gaza turned out to be a colossal failure in the minds of most Israelis during the years following this event. After the coup by Hamas against the Fatah leadership in Gaza in June 2007, and the emergence of Gaza as "Hamastan" with continual military support from Iran and from Hezbollah and other rejectionist groups, the Israeli leadership and the Israeli people realized, to their sorrow, that the experiment had failed. Not only did it not lead to a situation of peace between Israel and Gaza, but the exact opposite happened. Instead of peace, Israel ended up embroiled in three mini-wars with Gaza.[14] The Israeli mainstream viewed these operations as acts of defense designed to protect the lives of Israeli citizens threatened by *kassam* missile bombardments at first in the south and later all over Israel.

The Palestinians who lived in Gaza had a very different narrative. They saw Israel's so-called "defensive" move as just another form of occupation. Instead of soldiers on the ground in Gaza, there was complete control of Gaza from the outside, which the Palestinians viewed as a "siege". Until the siege would be lifted—and normal economic life in Gaza could return—they argued, "resistance" to the enemy would continue. In addition to blocking the coastline of Gaza, which caused severe economic hardship, Israel also prevented the development of a port stipulated in the Oslo Accords. Moreover, the Palestinian leadership constantly accused the Israel government of massacres and disproportionality since many more Palestinians were killed or wounded in these military operations, which Israel always referred to as "self-defense".

The Second Lebanon War, summer 2006

In addition to all these mini-wars between Gaza and Israel, there was also a major war against Hezbollah in Lebanon during the summer of 2006, under the leadership of Prime Minister Ehud Olmert. This war, which became known as the Second Lebanon War (the first one began in 1982 and lasted until 2000 when Israel pulled out of Lebanon), was against another Islamic rejectionist group, this time in the north. Like Hamas, Hezbollah saw the state of Israel as an illegitimate state, and rejected the idea of negotiating with this state about any kind of peace agreement. Supported too by Iran, Hezbollah only sought the destruction of Israel, and it was a powerful group within Lebanese society.

This war was highly unpopular in Israel as it dragged on for too long, with no clear purpose and since many Israeli soldiers were killed unnecessarily, especially towards the end of the war. It was another unfortunate milestone in what I am calling the "War Process", instead of the Peace Process. It succeeded in giving much of northern Israel a taste of existential threat, with hundreds of missiles from Lebanon raining down on towns and villages for several weeks. This only added to the sense of victimization and fear, already prevalent within Israeli society, which only lowered any interest upon the part of the public in Israel in returning to serious peace negotiations with the Palestinians, who were once again seen as being in bed with the enemies of Israel (including Hezbollah, Hamas, Syria, Iran, etc) rather than as a potential partner for peace.

The "Peace Process" limps on

Despite all the wars and violence, the international community, and especially the United States, continued to push, off and on, for a return to negotiations for peace between the state of Israel and the administration of the Palestinian Authority. However, all of the efforts from 2000-2017 by successive American presidents and the "Quartet" led nowhere. (The Middle East Quartet mediates the peace process. It is made up of the United Nations, the United States, the European Union, and Russia.)

- President Bill Clinton kept trying, until his last days as president in the year 2000, to seal a deal, but only got as far as establishing what are now known as "the Clinton parameters"[15], which were the last major statement of what the outlines of a peace agreement between Israel and the Palestinians might look like.
- President George W. Bush gathered the parties together in Annapolis, Maryland, on April 30, 2003, and called the ensuing declaration "The Road Map". This old/new plan, developed by the United States, in cooperation with the Quartet, was presented to Israel and the Palestinian Authority. It included clear phases, timelines, and benchmarks and involved reciprocal steps by the two parties in the political, security, economic, and humanitarian realms. However, this plan, which was just another name for the Oslo agreements, didn't succeed in advancing the cause of peace. On the contrary, after this meeting, both sides continued to stall and blame the other, as usual.
- Prime Minister Ehud Olmert held many meetings with President Abbas, the head of the Palestinian Authority, during 2008[16] and according to many commentators in Israel who look back on these days, it was as close as the state of Israel ever got to actually reaching a comprehensive agreement with the Palestinians. Many observers in Israel have conjectured that if Olmert had not been forced to resign due to his corruption scandals, he was the one who was actually ready to sign an historical deal with the Palestinians. In America, this would be called "Monday morning quarterbacking" since no one really knows if the Israeli side or the Palestinian side at that time would have been able to go through with it in actuality, mostly due to internal political opposition in each camp.
- Since the return of the Likud party and its leader Benjamin Netanyahu to power in 2009,[17] there has been mostly lip service and stalling with regard to renewing the political peace process. Despite repeated attempts by the American government led by President Barak Obama and Secretaries of State Hilary Clinton and John Kerry to broker a peace agreement, both sides have totally abandoned any notions of real compromise—one of the major pillars of the Oslo Accords. Each leader simply repeated for several years *ad nauseum* its demands and argued passionately, but not persuasively, why the other party is really the obstinate one.

The strange thing is that both leaderships gave lip service in principle, from time to time, but not all the time (and certainly not when speaking to their own people or their own political parties), to the two-state solution, but neither one of them showed any flexibility or creativity when it came down to the details of how to achieve this. Everyone knows that the devil is in the details.

The lack of any real peace process from 2000-2016—and the rise of what I have called "the war process", with one war and four mini-wars and lots of ongoing violence—led to a situation of political despair. No one seemed to see a way out of the quagmire. No one saw leadership that was ready to make the painful compromises needed to reach a peace agreement. As people on both sides increasingly despaired about the impossibility of reaching an agreement, the mood among both Palestinians and Israelis soured from day to day, week to week, month to month, year to year.

This situation of political despair is undoubtedly related to the fact that scholars of conflict resolution have referred to the Palestinian-Israeli conflict as an "intractable conflict".[18] The Palestinian –Israeli conflict falls under this category since it is characterized by many years, even decades, of failed attempts to achieve breakthroughs to peaceful resolutions. Indeed, one can see this when one examines the characteristics of intractable conflicts—such as "deep-seated identity issues, repeated cycles of violence, perception of the conflict by the protagonists as destructive, internalized long-standing grievances (serving as reasons for continuing the conflict), and institutionalization of the conflict."[19]

This led not only to despair but also to apathy. Why bother to lobby or demonstrate for peace if neither side had the political will to move forward? The so-called "peace camp" on both sides became smaller and smaller, and less influential in public opinion. For years I belonged to a group called "Peace NGO's", which at one time included 50 Israeli and 50 Palestinian NGOs all pursuing peace in one way or another, but over time fewer and fewer groups were involved and they exerted less and less influence on either Israeli or Palestinian society. People on both sides forgot completely about the euphoria and the high hopes for peace of the Oslo Process and began to talk a lot about a "one state solution", which, as far as I could tell, was just a statement about the frustration of the lack of progress of the two-state plan, rather than a real operational plan that would make the situation better.

As can be seen on the appendix at the end of this chapter, we have clearly gone downhill continuously since summer 2000, which saw the failure of the Camp David Summit and the beginning of the Second Intifada, and we are continually warned that things could get even worse. We could see a third even more violent intifada and a more violent counter attack by Israel, or we could see the whole region embroiled in a very dangerous religious war, if Jewish "religious" extremists were actually successful in carrying out any terrorist actions on Temple Mount (which the Muslims call Al-Haram al Sharif, one of their most holy sites). In short, this is the political and security context in which those of us involved in interreligious and intercultural dialogue found ourselves from 1991-2017.

We moved from the high hopes and the great euphoria of the peace process of the 1990s to the dashed hopes and political despair of the first decade and a half of the twenty-first century. Naturally, all of these developments—as they unfolded—influenced our ability and our motivation to enter into dialogue. In the good ol' days of the 1990s, there was much greater interest and motivation to be in dialogue with the "Other" since it seemed that our political leaders were on the road to reaching an historical agreement which could lead to an historic reconciliation process between our two peoples, the Jewish people and the Palestinian people. In contrast, in the war years since 2000, there has been much less motivation to enter into dialogue, and those who did engage in peace-building processes through interreligious and intercultural dialogue found the process much more difficult and challenging (see chapter four).

PEACEMAKING AND PEACEBUILDING

Since I have now brought in the concept of peacebuilding, I want to draw an important distinction between peacemaking activities and peacebuilding programs. This will help us understand what the purpose of interreligious dialogue is and should be in our particular political/security/peace context in Israel and Palestine in the second decade of the twenty-first century.

Peacemaking is the work of the lawyers, politicians and diplomats. The goal of those who engage in such work is to create peace treaties between governments, what one can call "pieces of paper". Professionals who do this work are usually trained in legal studies or international relations. While acknowledging the importance of these political/diplomatic processes, we need to be mindful of their limitations. They do not solve all the problems of a conflict. Rather, they prepare a legal framework for agreement on principles and practices to resolve the conflict.

Once these documents are prepared and agreements are reached, public ceremonies take place with lots of fanfare, publicity, and photo-opportunities. The signing of the Oslo Accords on the lawn of the White House in Washington D.C. on September 13, 1993, was one example of this. These public signing events are considered "historic" and offer new frameworks and possibilities for living together peacefully in the future for the peoples suffering through an intractable conflict for many years, even many decades.

After the agreements are signed, sealed and delivered, with considerable fanfare and ceremony, both sides spend the next several years, even decades, blaming the other for not living up to its part in the agreement. In the case of the Oslo Accords, this has been true for the past 24 years.

Peacebuilding,[20] on the other hand, is not the work of diplomats or politicians. Rather, it is the work of rabbis, imams, priests, educators, social workers, psychologists, architects and planners, youth workers, women's organizations, and other actors in civil society. It is these people—not the lawyers or the politicians—who bring people together to enter into dialogical and educational processes that are aimed at helping people figure out how to live in peace with each other. These processes—which are sometimes called "track two diplomacy" or simply "people-to-people programs"—involve long-term psychological, educational and spiritual transformation.[21]

There is, of course, a close connection between peace-making and peace-building processes. When there is momentum in the political realm—as there was in the 1990s with the Oslo Accords (1993), followed by the Fundamental Agreement between Israel and the Holy See (1993), the peace treaty between Israel and Jordan (1994) and the Wye River Agreement (1998)—then the existential and immediate need for people-to-people programs is more obvious and clear. Conversely, when there is a nearly total freeze in political progress, as has been the case in Israel/Palestine since the year 2000, with the exception of the efforts under Prime Minister Ehud Olmert to negotiate in good faith with the Palestinians, then the existential need for peace-building programs is perceived to be more distant and difficult.

Nevertheless, as I will demonstrate in subsequent chapters of this book, I believe strongly in the importance of peace-building programs—such as interreligious dialogue, education and action—even when the political peace processes are hardly functioning. These programs keep a flicker of hope alive in an ongoing conflict. They point the way to the future. They remind us that the goal of peace is normal relations, not separation. They train people for the possibilities of peaceful coexistence for the future, even if this is not the reality of the present moment.

One more theoretical note is in order here. The work that I have done for the past twenty-five years in interreligious dialogue, education and action is part of a growing field in the world known as "Religions and Conflict Resolution"[22]. The idea is that religions, i.e. their leaders and followers, can and ought to do their part to help resolve conflicts in various parts of the world, instead of only promoting extremist religious or nationalist doctrines.

Yet, in recent years, there has been much less focus on "resolution" (the word is hardly used any more) and much more focus on conflict mitigation, management or transformation. Indeed, the government of the United States began a program several years ago under USAID which it calls "Conflict Mitigation and Management (CMM)."[23] According to the USAID Guidelines:

Mitigating, managing, and responding to violent conflict are priority areas for
USAID assistance. This policy defines conflict mitigation as activities that
seek to reduce the threat of violent conflict by promoting peaceful resolution
of differences, reducing violence if it has already broken out, or establishing a
framework for peace and reconciliation in an ongoing conflict.

In other words, those who engage in peace-building programs are no
longer expected to solve the macro-political conflict. But, if they can reduce
hatred and violence, then they will be accomplishing something, at least in
the short-term.

Moreover, conflicts can be "transformed" from a violent phase to an
educational/social phase—as in the cases of Northern Ireland and South Africa—where the bloodshed has ended and all that needs to be done is to
overcome hundreds of years of hatred and separation! We in Israel/Palestine
will be happy to reach this stage, the sooner the better, in which the war will
have ended and we will be able to focus all of our societal energies on
educational, spiritual, and psychological transformation. But even though we
are not there yet, we need to begin wherever possible to bring people together
to experience and learn about the possibilities and benefits of living together
in the same country or same region.

As I argue in chapter five of this book, Interreligious dialogue, education
and common action is and will be needed more than ever before. There is an
existential need for a massive religious, spiritual, educational, and psychological campaign to change the hearts and minds of the people on both sides
of the conflict.

THE ADDITIONAL CONTEXT OF ARAB-JEWISH COEXISTENCE
WITHIN THE STATE OF ISRAEL

As part of the context for interreligious dialogue in Israel, it is also important
to discuss the historical and contemporary situation of "Arab-Jewish coexistence" within the state of Israel. This background is necessary since much of
the dialogue between Palestinian Arabs and Israeli Jews has taken place with
Palestinian Arabs who are citizens of the state of Israel.

Since the beginning of the state of Israel in 1948, there has been an Arab
minority living within the Jewish state. During and after the War of Independence, about 750,000 Arabs who had lived in what was to become the state
of Israel, fled the country (or were forced to flee), leaving about 156,000
Arabs[24] within the state of Israel (which represented about 12.5% of the new
state's population)[25]. For the first 18 years of the new state (1948-1966), this
Arab minority population lived under military rule, i.e. they could not move
freely within the state of Israel, since they were considered to be security

risks or part of a "fifth column" supporting those Arabs outside of Israel who sought the destruction of the Jewish state.

For most of this period, the Palestinian Arabs of Israel were called "Israeli Arabs" by the ruling powers in Israel. Their Palestinian identity was sublimated. But after the Six Day War in 1967—which created hundreds of thousands of refugees who settled in the nearby Arab states of Jordan, Syria and Lebanon, and in many Western countries—and with the rise of the Palestine Liberation Organization in the late 1960s, most Israeli Arabs also consider themselves to be "Palestinians" in that they see themselves tied to the history and hopes of the Palestinian people. Indeed, many of them have brothers, sisters, parents and cousins who live in the West Bank, Jordan, Gaza, Lebanon or Syria. In addition, many of the Palestinians who remained in Israel were displaced from their original towns and villages and became "internal refugees." and their lives were often defined by trauma, loss and tragedy.

In general, the Arab minority in Israel has lived for most of the past 69 years in some form of "coexistence" with the Jewish majority in the state of Israel. "Coexistence" was a term coined for the relations between the Jewish majority and the Arab minority within Israel. I feel that it is an unsatisfactory definition of the relationships between Jews and Arabs within Israel, but in fact it is much better than war or armed conflict, as is the case between Palestinian Arabs and the state of Israel within the West Bank or between Palestinians in Gaza and the state of Israel. What is implied by the term "coexistence"? I think that it means that one group lives over there—in their own communities—and the other group lives over here—in their own communities—and they don't kill each other! Given the reality in the West Bank –and in much of the Middle East—this is not bad. But is it enough?

I don't think so. The term is too neutral. What is needed, as I will argue in much of the rest of this book, is far more than mere "coexistence". What is necessary is mutual understanding and respect, as well as cooperation and constructive engagement, for the betterment of both communities, and for the benefit of Israeli society as a whole.

In recent years, the term "coexistence" has been called into question by activists and scholars in the field who argue that it is outdated, just as the notion of "Israeli Arabs" (without any mention of their Palestinian identity) is archaic in the contemporary reality. Other terms, such as "shared citizenship,"[26] have become more prominent in the discourse of those involved in trying to create better relations between the Jewish majority and the Palestinian Arab minority.

Those who don't like the "coexistence" model—particularly Palestinian Arabs of Israeli citizenship—have said to me many times in dialogue sessions that first they (the Israeli Palestinians) have to exist before they can co-exist. This means that the focus of many groups within civil society who are working on this issue has been on ending systematic discrimination and on promoting equality and equal opportunity for Palestinian Arabs in Israel in education, housing, infra-structure and employment, so that their daily existence is improved dramatically, certainly in comparison to the Jewish population. When this is achieved, they argue, then we can talk about "coexistence"!

Perhaps the biggest challenge to the old "coexistence" notion, came in October 2000 after riots in Israeli towns and villages in the wake of rioting in the West Bank and Gaza during the Second Intifada. For years, Israelis had lived under the illusion that "the Palestinian problem" existed only in the West Bank and Gaza. However, after severe rioting for about a week, which led to the killing of 13 Palestinian Arabs of Israeli citizenship by the Israeli security forces, both the Jewish population and the Palestinian Arab population were totally shaken up, and many illusions began to quickly disappear. This is when the term "coexistence" clearly wasn't working and new approaches (and a new terminology) needed to be developed.

Until now, there has never been a genuine systematic attempt by any government of Israel to come to grips with "the Palestinian problem" or how to integrate its Palestinian minority and at the same time allow them to preserve their unique cultural identity within Israel. As far as I can see, it remains an unresolved problem, even probably an intractable issue, since it poses a threat to the very definition of Israel as a Jewish and democratic state. Therefore, the question of how this Jewish state should relate to the Palestinian Arab minority within its midst in a serious, substantive, sensitive and fair way is always in the background of any discussion of the nature of Israeli society, and sooner or later the leaders of Israel will have to come to grips with this issue for the betterment of all of its citizens.

Part of the problem lies with the inability of Israeli leadership to grasp the fact that most Arabs who live in Israel now consider themselves part of the Palestinian people, and that the issue of how to relate to Palestinians within Israel is inextricably related to how to relate to Palestinians everywhere. There is still a great deal of denial around this issue, and many of our political leaders as well as ordinary citizens still prefer to categorize Palestinian citizens of Israel as "Israeli Arabs" or simply as Muslims, implying that they are all part of the enemy camp. This antiquated view is not only unrealistic but also counterproductive to understanding the complexity of the situation in which we live.

Many Palestinian Arabs in Israel whom I have met over the years through my work in interreligious dialogue tell me they have a dilemma since they are often forced to choose between their peoplehood (the Palestinian people) and their nationality (i.e., their citizenship as Israeli).[27] This puts them between a rock and a hard place. Even the most moderate Palestinian Arabs in Israel have in recent years insistently included their identification with the

Palestinian people as part of their identity. This is undoubtedly the result of the growing trend of "Palestinianization" of Israeli Arabs in recent decades.[28]

In short, I would say that the new way to relate to most Arabs who live in Israel is as Palestinian Arabs of Israeli citizenship. In so doing, we Jews should be cognizant about the Palestinian nature of their identity, rather than denying it or burying our heads in the sand or in the past. Accordingly, it should no longer come as a surprise to us that when Palestinians "on the other side", i.e., in the West Bank and Gaza, are involved in mini-wars and other violence with the State of Israel, that Palestinian Arabs of Israeli citizenship react viscerally and emotionally to their suffering. Just as Jews in Israel and around the world are affected both rationally and emotionally when their people suffer from Palestinian terror attacks or any other kind of violence, we should no longer be surprised when the same thing happens to members of the Palestinian people who live in Israel or in their Diaspora.

CONCLUSION

The multiple contexts that I have discussed and analyzed in this chapter help us understand the challenges and obstacles as well as the benefits of interreligious dialogue (which I will discuss in detail in chapter 4).

The peace process—or lack thereof—continues to influence the way that Jews view Palestinians in general, and in particular the way the Jewish majority in Israel has related to the Palestinian Arab minority within its midst. When the peace process flounders or is frozen (from 2000-2017!), people on both sides of the conflict despair and consider peace an impossibility.

It is important for us to keep in mind the difference between peacemaking and peacebuilding. People like myself who are involved in peacebuilding via civil society programs should not be expected to solve the problems of the macro peace process. This was, is and always will be the work of the politicians and diplomats. Their successes and achievements, as well as their failures and delays, continue to shape the context in which we live and work in Israel and Palestine. They create political hope or despair, which is inextricably linked to our ability to enter into and sustain interreligious dialogue successfully over time.

With this context in mind, the next chapter looks in detail at the nature of Palestinian identity within the state of Israel, as well as within the Territories (primarily East Jerusalem and the West Bank), and its implications for more profound dialogue and cooperation with the Jewish people in Israel.

APPENDIX: THE UPS AND DOWNS OF THE PEACE PROCESS

THE PERIOD OF   **THE PERIOD OF**

THE "PEACE PROCESS"   **THE "WAR PROCESS"**

THE 1990s

2000-2017

2000, July 11-24
Camp David II
meetings fail

2000-2003
The Second "Intifada" (Uprising)

1998, Oct. 23
Wye River Memorandum

2002-2006
Building the Security Fence/Separation Wall

1995, November 4
Assassination of
Israeli Prime Minister Yitzhak Rabin

2005, Aug.15-Sept. 12
Disengagement of Israel from the Gaza Strip

2006, July 12-Aug. 11
Second Lebanon War

1994, Oct. 24
Israel-Jordan
Peace Treaty

2008, Dec. 27 – Jan. 18, 2009
Gaza military operation "Cast Lead"

2012, Nov. 14-22
Gaza operation #2 "Pillar of Defense"

1993, Dec. 30
Agreement between
Israel and the Vatican

2014, April
Kerry Diplomatic Initiative Ends after Nine Months

1993, Sept. 13
Oslo Accord
between Israel and the PLO

2014, July 8-Aug. 5
Gaza military operation #3 "Protective Edge"

1991, Oct. 30-Nov.1
Madrid Conference

2015-2017
No wars and no peace talks

Ongoing sporadic violence and counter-violence

NOTES

1. For a full account of how and why the leaders of Israel abandoned their policy of rejecting the Palestinian Liberation Organization (PLO) as a terrorist group bent on Israel's destruction and exchanged it for a diplomatic approach founded on the belief that the PLO and its longtime leader, Yasser Arafat, were essential partners in peacemaking, see David Makovsky, *Making Peace with the PLO—The Rabin's Government's Road to the Oslo Accord.* Westview Press, Boulder, Colorado, 1996, p. 22.

2. Makovsky, *Making Peace with the PLO*, p. 22.

3. *Ibid*, p. 223.

4. *The New Peace Atmosphere in Israel,* in *Palm Beach Jewish Journal South,* Sept. 14, 1993, p. 5A, also appeared in the *Dade Jewish Journal,* Sept. 16-22, 1993, p. 5.

5. UN Resolutions 242 and 338 refer to UN Security Council Resolutions that lay the foundation for the Israeli-Palestinian political process, based on territorial compromise and a solution to the problem of Palestinian refugees. The two resolutions were approved by the UN Security Council. Resolution 242 was approved after the 1967 war (November 1967) and Resolution 338 was approved during the 1973 war (October, 1973). These resolutions call for the peaceful resolution of the Arab-Israeli conflict through territorial compromise.

The main points of Resolution 242 (11/67) call for:

* Withdrawal of Israeli armed forces from territories occupied in the 1967 war.
* Termination of the state of belligerency.
* Mutual "acknowledgement of the sovereignty, territorial integrity and political independence of every State in the area, and their right to live in peace within secure and recognized boundaries free from threats or acts of force."
* Achieving a just settlement of the refugee problem.

Resolution 338 (10/73) reiterates the importance of Resolution 242, and calls upon the sides to begin negotiations with the aim of achieving a just and durable peace. www.reut-institute.org.

6. www.israel.org/MFA/ForeignPolicy.

7. Uri Savir, *The Process. 1, 1,000 Days That Changed the Middle East,* New York: Random House, 1998.

8. www.vatican.va.

9. Based on personal discussions with Msgr. Sambi in 2001, in preparation for a film entitled *I am Joseph Your Brother*, produced by the Interreligious Coordinating Council in Israel, that same year.

10. As stated on the Israeli government website (www.mfa.gov.il), the official name of the treaty is "the Treaty of Peace between the State of Israel and the Hashemite Kingdom of Jordan".

11. Sixteen months after Egyptian President Anwar Sadat's visit to Jerusalem, on March 26, 1979, Israel and Egypt signed a peace treaty on the White House lawn.

12. The preamble to the Wye River Memorandum can be found on the website of the Israeli Ministry of Foreign Affairs.

13. Camp David I took place during 13 days from September 4-17, 1978 with President Jimmy Carter, Egyptian President Anwar Sadat and Israeli Prime Minister Menachem Begin, and it led to the peace treaty between Israel and Egypt, signed in Washington DC, on March 26, 1979.

14. Operation "Cast Lead" in December 2008 - January 2009; Operation "Pillar of Defense" in November 2012; Operation "Protective Edge" in July – August 2014.

15. In a last ditch effort to revive the peace process, President Clinton invited Israeli and Palestinian negotiators to Washington for talks. In December 2000, they met for two days separately with American officials. Following this, Israeli Foreign Minister Shlomo Ben-Ami and PA negotiator Saeb Erekat met with President Clinton who presented the sides with his parameters for a final status agreement. www.jewishvirtuallibrary.org.

16. Palestinian Authority President Mahmoud Abbas shed new light on the breakdown of a potentially history-altering round of 2008 peace talks, saying that he rejected an offer from Israel's Ehud Olmert because he was not allowed to study the map, as reported by Josef Federman in *The Times of Israel*, November 19, 2015.

17. Benjamin Netanyahu was sworn in as Prime Minister on March 31, 2009.

18. Galia Golan. *Israeli Peacemaking Since 1967: Factors Behind the Breakthroughs and Failures,* London and New York: Routledge, 2015, chapter one, pp. 1-8.

19. *Ibid,* p. 1. Golan credits Louis Kreisberg and Peter Coleman for suggesting these characteristics of intractable conflicts. See Kreisberg, Louis and Bruce Dayton, *Constructive Conflicts: From Escalation to Resolutions.* Maryland: Rowman and Littlefield, 2011.

20. According to Catherine Morris ("What is Peacebuilding? One Definition", 2000, revised 2013, see www.peacemakers.ca), "The term *peacebuilding* came into widespread use after 1992 when Boutros Boutros-Ghali, then United Nations Secretary-General, announced his Agenda for Peace (Boutros-Ghali, 1992). Since then, *peacebuilding* has become a broadly used but often ill-defined term connoting activities that go beyond crisis intervention such as longer-term development, and building of governance structures and institutions. It includes building the capacity of non-governmental organizations (including religious institutions) for peacemaking and peacebuilding.

21. Peacebuilding involves long-term processes and the transformation of human relationships, according to John Paul Lederach, *Building Peace: Sustainable Reconciliation in Divided Societies,* Washington, DC: United States Institute of Peace Press, 1997, pp. 82-83.

22. See for example the works of Marc Gopin, especially *Holy War, Holy Peace, How Religions can bring Peace to the Middle East,* David R. Smock, editor, *Interfaith Dialogue and Peacebuilding,* and S. Ayse Kadayifci-Orellana, *Interreligious Dialogue and Peacebuilding.*

23. www.usaid.gov.

24. Elan Peleg and Dov Waxman. *Israel's Palestinians: The Conflict Within,* Cambridge University Press, NY, 2011, p. 49.

25. Kimmering and Migdal, *The Palestinian People,* p. 172.

26. For example, the Shared Citizenship Model is based on core concepts developed by the founder of Merhavim, Mike Prashker in 2006. Merhavim is a non-profit educational organization in Israel working to educate all sectors of Israeli society about how to live together in a shared society. www.machon-merhavim.org.il.

27. See Issa Jaber in his article, "Is Arab-Jewish Coexistence in Israel Still Possible", from *Coexistence and Reconciliation in Israel,* Ronald Kronish, ed. Paulist Press, 2015, pp. 160-168.

28. An in-depth analysis of the situation of Palestinian Israelis can be found in Elan Peleg and Dov Waxman's, *Ibid,* p. 27.

Chapter Two

Palestinian Arab Identity— Religious and Cultural Diversity

INTRODUCTION

In my more than two decades of involvement in interreligious and intercultural dialogue with local Palestinians—inside Israel, in East Jerusalem and in the West Bank—I have become intensively acquainted with their complex religious, national, civic and cultural identities, which are more diverse and different than is generally understood in Israel and the Western world. Palestinians—whether Muslim (the majority) or Christian (the minority)—live among the Jews, whether in Israel, within the "Green Line"[1], or in the region. Accordingly, I have come to the conclusion that the Jews of Israel, and beyond, must learn to substantively and sensitively come to understand the identities of their Palestinian Arab neighbors, if we are going to live together, now and in the future.

It is no surprise that the overwhelming majority of Jews in Israel—not to mention both Jews and others from abroad—have never met Palestinian Arabs in any meaningful or substantive way. They know very little about their personal identity, culture, religions, history, or psycho-social situation as a minority group in Israel, and unfortunately often they don't care to know. Ignorance is bliss. Rather, Palestinian Arabs, whether they are Israeli citizens or residents of East Jerusalem, or of "Palestine"[2] (the West Bank and Gaza), are all too often perceived as the "enemy", certainly as long as the Israeli-Palestinian conflict persists. Note that I use the term "Palestine" for the area which the Palestinians control and over which they have quasi-statehood, what is called officially the "Palestinian Authority" or the "Palestinian National Authority", i.e. the West Bank and Gaza. Some Palestinians and the international community also refer to East Jerusalem as part of "Palestine" but this is not yet the case. "Palestine" is also referred to variously as the Territories or the disputed territories, or the Occupied Territories, "the West Bank and Gaza", or "Judea and Samaria."

A very small minority of Israeli Jews have come to know Palestinian Arabs in Israel well. I have come to know them not only through my professional work in interreligious and intercultural dialogue, but also through visiting them in their homes and villages all over Israel, as well as through reading and research. Unfortunately, most Jews and Arabs in Israel live separately and hardly interact with each other. I have found that by transcending boundaries, one can actually get to know one another well. In this chapter, I will discuss their identity, which is a complex and fascinating one.

In addition, I will also describe the identity of Palestinians who are not citizens of Israel, with whom I have interacted over the years, especially the Palestinians of East Jerusalem, many of whom have become my colleagues. Palestinians who are not citizens of Israel—and who live under what they perceive, along with much of the international community and much of the population of Israel (including myself) to be "occupation"—have developed different identities than those in Israel, although they have much in common.

PALESTINIAN ARAB CITIZENS OF ISRAEL

Palestinian Arab citizens of Israel (including East Jerusalem Arabs) make up about 20.7% of the citizens of the state of Israel, according to the latest statistics.[3] In conversations with them over many years, I have learned that they have a four-dimensional identity[4]:

1. They Are Arabs in Terms of Culture.

In their schools and communities they speak and learn in the Arabic language. They feel that they are part of the Arab world, its history and its contemporary struggles. They read Arabic literature, partake of Arabic culture (song, dance, literature, arts), watch Arabic television stations (especially Al Jazeera), and follow events in the Arab world closely, especially in the region of the Middle East, particularly in the countries that border and are very close to Israel (Egypt, Jordan, Lebanon, Syria, and Iraq). In previous decades they were generally referred to by the Israeli establishment as "Israeli Arabs", i.e. they were Arabs living in the state of Israel, without any "Palestinian" identity; but in recent decades, many local Arabs, especially among the younger generation, have added the Palestinian identity element to their Arab identity.

2. They See Themselves as Part of the Palestinian People

Even though they live as citizens in the state of Israel—and want to continue doing so for the foreseeable future—they identify with the struggle and the goals of the Palestinian People in their desire to have a Palestinian state side-by-side with the state of Israel. Moreover, much of their culture is perceived to be not just "Arab" but also "Palestinian", including history, art, dance, music, literature, food and dialect, since they see themselves as indigenous to this land. While most Jews see this as an oxymoron, the Palestinian Arabs of Israel see their complex identity as combining both Palestinian and Israeli elements.[5] This is the result of the "Palestinianization" of Israeli Arabs that has been going on since the Six Day War of 1967 and especially since the Oslo Accords of 1993.[6]

3. They Are Israeli Citizens

As citizens of the state of Israel, they vote in national and local elections (in large numbers!)[7]; they participate in the democracy of the state of Israel through their own political parties and through civil activism via non-governmental organizations. In addition, they send their children to schools which are supervised by Israel's Ministry of Education (through a division called "the Arab sector") and more and more of their children are graduating Israeli high schools and going on to higher education in Israeli universities[8]. Indeed, most of the Palestinians of Israel with whom I have been in dialogue over the past 25 years have at least a B.A., and many have second and third degrees from Israeli or foreign universities.

Moreover, most Palestinian Arab citizens of Israel know Hebrew as a second language. They can read and speak Hebrew well, and when they go to Israeli universities, they write their papers in Hebrew, such that their written Hebrew often surpasses their written Arabic. Many read Israeli newspapers, view Israeli news (and sports!) on Israeli television stations, engage in commerce in Israeli malls and shopping centers, and speak Hebrew to the doctors and nurses in Israeli health care clinics and hospitals, where they also work side-by-side in very high numbers with Jewish Israelis. Also, they travel abroad on Israeli passports.

While there is much divergent opinion on how much they like or enjoy being "Israeli", there is no doubt that they are Israeli citizens who share most of the responsibilities (observing the law, paying taxes, etc.) except for serving in the army, of being a citizen of this state. Despite this, they do not get their fair share of budgets and infrastructure in their towns and cities, and consider themselves treated as "second-class citizens."

4. They Are Religious, Primarily Affiliating with Islam or Christianity

It is amazing to me that over the decades, Palestinian Arabs in Israel have been labeled only as "Arabs", which ignores their religious identity as either Muslim (the majority, including Druse and Circassians, which are offshoots of Islam) or Christian. Indeed, most people in Israel see Arabs only in their ethnic or national identity, and most people have ignored the fact that they are also usually religious.

I would argue that it is impossible to understand Palestinian Arabs in Israel without understanding something about their religious identity. To do so would give an incomplete picture, yet most observers of Arab society in Israel continue to miss this point. Perhaps this is because so many of them are secular and see the world through a secular lens. Or, it may be that they see religion and religious identification as part of the problem and not part of the solution in Israel and the region, so they continue to ignore it and deny its importance.

Much of my work in dialogue with Jews and Arabs in Israel over the past twenty-five years has been devoted to emphasizing this element of Palestinian Arab identity in Israel since it is so often avoided or downplayed. I have learned in my many encounters with Palestinian Arabs that their religious identity is very important to them, whether they are devoutly religious or only moderately observant or even cultural or secular in their outlook. This is perhaps more salient with Muslims than Christians, as I will explain below, but in both cases it is impossible to understand Palestinian Arabs merely in ethnic or national terms.

THE MUSLIM COMMUNITY IN ISRAEL

The overwhelming majority of Palestinian Arabs in Israel are Sunni Muslims.[9] Muslim identity in Israel—like Jewish identity—can roughly be divided into four categories: extremist/fundamentalist, moderately religious, traditional and secular.

Some Muslims in Israel hold fundamentalist religious views of Islam, even though their extremism is only verbally, not physically, violent. According to one Palestinian Muslim observer of Muslim religious behavior in Israel, Dr. Aziz Haidar, a research fellow in sociology at the Van Leer Jerusalem Institute and a lecturer at Al Quds University in East Jerusalem:

> Most Muslims who are 'fanatically' religious are those who perform prayer five times a day, who visit Mecca more than once in a lifetime, and who keep Islamic life in the most traditional way. The women cover their faces and wear long clothes and keep a distance between themselves and others.[10]

The core division between the extremists and the common people is based on strictness of religious observance and attitudes toward the Western world. Religiously extreme Muslim Palestinians who live in Israel are more pious, increasingly strict in religious observance, more traditional in dress, and more immersed in the religion and culture of Islam than non-observant Muslims. This is mostly related to their behavior rather than their theologies, since it seems that they do not have well-developed theologies. I would say that they are more "orthoprax" than "orthodox", i.e. they practice the rituals and customs of their religion even though they do not necessarily have a well-worked out theology or belief system about God.

According to Dr. Haidar, the number of Muslims in Israel who are extremely religious is very small, in fact, no more than 5-7% of the Palestinian Muslim population are extreme in their religious observance and most of them are concentrated in the "Triangle" area[11] in central Israel, northeast of Tel Aviv.[12] As we will see, the Islamic Movement (discussed below) did not succeed in engendering a real religious revival among Muslims in Israel or in returning Muslims in large numbers to a fully religious Muslim way of life.[13]

The Islamic Movement

Although Islam is basically a religion and not a political movement, the Islamic Movement in Israel, which first emerged in 1971, combines the two. The movement was founded by a charismatic imam by the name of Sheikh Abdallah Nimer Darweish of the village of Kafr Kassem, who had studied Islam in Nablus, in the heart of the northern West Bank, where he became friendly with people from the Islamic Brotherhood and adopted many of their beliefs. Upon his return to the Triangle area in central Israel, which is populated mostly by Sunni Muslims, he recruited students and other followers to his new movement. Among his most important students were Sheikh Ibrahim Darweish, who grew up in the same village of Kafr Kassem, Sheikh Ra'ed Sallah (who had studied Islam in Hebron, the largest Palestinian city in the southern part of the West Bank) and Hasem Abdel-Rahman, all of whom became leaders of the Islamic Movement in the large Israeli Arab town of Umm el-Fahm, which is in the northern area of the Triangle in central Israel. Upon returning to his village, Sheikh Abdallah developed a synthesis of religion and politics which can be called "political Islam."[14]

Muslims whom I have interviewed argued that there is a distinction between degree of religiosity and involvement in politics among Israeli Muslims. According to one observer,

> There are many pious Muslims not involved in politics who are very religious out of love for God. If a Muslim is involved in politics, it is because he or she likes it, not because he or she is a Muslim. There is a difference between a Muslim and a politician.[15]

In other words, some very observant Muslims are involved in politics and some are not. Those who are drawn to politics are often involved in the Islamic Movement.

One can say that the Islamic Movement incorporates adherence to strict religious observance and opposition to Western culture into a political movement, which focused on a new analysis of the situation of the Palestinian Arab minority in Israel. Their slogan was: "Islam is the solution for everything."[16]

Unlike the Palestinian radical Islamic organization Hamas, which operates in the West Bank and Gaza (but not in Israel), and whose members are mostly refugees who fled Israel (or were expelled) in 1948 or 1967, the Islamic Movement is basically nonviolent (although I would argue that it is often verbally violent) in its orientation and is led and supported by Palestinian Arabs who are Israeli citizens. Some of its leaders publicly denounce acts of violence by Hamas and other similar groups, stressing that they believe that Islam is a religion of peace, i.e. the world "salaam" actually means "shalom" or peace. On the other hand, some of its leaders, especially those of the Northern branch of the movement, sound very much like Hamas leaders when they denounce alleged Israeli attempts to undermine the foundations of the Al Aksa mosque or when they say that the ancient Jewish Temple never existed on the Temple Mount and therefore only Muslims should have access to pray there.[17]

The city of Kafr Kassem became famous, or infamous, depending on one's point of view, for the well-documented massacre that took place there in 1956 on the eve of the Sinai Campaign, a mini-war between Israel and Egypt. At that time, a strict curfew was imposed on Israeli Arab villages, and Israeli security forces shot and killed 48 citizens of Kafr Kassem[18], ostensibly for breaking the curfew. Later on, Israeli courts found some members of the security forces guilty of the crime, but their sentences were not serious and were never imposed.

I have taken Israeli and foreign groups, including rabbis and community leaders, to Kafr Kassem several times over the years, to meet with local leaders, to visit the local museum which commemorates this massacre and to express interreligious solidarity with the local citizens.[19] Each time I noticed how much the local citizens appreciated these solidarity visits and how much the attendant Jews felt a need to express empathy with the people of this Israeli city.

According to Sheikh Ibrahim Sarsur (who graciously hosted me in his book-lined study in his beautiful home for a long interview), what distinguishes the Southern branch from its Northern counterpart is more political than religious. I have known Sheikh Sarsur for many years and often visited him in his office when he was a member of Knesset. I always found my conversations with him fascinating, especially since he was a serious parliamentarian who constantly strove to improve conditions for Palestinian Arabs of Israel, while at the same time being an eloquent spokesman for Palestinian national identity. When I invited him to speak to interreligious dialogue groups which I supervised, he was always gracious in accepting and delivered thoughtful and sensitive talks. Now retired, Sheikh Sarsur is writing a history of the Islamic Movement in Israel and remains active in the Southern branch of the movement as an elder statesman.

The famous big split within the Islamic Movement was preceded by internal political developments. From 1972-1996, there was only one Islamic Movement. In 1990-91, the members of the movement began to think about entering national Israeli elections and not just local ones—they had been involved in local elections since 1989, when Sheikh Sarsur, on behalf of the Islamic Movement, was elected mayor of Kafr Kassem at the age of thirty. In that same year, the movement decided to run candidates for mayor in ten local Israeli Arab councils, and won seven out of the ten.

When they began to think about entering national elections in 1991, the majority of the movement stood behind the idea. But a vocal minority, led by Sheikh Ra'ed Sallah and Sheikh Kamal Hatib, both from Umm el-Fahm, formed an opposition group. Sheikh Abdallah Nimer Darweish, who had been the widely-respected founder and leader of the movement from the beginning, for a long time preferred unity, but in the end his efforts and those of other leaders of the movement to convince Sheikh Ra'ed Sallah to stay within the movement failed, and Sheikh Ra'ed set up the Northern branch in 1996. When the religious leadership of the movement voted to run for national elections, they recommended this to the General Assembly of the movement. This is the moment at which Sheikh Ra'ed and his followers split from the main body of the movement.[20]

In prayer and social activities the Islamic Movement's Northern branch is very similar to that in the South. But the rhetoric of the Northern branch is much louder and more provocative. The leadership in the South is more pragmatic, which is why I was able to work with them for many years. It is important to note that the terms "North" and "South" are not accurate, since both wings of the movement operate all over the country. The mother movement, which is the Southern branch, is active in 95% of the Muslim communities in the Negev, and they are active in most of the towns of the southern Triangle as well as in some parts of the Northern Triangle, as well as in the Galilee. According to the former leader of the Southern branch, they are much more practical than their Northern counterpart. Nevertheless, both branches of the movement function in accordance with the laws of Israel; both are against violence and refrain from acts of terror.[21]

I have had the privilege and pleasure of working with Sheikh Sarsur and his colleagues over many years. I greatly value our relationship and I believe that the feeling is mutual. I have also worked closely with one of his colleagues, Sheikh Kamal Rayan, the youngest ever mayor of his Israeli Arab village, Kafr Bara near Kafr Kassem, where he served as mayor for three consecutive terms. Sheikh Rayan was a valued partner in a unique interreligious program called "Kedem—Voices for Interreligious Reconciliation", which we co-directed for six years.[22]

Since the split in 1996, the Northern branch has been led by Sheikh Ra'ed Sallah, a verbally provocative leader who has been jailed by the Israeli authorities several times for his hate-filled rhetoric, especially his inflammatory statements that the state of Israel was seeking to sabotage the al-Aksa Mosque on the *Haram el-Sharif* (literally, Noble Sanctuary). Indeed, his campaign to wrest control of the *Haram al-Sharif* (Temple Mount) from Israeli control has alienated most Israeli Jews,and many of his Palestinian Arab fellow citizens as well. His militant radicalism grew to such proportions that in 2015 the Northern branch of the Islamic Movement was declared illegal by the (right-wing) government of Israel.[23] The government based its decision to outlaw the Northern branch of the Islamic Movement on the argument that for the past years the movement had been conducting a mendacious campaign of incitement, accusing Israel of planning to damage the al-Aksa Mosque. A large part of the Israeli public, most of which supports an iron-fist policy toward Arab protest movements, supported this decision, as did all the Zionist parties in the Knesset. In contrast, Israel's politically variegated Arab population reacted angrily to the decision, which they see as the suppression of a legitimate political movement and a violation of their freedom of speech and right to organize.

The split of the Islamic Movement into Northern and Southern branches had more to do with politics than theology. The Northern branch rejects the idea of participating in national elections in Israel since it sees this as a form of collaboration with the Israeli government. However, they do participate in local elections in Arab communities in Israel, especially in Umm el-Fahm, where they control the local government, which they have dominated for many years.

Several years ago, on a visit to Umm el-Fahm with a group of scholars from the Hebrew University of Jerusalem, I saw for myself how the Islamic Movement controls most of the key institutions in that town. We visited Islamic Movement institutions including a local seminary for the training of imams to serve "independent" mosques (not recognized or supported by the state) all over Israel, a new local high school for the sciences, a high school for girls, and a local art gallery. Also, contrary to popular wisdom, everyone we met in the town spoke to us in moderate and soft tones and were extremely welcoming.

The principal of the Islamic high school held a doctorate from the Hebrew University, as did the director of education for the town, who had recently returned to Israel after spending three years as a post-doctoral fellow in

Berkeley, California. In addition, the religious faculty members of the Islamic seminary whom we met were all tolerant and open about their humanistic religious beliefs and asked the professors from the Hebrew University who were with me for their help in getting them recognized as an institution of Higher Education in Israel.

My experience there points to the fact that despite their Palestinian and Muslim identities, the local Arabs there sought more rather than less integration in Israeli society, a fact that is not well-known by the Jewish majority, who tend to see them only through the eyes of the negative mainstream media, which portrays them as flaming anti-Israel fundamentalists.

Moderate Orthodox Israeli Muslims

It is important to point out that, contrary to the conventional wisdom in Israel as revealed in the tabloids, on television and on the internet, not all Palestinian Muslim Arabs in Israel are members of the Islamic Movement, nor are they extremists or fundamentalists. On the contrary, the majority of Muslims in Israel are in fact either moderately religious, or "traditional", and some are even secular!

The moderately religious Muslims are parallel to Modern Orthodox Jews in Israel. They practice most of the rituals and observe the Muslim sabbath (on Friday) and the main Muslim holidays in religious ways, i.e. by prayer, fasting throughout the 30 days of Ramadan, eating festive meals with family and friends, giving charity, and going on pilgrimage to Mecca at least once in their lifetime if possible. However, they dress and think in modern ways, and are very much part of the contemporary world in terms of fashion, political outlook (democracy), and education (which includes sciences and humanities as well as religious studies). According to Dr. Aziz Haidar, probably 40-50% of Muslims in Israel live according to Muslim standards in some ways and Western standards in other ways. They give more freedom to women and to their children; they go to movies, to the beach and to university.[24] Indeed, Muslims in Israel have become more and more "Western" or "modern" or "secular" in their lifestyles in recent decades.[25]

Probably the best exemplar of moderate religious Islam is Kadi Iyad Zahalka, the kadi (Muslim judge) of the Shari'a Court of the State of Israel in Jerusalem, the head of the Shari'a courts of Israel and a sought-after lecturer in Islamic thought and Israeli Arab society at Tel Aviv University, Bar Ilan University, and at Emek Yizrael College. He is the first religious Muslim in Israel to obtain a doctorate in contemporary Muslim thought from the Hebrew University of Jerusalem. Zahalka adapted his doctoral thesis into a book which was published in recent years in Hebrew and English[26] and which explains clearly and comprehensively how he sees Islam adapting to modernity. In addition, he clarifies for readers in Israel and all over the world why Islam, according to his research and belief system, is a humanistic, peaceful and tolerant religion. This, of course, runs contrary to popular wisdom these days in Israel and the West where one sees only political Islam or radical Islam on one's television or computer screens.

I have spoken publicly with Kadi Zahalka on many panel discussions in Israel and abroad, and have invited him to speak at conferences and seminars that I have organized. The audience—whether Jews, Christians or Muslims—always come away inspired by his rational and reasonable approach to Islam, which he sees as a religion that is adapting to contemporary life and offers a way of life to its adherents which is not only to their benefit but to the benefit of all humankind. He is a proponent of a modern orthodox Islam which is understandable and accessible, and which offers hope for the future. It is a version of Islam which not only helps Muslims integrate successfully into Israeli society, but into the international community, especially in places in the Western world where Muslims live as minorities.[27]

In addition to my work with Kadi Zahalka, I have come to know several of the other leading kadis in Israel, who share the same modern orthodox world view of contemporary Islam. Four kadis participated in our "Kedem" program for religious leaders; one of them, Kadi Abedlhakeem Samara, was always the moral voice of the Muslim religious leadership, a fact which deeply impressed his Jewish colleagues in the dialogue.

Through their work in the Shari'a courts of the state of Israel, these kadis—who are highly educated, often with second and third degrees, in addition to their first university degree—are trying their best to adapt Islam to contemporary circumstances, especially when it comes to issues relating to family life, such as marriage and divorce, inheritance and custody of children. They have adopted a liberal approach to Shari'a law within the constraints of their orthodox understanding of Islam and they also remain sensitive to the complexities of traditional Arabs living in contemporary culture.

Traditional Muslims

In contrast to the minority of Israeli Muslims who are modern orthodox, most Muslims in Israel are simply "traditional" (as is also the case for many Jews in Israel). They observe many rituals and holidays even though they don't come to religious practice out of belief in God but rather for sociological reasons. They observe many of the practices of their religion since they have a positive attitude to "tradition", whereas they might see "religion" *per se* as coercive. So, for example, they would fast during the thirty days of Ramadan or give charity during Ramadan since it is the traditional normative thing for Muslims to do, not because they feel commanded by God to do so. But they would not pray five times every day, nor would they necessarily eat exclusively "hallal" food (the Muslim version of "kosher"), nor would they be interested in finding the time and money to make a pilgrimage to Mecca even once in their lifetime.

In terms of identity, this traditional group of Israeli Muslims is mostly nationalist since they define themselves more as Palestinian or Arab than as Muslim. At the same time, they observe some Islamic traditions.[28] In my experience, the best parallel to this middle-of-the-road Muslim group are traditional (*masorti*) Jews in Israeli society, who often identify more as "Israeli" than as "Jewish" and who do not strictly or consistently observe the Jewish Sabbath and other holidays, but maintain some degree of traditional observance in their homes.

Sufi Muslims

One other group of Muslims in Israel with which I have interacted meaningfully over the years are Sufi Muslims. Sufis are Sunni Muslims, but they have preserved their own special brand of Islam which is based on mystical Muslim thinkers of the Middle Ages, such as Rumi and Ibn Arabi. There are many small Sufi sects in Israel but the one I worked most consistently with, the Kadiri order, is based in Nazareth. It was led first by the father, Sheikh Abdel-al Salaam Manasra, and later by the son, Ghassan Manasra, who left Israel in 2015 for the USA for personal reasons.

Sheikh Ghassan Manasra, well known in Israel for pursuing a progressive and pluralistic form of Islam, and highly engaged in interreligious dialogue and in the interrelated field of education for Arab-Jewish coexistence, upset some Muslim extremists through his overly open and moderate stance. For decades, the Sufis in Nazareth have celebrated Islam through music and poetry without considering themselves in danger. But in recent years, local Salafis, who practice a more conservative and coercive Islam, bully and beat Sufi leaders to deter them from their practices.

In an interview for a major Israeli newspaper in 2012, Sheikh Manasra said:

> We visit tombs of holy peoples and they say it is forbidden; we chant and they say it is forbidden to use instruments.[29]

Sufis in general are well-known in the world as "whirling dervishes", but the Nazareth Sufis do not practice this tradition. They observe Islamic law, but include in their worship special prayers which they feel enhance their spirituality. In addition, they engage in chanting (zikr), and they use musical instruments and poetry in their prayer. A mystical order, they are often compared to Jewish Kabbalists. The greatest *jihad* of Islam, according to the Kadiri order that Manasra and his father Abdel-al Salaam head, is to overcome ego, hatred and violent speech and behavior.[30]

Manasra has often expressed his view that interreligious dialogue and cooperation were the Prophet Mohammad's ways and that later it was the tradition of Muslim and Jewish mystics in medieval Cairo, Baghdad, Damascus and Morocco. He has also said that dialogue can be helpful to local Arabs:

> We need to talk [with Jews] about the problems of Arab rights in Israel and Palestinian rights. Muslims can also teach Jews the cultural codes of peace-making in Islam—politics alone cannot build trust. [31]

Sheikh Manasra was involved with me in interreligious dialogue for many years, first as a group facilitator with our Kedem program and later as a lecturer, especially in a course that I sponsored at the education center of my organization called "Israeli Islam—According to Muslim Religious Leaders in Israel." In addition, he twice travelled with me on lecture tours to the USA and Canada, during which time he shared both his ideas on Sufi Islam as well as his views about the importance of interreligious dialogue as a means of maintaining and fostering Arab-Jewish coexistence in Israel.

I came to regard Sheikh Manasra not only as a knowledgeable religious Muslim leader in Israel—he studied for a doctorate in Islamic thought but unfortunately never completed it—but as a sincere believer in the value and centrality of dialogue, from the point of view of his Muslim tradition, and for the sake of peaceful living in Israel. He served as a facilitator for me for a few years for our Kedem religious leaders program, and he always brought a soft voice of commitment to mutual understanding to the discussions. In addition, when he and I were in Spain for a seminar in 2007, he gave an outstanding lecture on the famous Muslim philosopher Al-Ghazali[32], which he did without notes and with great enthusiasm, leaving a positive impression on everyone in the group, especially the rabbis. He is the living embodiment of his philosophy of Sufi Islam, which is the cornerstone of his contemporary identity as a Muslim.

Secular Muslims

A small minority of Muslims in Israel identify themselves as secular. Yet, even these Muslims are probably closer to being "traditional" than "secular" in their lives. For example, Howla Sadi, who served as director of the Curriculum Department for the Arab sector of the Israeli Ministry of Education, defined herself as secular because:

> I try to give some Muslim things new meanings for this life. I do the things that I believe in. I do some of these things to be part of the community. When I was a student in the university, I didn't have time to observe, so I stopped.

Then, when I had children, I began again to pray and fast. And I never tell my children to do that. It's their choice.[33]

Moreover, when asked about the modern significance that she attaches to Muslim traditions, she responded:

Let us take fasting. For me, the social meaning is to feel like the poor people everywhere . . . it makes you more aware to help these people. You bring the family together . . . and feel a part of the Islamic community everywhere.[34]

Thus, even though Sadi considers herself to be secular, she still observes select Muslim rituals, according to her own criteria. She does so for the sake of cultivating social consciousness, family togetherness, and links to Muslims worldwide, rather than out of a sense of religious obligation.

The idea of a "secular Muslim" is rejected in principle by many Muslims in Israel. Indeed, there is not really an ideological group of secular Muslims which could be compared to secular Jews or Christians. One of the Israeli Muslims with whom I talked put this succinctly:

If you say, you are secular, you can still be Jewish . . . If I take this model and try to put it in Muslim ideology, it does not work because if you are secular, you do not belong. From the religious point of view, you cannot be a Muslim if you are secular. If a Muslim says that he is secular, he does not understand Islam; he is thinking in the language of Judaism or Christianity.[35]

From other interviews that I have conducted, there was a consensus that there is no concept of secularism among Muslims in Israel. Similarly, there seems to be no notion of ethnic Muslim identity among the Palestinian Arab Muslims of Israel. Thus, on a theoretical level, there appears to be a mutually exclusive, either/or relationship between secularism, often defined as "non-believing" and Islam as a religion, i.e. "believing." Indeed, one of my good friends and colleagues for many years in the Muslim community in Israel told me once: "We have no religious or secular people, only very good Muslims or less good Muslims."

However, from a more pragmatic *de facto* perspective, it seems that there are in fact some contemporary Israeli Muslims who both behave as secular people and at the same time self-identify as Muslims. Many of these people are almost totally secular in their lifestyle and behavior. One prominent Muslim educator put it this way:

Because of political and social circumstances, I can in a practical way behave as a secular person, but I cannot declare myself as one because "secular" in Islam means that you are not just out of Islam, it's also understood as beginning a path that is anti-Muslim.[36]

Because of the social complexities involved in this matter, it appears that secular Muslims are generally a silent minority. As such, they are not part of contemporary Muslim consciousness in Israel; indeed, many Muslims do not know that they exist or do not recognize their existence. Though they do not participate in communal religious events, they do participate in the social sphere. If you ask these Muslims to explain who they are, many say that they are just "human beings" or that they are "Arab" or "Palestinian", which means that they identify and share a common destiny with fellow Arabs as part of a pan-Arab nationalism, or with Palestinians as part of the growing consciousness of Palestinian peoplehood among Muslim Arabs who live in Israel.

In my discussions and interviews with Muslim Israelis over the years, I have encountered secular Muslims very often. One of them, Aziz Haidar, was born and raised in a Muslim village in the Galilee, but has lived and taught at various academic institutions for most of his adult life. In an interview, he told me that his complete lack of attachment to Islam as a religion is unusual for Palestinian Arabs in Israel because some vestige of belief in Islam as a religion persists for most Muslims. For example, secular Muslims may turn to Islamic concepts when struggling to explain metaphysical questions of life and death, and they often resort to traditional Muslim practices when there is a death in the family. (In my experience, this often happens with non-observant Christians and Jews as well!)

Estimated percentages of Muslims in Israel who lead completely secular and totally nonobservant lifestyles (they don't pray daily or even during Ramadan and they don't fast during Ramadan) range from 10 to 20%. According the Dr. Haidar, many of them are university-educated. Geographically speaking, secular lifestyles tend to be more pervasive among Muslims in the Galilee than in the Triangle area of central Israel.[37] In fact, the overwhelming majority of Muslims in Israel lead very secular lifestyles in their daily lives when it comes to clothing, weddings, entertainment. On vacations, they go to regular hotels in Eilat or Tiberias or Antalya (Turkey) where they participate fully in the contemporary culture.[38]

A Palestinian Arab Israeli Muslim woman whom I got to know well in the course of many dialogue programs organized by the Interreligious Coordinating Council in Israel, and who gave lectures to some of our groups from time to time (who prefers to remain anonymous), also defines herself as a secular Muslim. She does not practice the rituals of the religion, nor is she a believer. A secularist and a feminist in her outlook on life, she believes that more and more young Muslim women who are educated in Israeli universities (she studied for her first and second degrees at the Hebrew University of Jerusalem and is pursuing a PhD there as well) are leaving the religious fold in order to advance their careers, and be active in social and educational issues in Israeli society and within Palestinian communities within Israel. However, she readily admitted that for now she is the exception rather than the rule and that many of the young people with whom she grew up in the all-Muslim village of Baka al-Gharbiyah remain traditional in their lifestyles and continue to live in the village where they were born and raised, close to their extended families.

It seems clear to me that the intersections of Muslim, Palestinian, Arab and Israeli dimensions of their identity are particularly complex for secular-identified Muslims.[39] Living as a citizen within a modern democratic Western-oriented state that also defines itself as a "Jewish state" or as "the nation-state of the Jewish People" sometimes seems to facilitate both the adoption of a secular free-thinking lifestyle and the inclusion of "Muslim" in one's own self-definition. Also, for some Muslims in Israel, being secular means that religion is a private matter and that state and religion should be separated.

In addition, Muslims in Israel may also be influenced by diversity within the Israeli Arab minority, which includes a mix of Christians, Muslims, Druse and Circassians, all of whom have greatly diverging identities. Some observers have argued that this internal religious diversity makes for more of a tendency toward secularism because unlike Arabs in Islamic states, Arabs in Israel do not always connect on the basis of shared religion, but rather on shared ethnicity or pan-Arab nationalism.[40]

Islam in Israel or "Israeli Islam"

As most of my professional interreligious work was with Muslims in Israel, I have come to know Islam in Israel quite well, according to the diversity outlined above. I have discovered that Islam in Israel, or as I have come to call it "Israeli Islam" is a unique phenomenon, not only in the Middle East but in the Western world as well. Let me explain.

A good example of this can be found in the way that Israeli Muslims celebrate their holidays in Israel. For example, I was particularly mindful of how they celebrated one of their major feasts last year, the holiday of Eid al-Adcha—the Festival of the Sacrifice—one of the main religious and cultural holidays in the Muslim calendar. During a visit to the Israeli Arab town of Abu Ghosh, my Arab colleagues were talking about how they and their families are planning to celebrate their holiday. They told me that lots of families from Abu Ghosh go on vacation to the Israeli port city of Eilat for the week, as do thousands of Muslim families from all over the country.

Later that day I spoke to another religious Muslim colleague with whom I work often, and he told me something similar. He added that his family would take day trips to nearby Israeli towns, like Haifa (Israel's leading mixed Arab-Jewish city), since they like vacationing inside Israel.

After this, I happened to visit two Jerusalem malls. In each mall, I saw hundreds of Muslim families out shopping for food and clothing and gifts for the holiday. No-one blinked an eye. No-one said a word. No-one harassed them. It seemed that no-one even noted their presence. It appeared to be totally normal and acceptable. This was a great contrast to the way most Muslims are treated at security checkpoints and at the airport, but it was nevertheless a positive sign of coexistence in daily life.

And I wondered why. How is it that Israeli Muslims enter Jewish malls without fear? How is it that thousands of Israeli Muslims travel to vacation spots all over Israel, without trepidation?

I think that there are three answers to these questions.

Firstly, Palestinian Muslim Arabs of Israeli citizenship feel somewhat at home in Israel. After all, they are Israeli citizens. It says so clearly on their identity cards and their passports. And, some of them even enjoy that status. They feel comfortable here. They speak the language, share the workplace with Jews, especially in industries such as health and tourism, and they know the geography well. They are part and parcel of the landscape and of civil society, despite the difficulties of segregation and inequality that they often suffer as an indigenous group that has become a distinct minority group.

Secondly, Muslims who live in Israel have complete freedom of religion. The democratic structure of the state of Israel allows them to practice Islam fully and freely. Unfortunately, the same cannot be said for Palestinian Muslims who live under occupation in the West Bank and East Jerusalem, for whom it is often more difficult to pray at the al-Aksa mosque in Jerusalem for security reasons and who suffer the lack of freedom that comes with the occupation.

Thirdly, Israel is becoming more of a multicultural country, like most countries in the West, whether the old guard likes this or not. In addition to the great diversity among the Jewish majority—with immigrants and their descendants from more than 70 countries all over the world—Israel has a growing non-Jewish minority, which comprises almost 21% of its population. This non-Jewish minority is made up of Muslims, Druse, Circassians, and many Christian denominations, including tens of thousands of Christian asylum seekers from Africa who reside in Tel Aviv and other cities. Israel is no longer the "melting pot" of the 1950s but a richly diverse and colorful mixture of religions and races.

Within this mosaic, Islam in Israel is also diverse and fascinating. Similar to the Jewish population, we find within the Arab population Muslims of different worldviews and practices: ultra-Orthodox, Modern Orthodox, traditional, cultural and secular Muslims. And there are many fascinating Sufi sects which are more mystical and pluralistic. All of these versions of Islam are alive and well in Israel, and they greatly outnumber the small groups of "radical Islam" or "political Islam".

ISLAM IN EAST JERUSALEM AND THE WEST BANK

In stark contrast to Israeli Islam, the expressions of Islam that one finds in East Jerusalem are much different as a result of the vastly different political, sociological, cultural and security context. Muslims who live in the West Bank see themselves as living under Israeli occupation. As such, they do not live in a free and democratic environment and they are not seeking integration into Israeli society. In the West Bank, integration into Israeli society is not an option. However in East Jerusalem, Palestinians actually do seek some forms of integration while at the same time resisting the occupation, because they are pragmatic and they are able to do so. Nevertheless, most Muslims in East Jerusalem and the West Bank spend much of their time and energy in resisting the occupation and in working to establish an independent Palestinian state, a fact which is both physical and psychological in that it often consumes their lives.

In my experience, I have discerned that there are two main kinds of Islamic identity in East Jerusalem and the West Bank. The first is ultra-Orthodox political or radical Islam, most closely identified with Hamas, the Islamic branch of the Muslim Brotherhood, headquartered in Gaza (which is ruled by Hamas) and which operates all over the West Bank and East Jerusalem, often underground, since both the Palestinian Authority and Israel's security services frequently hunt them down on account of terrorist activity. This brand of Islam is political as well as religious. Verbally and physically violent, it encourages the overthrow of Israel as a Zionist state and engages in armed resistance. Politically, it allies with the Muslim Brotherhood in Egypt and with radical Islamic forces in Lebanon, Qatar and Iran, all of which are uncompromisingly anti-peace, anti-modernity, and anti-Israel. It is fundamentalist in its religious worldview and practice, with no liberal tendencies whatsoever, and as such, it has not adapted Islam to the modern world, but practices a pre-modern form of Islam.

Yet, according to Dr. Haidar, most Muslims in the West Bank live their daily lives as modern secular people, even though many of them do pray daily, mostly for social reasons. But they do not have a religious worldview. They pray and fast for nostalgic reasons rather than because of theological imperative. They have not adopted the religious ideology of political or radical Islam, even though they may vote for Hamas and support the organization emotionally.[41]

The second kind of Islam in East Jerusalem and the West Bank is secular Islam, much like the Islam that I described above. However, this secular Islam is also political in that it identifies with the ruling Fatah party of the Palestinian Authority in the West Bank. It seeks to create a secular independent Palestinian state, not one that would be ruled by medieval versions of Islamic law, and it operates in strong and consistent opposition to Hamas, which it regards as its internal enemy. These secular Muslims do not dress in fundamentalist garb, nor do they necessarily share the core beliefs and practices of religious Muslims. In many cases, they are avowedly anti-religious or non-religious since they see Islam—especially radical political Islam—as the source of the ongoing conflict rather than as part of the solution. One finds many of these secularists in the civil service of the Palestinian Authority or in the universities in East Jerusalem and the West Bank (there are six Palestinian universities in East Jerusalem and the West Bank). They are teaching modern ideas and modern culture in their universities and through their civil service institutions they are struggling to set up and maintain a democratic culture (not too successfully) and a form of governance in an area of the world in which this hardly exists, except for Israel. [42]

There is a variation on the secular Muslim that is important to mention. I would call it the "secular-cultural Muslim". This person knows and venerates Muslim history and culture even if he or she is not a believer, and therefore not considered by himself or herself, or others, as religious. Perhaps the best example of this type of person is Professor Sari Nusseibeh, former president of Al Quds University in East Jerusalem, and a well-known scholar of Islamic thought. Professor Nusseibeh, whom I had the privilege and pleasure of meeting several times, is an erudite intellectual. [43] When I was with him at an interreligious conference sponsored by a Catholic group in Palermo, Sicily, Italy, many years ago, he impressed audiences with his frank and his forthright stance on many issues, including the Israeli-Palestinian conflict. [44] On another occasion, I visited him in his office once when he was president of Al Quds University in Jerusalem, when he issued an important statement during the Second Intifada (Palestinian uprising from 2000 to 2003) against suicide bombing, which I felt was an important moral declaration from a unique Palestinian cultural leader.

As a result of my encounters in dialogue, I would posit that there is one further type of "secular" Muslim in the West Bank which I would call traditional. Similar to their co-religionists in Israel, traditional Muslims live mostly secular lives but they do fast during Ramadan and observe the main Muslim feasts, even though they do not share the radical theology of Muslim fundamentalists. However, it is impossible to say how many of the Muslims in the West Bank would agree to call themselves "traditionalists" because it might not be culturally acceptable.

MODERATE ISLAM IN EAST JERUSALEM
AND THE WEST BANK—A UNIQUE CASE

There is a prominent secular-cultural Muslim, who has become quite famous not only for his views on Islam as a religion or culture of moderation and tolerance, but also for his forthright statements and writings in favor of reconciliation and peace. Professor Mohammed Daoudi Dajani is one of the few Muslim intellectuals still around who rejects anti-normalization among mainstream Palestinians and believes that the path of dialogue and peace is the one that can lead to reconciliation with Jews in Israel (and abroad). Several years ago, he founded a movement in East Jerusalem and the West Bank called "Wasatia" (Arabic for "the Middle Way"), which endeavors to spread the message of tolerance and reconciliation at the heart of the Koran. Wasatia, a Palestinian NGO founded in 2007 under his leadership, works "to ensure that Palestinian children will grow up in a culture where they can coexist in peace, prosperity and harmony."[45]

I have known and worked with Professor Dajani for many years. I frequently invited him to address interreligious groups visiting or living in Israel, and we have spoken abroad together. In addition, I have read many of his articles and pamphlets about Wasatia,[46] so I am quite familiar with his teachings and his approach.

Professor Dajani—who has been involved in dialogue and education for a long time—is now going beyond dialogue and talking more about "reconciliation". According to him, "this war will be over some day, and we will need experts in reconciliation to maintain the peace."[47] In order to do this, one needs to learn how to effect reconciliation. Accordingly, Professor Dajani is now setting up a graduate program in Palestine, in cooperation with a university in Germany—the Fredrick Schiller University—to train experts in reconciliation who can teach in Palestinian and Israeli universities and work for their ministries of education.

Professor Dajani believes that Palestinian society is ready for this message. He feels that 70-80% of Palestinians in the West Bank are in the "moderate middle" and are tired of the fanaticism of Hamas and the corruption of Fatah, and they would appreciate a new way that might enable them to lead a normal life. He vividly recalls that in the 1950s, when he was growing up in Jerusalem, the kind of either-or Islam of Hamas or Fatah was nonexistent. In contrast, the Islam of his childhood was moderate. He never heard anti-Jewish or anti-Semitic interpretations of the Koran as can be heard every day by Islamic preachers. In his view, it is only during the last 20 years that the interpretations of the Koran by radical Islamic religious leaders have dominated what passes for religious Islam in East Jerusalem and in the West Bank, and he still believes that he and his followers in the Wasatia movement can reverse this trend.[48]

One of the reasons that he feels that he can do this is that he references the Koran in all of his writings, lectures and workshops. He says that he believes in God, even though he does not observe the religious practices of Islam, according to Shari'a law. Moreover, he sees himself as a "secular-religious" person (a new category that he invented!) since he relies heavily on the

Koran, although he deduces his own unique and important ethical conclusions for living a moral way of life.[49]

His interpretation of Islam as a religion of peace, ethics, justice and tolerance, reminds me a great deal of Reform Judaism (with which I identify as a Reform rabbi), with its emphasis on personal ethics and social justice, as opposed to ritual and religious observance—and of the Society for Ethical Culture, which rational non-observant Jews established in New York at the end of the 19th century and which still exists today, although it is very small.[50] Indeed, Professor Dajani seems to be much more comfortable with liberal-minded Jews than Orthodox or ultra-Orthodox ones, since we clearly share the same overall world view.

Professor Dajani became famous—or infamous, according to extremist Palestinians who opposed him—for taking Palestinian students to Auschwitz for a seminar, to learn about Jewish suffering, just as he took Jewish students to Palestinian refugee camps to learn about Palestinian suffering (with a stark awareness, in my view, of the radical differences in the amount and quality of the suffering). He has written about this experience extensively on social media and in booklets; and he has been interviewed by the mainstream media several times.[51] He called this project "Hearts of Flesh - Not Stone", a reference to a passage in the book of Ezekiel, which is significant for Jews, Christians and Muslims, which reads: "I will give you a new heart and put a new spirit in you: I will remove from you your heart of stone and give you a heart of flesh." This metaphor encapsulates for Dajani what Wasatia and his journey to Auschwitz is all about, i.e., "the transformative process of opening yourself up to peace and reconciliation."[52] Moreover, he co-authored an op-ed for the *New York Times* with a Jewish colleague about why Palestinians need to learn about the Holocaust[53].

Over the years, I have developed great respect and admiration for Professor Dajani's idealism and perseverance against great odds. In fact, I found him to be practically the only reliable and relevant Muslim religious/cultural leader from East Jerusalem or the West Bank, with whom I could work in honest cooperation. He is genuinely devoted to the cause of dialogue, reconciliation and peace, and does not intend to give up any time soon. I only hope that his diagnosis of the willingness of Palestinian society to hear and welcome his message is correct; it is refreshingly optimistic and echoes my diagnosis of Jewish-Israeli society. There is no question that Professor Dajani and his Wasatia movement—through their publications, programs and their active presence on social media—offer hope and inspiration not only for Palestinians, but for people all over the world.

IMPLICATIONS OF MUSLIM DIVERSITY FOR INTERRELIGIOUS AND INTERCULTURAL DIALOGUE AND EDUCATION

Exploring religious and cultural diversity among Muslims of Israel has important implications for interreligious dialogue. The multiple complex dimensions of Muslim identity, as discussed above, provides much food for thought which contradicts the distorted Western and Israeli media presentations of Muslims as fanatic fundamentalist terrorists. Also, it will help to erase the well-documented tendency in social psychology to view "out groups" in a homogenous or one-dimensional manner.

For Jews in Israel, like myself, the discovery of Muslim diversity within our society has been not only helpful personally, but also professionally. It gave me a new consciousness and awareness of my Muslim neighbors and it transformed the nature of my dialogue with them from one-dimensional to multi-faceted. If more Jews could be mindful of the fact that any single Muslim Israeli is but one in a diverse group of individuals who often speak with different voices about their common religion and culture, they would be able to enter into dialogue with fellow Muslim citizens without preconceived notions or outdated stereotypes.

Jews who engage Muslims in serious, systematic and sensitive dialogue—as I have done for the past 25 years—are now able to do so with a greater awareness of diversity within Islam in Israel than was heretofore the case. Moreover, they will find many parallels to Jewish diversity in Israel, which also contains a great variety of identities, from secular and cultural to traditional, Modern Orthodox (both moderate and extreme nationalists) and ultra-Orthodox. Indeed, it has been amazing to discover that virtually the same breakdown of sub-identities exists *de facto* among Muslims in Israel as among the Jews of Israel.

An additional implication that arises out of the awareness of Muslim diversity within Israel, is the need for Jews in the Jewish majority to come to know their Muslim neighbors in more serious and systematic ways, rather than living with so many worn out stereotypes. This can be accomplished by more sensitive and substantive dialogue. More and more Jews will realize that it is impossible for us to understand fully our Palestinian Arab Muslim neighbors if we only view them in ethnic or nationalistic or political or cultural terms. Rather, we need to be aware of the fact that the religion of Islam, in all of its diversity, plays a central role in their lives. Accordingly, I have come to believe, after many years of dialogue with Muslims, that it is incumbent upon Jews (in Israel and abroad) to do much more to try to understand how Islam is actually understood and practiced in Israel in order to be able to live in peaceful coexistence now and in the future.

THE CHRISTIAN COMMUNITIES IN ISRAEL
AND IN THE WEST BANK

Within Israel

The Christian community within the state of Israel is more diverse than the Muslim community even though it is much smaller. The Christians of Israel make up only about 2% of the citizens of Israel[54], and only 9% of the 21% minority of Palestinian Arabs in Israel.

Within the state of Israel, the Christian population has been steadily growing since 1948. At that time, the Christian population was 34,000 and by 1967 it was 71,000, and by 2009 it had grown to 151,700. This represents a growth of 346% since 1948 and 114% since 1967.[55] During many of these years, Christian growth outpaced Jewish growth.[56]

The latest figures on the Christian population reveals that there are 163, 500 Christians in the state of Israel.[57] This includes Palestinian Arab Christians as well as non-Arab Christians. One Palestinian sociologist points out that Israel has inflated the number of Christians in the country by adding to the number more than 30,000 Russian Orthodox Christians who came to Israel as "Jews" under the Law of Return (but who actually live their lives as Christians) and that therefore the real number of Palestinian Christians in Israel is closer to 120,000.[58] Therefore, even though the state of Israel likes to claim that the Christian population is growing within Israel in recent years, the local Palestinian Arab Christian population is not growing. Rather, the number of Palestinian Christians in Israel is stable.[59] To give these numbers an even broader context, one should be aware that 27.5% of all Palestinian Christians in the world (500,000-600,000) live in Israel (120,000) and in Palestine (50,000 in the West Bank, which includes East Jerusalem, plus another 2,000 in Gaza).[60]

Over the past decades, Christians from Israel and Palestine have been emigrating in large numbers to the West. The reasons are multiple and diverse, depending on historical circumstances. During the Ottoman Empire, especially between 1900 and 1918, practical issues led many Palestinian Christians to emigrate. Conscription of the eldest sons of the family to the armies of the Turks was one of the major reasons. For example, many Palestinian Christians, especially those who came from affluent families, left the villages of Beit Jala and Bet Sahour (villages adjacent to the city of Bethlehem) to go to live in Chile. I once met the ambassador of Chile to Israel at a conference and she told me that there are more than 300,000 Palestinian Christians who live in Chile and that the locals call them "Turkos" since they came from the Holy Land during the period of the Ottoman Empire! It was good to discover that the Israeli occupation was not the sole historical reason for the emigration of Palestinian Christians!

During the British mandatory period, there was less emigration of Palestinian Christians from the area on account of the fact that the British invested in and developed the society. But, towards the end of the period and in the lead up to the 1948 war and establishment of the state of Israel, Palestinian Christians suffered a great deal. Indeed, in 1948, 50-60,000 Palestinian Christians became refugees (of the approximately 700,000 total refugees), which was a big blow to the Christian communities in the land.[61]

Among the Arab Christians within the state of Israel, the largest community is the Greek Catholic - about 40% (48,000), then Greek Orthodox about 30%, Latins (Roman Catholics) about 15% (24,000) and Maronites about 8% (8,400), all the other communities are very small.[62] Among the non-Arabs, the overwhelming majority are Russian Orthodox, and there are about 1,000 Roman Catholics. In addition, quite a few have joined Evangelical and Messianic congregations.[63]

Christians in the Galilee

Most of the Christians who live in Israel live in the Galilee[64], mostly in Nazareth, the largest Arab city in Israel, and also in mixed villages with Muslims and Druse, who are all considered "minorities" by the Jewish Israeli mainstream; in two cases there are all-Christian villages—Me'ilya and Fassuta. The largest denomination of Christians in the Galilee is Greek Catholic (also known as "Melkite"), which is an amalgam of "Orthodox" and "Catholic" traditions, with the church loyal to the Pope. They represent about 50% of Christians in the Galilee. The second largest group are Greek Orthodox (about 30%), and the remaining Christians are Copts, Maronites, Anglicans and Baptists.[65]

In my dialogues with Christians from the Galilee, I discovered that they have a unique Christian identity among the Christians of Israel. While they are Arabs—and many identify themselves as "Palestinian Christian Arabs of Israeli citizenship"—they are mostly content with their lot in Israel and do not engage in demonstrations against the government very often. Rather, they tend to work with the government and its officials to ensure the stability of their churches and educational institutions rather than getting involved in conflict situations with the Israeli authorities.[66] In general, I would say that Israeli Christians are generally perceived by the Jewish majority in Israel as being more friendly and accommodating and less vituperative and confrontational than their Muslim counterparts. This is attributable to the fact that the Crusades are over[67] (Christians are no longer at war with Jews), and it is a result of the mainstream formal dialogue process between Christians and Jews of the last 50 years since the famous Vatican Declaration, "Nostra Aetate" ("In Our Time"), which I discuss in the next chapter.

I have encountered what I might call a "pre-Church Christianity", one that believes in and spreads the message of love of the Gospels, without all the Church history that came after the time of Jesus. One of the best examples of this is Fr. Nadeem Chacour, a Melkite priest from the village of Me'ilya (one of the all-Christian villages of the Galilee), who formerly served a Greek Catholic Church in Shfaram in the Lower Galilee (a mixed Christian-Muslim-Druse town). Fr. Chacour was one of the most prominent Christian ministers to participate in my Kedem Interreligious Dialogue program.[68] Over six years he contributed the voice of a Galilee Christian to our dialogue, always referring to the Gospels, in our discussions.

Another excellent example of the Christianity of the Galilee whom I came to know is embodied in the figure of Fr. Elias Chacour, who became the leader of the Melkite community in Israel. Before becoming the head of his church, he had been the Archbishop of Akko, Haifa, Nazareth and All Galilee of the Melkite Greek Catholic Church and the head of the Mar Elias school in the Israeli Arab village of Ibillin in the lower Galilee. In this capacity, he built up one of the most successful and prestigious Christian schools in Israel, which I visited many times. I recall that on one of my visits to the school, he took me to see a little memorial on the campus, which was a model of two tombstones—one for an Israeli child and one for a Palestinian child—which was his way of indicating that he cared for the lives of both Palestinian and Israeli children. Indeed, in his younger days, he was an anti-war, pro-peace activist, which got him into trouble when he was too vocal with some of the Israeli authorities. But later in life, he mellowed and became part of the team of Israeli rabbis and Christian leaders who engaged in a formal dialogue process with religious leaders from the Vatican. Father Chacour has always been a strong believer and participant in interreligious dialogue.

According to a website called "Pilgrims of Ibillin," Father Chacour has been a major force for good in the Galilee in general and in his village of Ibillin in particular:

> A three-time Nobel Peace Prize nominee, he retired after serving since 2006 as the Archbishop of the Melkite Catholic Church and is living again in Ibillin where he continues to read, write, pray, and meet pilgrim groups to share his story of "Building Peace on Desktops." He was born to a Palestinian Christian family in the village of Biram in Upper Galilee in 1939. Along with his whole village he experienced the tragedy of eviction by the Israeli authorities in 1948 and became a refugee in his own land. He and all his family members became citizens of Israel when the state was created. Ibillin is a small Arab village in the Galilee region, near Nazareth, where Christians and Muslims have lived together peacefully for hundreds of years.[69]

Christians in the Galilee are doing rather well. They are usually cooperative with Israeli governments and they get along well with people from other
religions who live in the Galilee, including Jews, Muslims and Druse. In my
experience, they are generally part of the solution and no longer part of the
problem when it comes to living as a successful minority in the Jewish state.
Their problems these days are much more with Islamic fundamentalism than
with the limitations of Israeli democracy.

Diversity vs. "Christian Unity"

In short, indigenous Christian communities in Israel are small but diverse.
And, they all do not agree on everything, to say the least. In my dialogues
and interactions with local and expatriate Christians who live in (and who
visit) Israel, I have become acutely aware that there is no such thing as "The
(with a capital T) Christian Community". Rather, there are many Christian
communities, with many differing religious, cultural and political points of
view.

Nevertheless, there have been some attempts at "Christian unity" on some
matters. For example, there is a committee of church leaders called the Council of the Patriarchs and Heads of Churches, which was formed in 1994,
shortly after the Oslo Accords. It comprises the thirteen historic churches—
which includes all churches mentioned above and the Custody of the Holy
Land—and is chaired by the Greek Orthodox Patriarch, who is considered
the first among equals of all the Christian patriarchs in Jerusalem. The council is an attempt on the part of the Christian Church leaders in Jerusalem to
deal with issues of common concern to the Christian communities in Jerusalem and in Israel. It meets about five to seven times per year. Fr. Hosam
Naoum, Dean of St. George's Cathedral in Jerusalem, serves as the secretary
of the Council.[70]

Among the common issues that this council deals with are:

* Obtaining visas from the government of Israel for visiting clergy and
  volunteers
* Maintaining Christian holy sites, according to the historic *"status quo"*[71]
  and formal (diplomatic) relationships of the Christian communities with
  the governments of the region, i.e., Israel, Jordan and the Palestinian Authority
* Vandalism against Christian churches by Jewish extremists
* Taking stands on public issues, such as the future of Jerusalem.

Christians in East Jerusalem[72]

A famous public statement was issued on November 14, 1994 by the council on "The Significance of Jerusalem for Christians."[73] This statement elaborated the consensual views of the heads of the Christian communities as to the holiness of the city for all the monotheistic religions—Judaism, Christianity and Islam—as well as the need to consider carefully the status of Jerusalem in the peace process. In particular, the memorandum outlined in great detail the Christian vision of Jerusalem. Among other things it said:

> The Significance of Jerusalem for Christians thus has two inseparable fundamental dimensions: 1) a Holy City with holy places most precious to Christians because of their link with the history of salvation . . . 2) a city with a community of Christians which has been living there since its origins. Thus for the local Christians, as well as for local Jews and Muslims, Jerusalem is not only a Holy City, but also their native city where they live, whence their right to continue to live there freely with all the rights which obtains from that.[74]

The heads of the Christian communities were clearly making a clarion call to not be forgotten by the politicians and diplomats who were busy thinking about practical political solutions for Jerusalem as part of the peace process which assumed momentum after the Oslo Accords of 1993 (see chapter 1). They did not want to be ignored. Therefore, they issued this important memorandum which called for a special status for Jerusalem, and guarantees by the international community to preserve the stability of Jerusalem.

In 2006, a similar but shorter statement on Jerusalem was issued by the heads of the thirteen historic churches. It emphasized that Jerusalem should be shared, not divided by the three major monotheistic religions—Judaism, Christianity and Islam—and the two nations—Israel and Palestine—and it called for respect for the historical *status quo* in Jerusalem.[75]

Clearly the Christian communities of Jerusalem see this city as holy and as central to their Christian identity. They are certainly worried about the declining numbers of Christians in the city[76] over the years as well as the increase in anti-Christian activity –such as vandalism against church properties in Jerusalem and other places in Israel and spitting by extremist Jewish "religious" Orthodox or ultra-Orthodox Jews in Jerusalem, as church leaders move through the Old City of Jerusalem on their way to prayers, especially on their way to visit the Holy Sepulcher.

I have had the opportunity to come to know many of the Christian leaders in Jerusalem over the years as part of my professional work in interreligious dialogue. Many of them have become good friends, as well as trusted partners in dialogue. Because of my ongoing contacts with Christian leaders and institutions over the years, I have often been one of the "first responders" after their churches or seminaries were vandalized by Jewish extremists. At different times, I made solidarity visits—often with the members of the "Light Tag" forum[77] —to the Armenian Church in the Armenian Quarter of the Old City of Jerusalem, where I worked in common cause with Archbishop Aris Shirvanian, and to the Dormition Abbey on Mount Zion, a place that became a source of much friction between Jews and Christians (and Muslims) due to the presence of an extremist Jewish group on Mount Zion.

Over time, I developed very good relations with the leaders of the Catholic, Anglican, Lutheran, Armenian and Greek Orthodox churches in Jerusalem. In fact, one of the changes that I tried to make in the field of Jewish-Christian relations in Israel was to focus on conversations with local indigenous Christians. (Previously, the dominant pattern in Jewish-Christian relations had been to dialogue exclusively with expatriate international Christians who happened to be living in Jerusalem for various periods of time). In so doing, I learned a great deal about what local Christians are thinking and feeling, not only theologically but also politically and practically. Accordingly, I came to know that they are sincerely concerned about the dwindling Christian population in Jerusalem, and that they are intimately and personally very concerned with anti-Christian sentiments expressed by Jewish extremists, as well as with the ongoing Israeli military occupation of East Jerusalem and the West Bank and its deleterious effect on their communities.

One of my main partners in dialogue on the local level for many years has been Bishop Munib Younan, the bishop of the Evangelical Lutheran Church in Jordan and the Holy Land since 1998, and president of the Lutheran World Federation since 2010. Together, we co-moderated a group which we called "The Jonah Group" for more than 10 years. It was comprised of local Christians whom he would bring from the Armenian, Catholic, Anglican, Lutheran and Greek Orthodox churches and Jewish clergy (rabbis) and educators whom I would bring from diverse denominations in Jerusalem, including Modern Orthodox, Conservative, and Reform Judaism.

The group would meet often for the study of Jewish and Christian sources on contemporary themes, such as justice, peace, and reconciliation, as well as for conversations on contemporary concerns, such as the ongoing conflict between Palestinians and Israelis, the desecration of holy sites in Jerusalem and in other places in Israel and the West Bank, and the need for more education for peaceful coexistence in our communities. All of our conversations were off-the-record, discrete, honest and candid. We developed a great deal of trust in each other over the years, so that we could genuinely share our concerns about issues which were of such great importance to us.

In addition to our dialogue sessions, we have developed a long-standing personal friendship that stresses open and frank discourse that has lasted many years. Together with my wife, I attended the wedding of one of his children in Nazareth and another one in Jerusalem, and he attended the wedding of one of my daughters nearby Jerusalem. Moreover, we travelled together to the United States for ten days in January 2002, with a Muslim colleague, at the height of the Second Intifada during which time we addressed Jewish, Christian and interreligious audiences in several cities in the USA in persuasive public dialogue sessions which were candid and non-confrontational, and which demonstrated our joint commitment to peaceful coexistence through genuine openness and dialogue.

Bishop Younan grew up in Beersheba as the child of Palestinian refugees from the 1948 Israel War of Independence, and holds UNWRA (United Nations Relief and Works Agency) refugee status. Souha, his wife, grew up in Haifa, where there remains a strong Christian Arab presence until this day. After completing his primary and secondary education, Younan studied to be a Lutheran minister in Finland, where he also earned a master's degree and wrote a thesis on Deutero Isaiah. In 1976, he was ordained a Lutheran priest at the Church of the Redeemer in Jerusalem, following which he served the Lutheran Church in Jerusalem and the region in areas of pastoral leadership, youth leadership and Christian education. In 1988, he was appointed bishop of the Evangelical Lutheran Church in Jordan and the Holy Land.

I vividly remember his investiture in the beautiful Lutheran Church of the Redeemer in the Christian quarter of the Old City of Jerusalem since I was one of the few Jews invited to this event and I sat in the front row. In his inspirational sermon on that day, he called upon both Palestinians and Israelis to seek peace, since the end of violent conflict is in the interests of both peoples. This is a position that has been a constant mainstay of his religious outlook vis-a-vis the Israeli-Palestinian conflict. I remember vividly how he called to wish me a *Shanah Tovah* (happy Jewish new year) in late September of 2000 during the Second Intifada while he was caring for wounded Palestinians at the Augusta Victoria hospital on the Mount of Olives in East Jerusalem (a hospital that is operated under Lutheran auspices). From then on, he made it a habit to call me before every major Jewish holiday to wish me holiday greetings and I would call him before Christmas and Easter each year. One year he even attended our family Passover Seder. Moreover, we would often meet for coffee or breakfast to discuss issues of common concern and seek ways in which we could help each other. We continue to do this to this day.

It was no accident, therefore, that when I did a series of public programs in Jerusalem, at the Van Leer Jerusalem Institute on meeting Christian leaders in Jerusalem, Bishop Younan was the first person that I asked to speak. In 2014, he gave a compelling talk in which he presented background information on the Lutheran community in Jerusalem as well as presenting his views on the key issues facing Jewish-Christian dialogue in Jerusalem in recent years. In this speech, he clearly outlined the approach of the Lutheran Church to the Palestinian-Israeli conflict. Among other things, he said:

With other Palestinians, I seek the just establishment of a Palestinian state alongside Israel, a just resolution to the status of the Israeli settlements, and a just resolution to the chronic crisis of Palestinian refugees. It is my hope that the state of Palestine would be a non-militarized state, with the funding traditionally given to that pursuit to be invested in educational pursuits. [78]

Bishop Younan has remained one of the key Palestinian Christian religious leaders who is devoted to peace through dialogue. For several years, he has been one of the most consistent participants in the dialogues of the Council of Religious Leaders of the Holy Land.

In an interview, [79] I asked Bishop Younan about how he sees Christian identity in Israel. In his view, the religious attachments of Christians in Israel to their church communities remains paramount in their identity. Their religion—which includes a religious culture of weddings, funerals, food and feasts—is essential to who they are as Christians.

Through my dialogues with Bishop Younan and others, I have learned that Palestinian Christians in Israel see themselves as part of the Palestinian people. Even though they no longer live under occupation (except for those who live in Jerusalem), they remember well the military rule which governed their lives from 1948-1966. And, even though they are Israeli citizens, Palestinian Christians in Israel identify with the struggles and sufferings of Palestinians in East Jerusalem, the West Bank and Gaza.

However, there is a major difference between Christians who live in the West Bank (including East Jerusalem) and those who live as citizens within the state of Israel. According to Bishop Younan, Palestinian Christians in the West Bank—who have been part of a refugee community since the wars of 1948 and 1967—ask themselves: "what does the Church do for us"? On the other hand, Christians within Israel, particularly in the Galilee, ask "What can I do for the Church?" Their situations are clearly very different and the way that they relate to their established churches is also different. [80]

One of the main ways that the Christian identity of Palestinian Christians in Israel is preserved is via their schools. All of the main Christian denominations—Lutheran, Latin Catholic, Greek Catholic, Franciscan and Orthodox—operate schools in Israel. These schools help preserve Christian identity by teaching ethics and values that are central to Christianity as well as providing an education in Christian culture and community. [81]

Another Christian leader in Jerusalem with whom I have worked closely in recent years is Father Hosam Naoum, Dean of the Cathedral of St. George in East Jerusalem. He too can attest to the importance of education within the Anglican Church, which sponsors two schools in Israel, one in Ramallah and a large primary and secondary school in Jerusalem, where he served as acting headmaster from 2013 to 2015. Fr. Hosam is a relatively young Anglican priest (in his mid-forties), who sees himself not only as a local priest and pastor for his own people, but as someone who actively pursues dialogue and reconciliation as part of his ministry. Personally, he is an amalgam of Israeli and West Bank identities, since he was born in the Israeli Palestinian Arab town of Shfaram, in the lower Galilee, and served an Anglican congregation for 10 years in Nablus in the West Bank, as well as marrying a Christian woman from Nablus. Accordingly, Fr. Hosam has a very good understanding of Palestinian Christian identity both within Israel and within the West Bank.

Not all Christians in Jerusalem are "Palestinian" Christians. For example, the Armenian Orthodox Church which has been in Jerusalem for a very long time, represents the interests of Armenian Christians, whose national identity is Armenian and their homeland Armenia. One of my trusted colleagues and friends for many years in Jerusalem is Archbishop Aris Shirvanian. He served on the board of directors of ICCI for many years, and he often spoke with me (and other colleagues) and to visiting groups about diversity within Christianity in Jerusalem, where he talked about the uniqueness of the ancient and contemporary Armenian community in Jerusalem. Indeed, one of the four quarters of the Old City in Jerusalem is the Armenian quarter, where the Armenian patriarchate, the Armenian seminary and the historic cathedral of St. James are all located.

Bishop Shirvanian and I also worked in common cause on issues of discrimination against Christians in Jerusalem. When many of the Armenian priests were spat upon by young ultra-Orthodox Jewish youth—in hate crimes which were largely ignored by the police—I and my colleagues organized solidarity visits to the Armenian community in Jerusalem to explain to them that normative Judaism rejects and denounces these acts. In short, I worked with many of the Christian leaders in East Jerusalem over many years, and became a trusted partner in dialogue. This list also included Msgr. Michel Sabbah, the former Latin (Roman Catholic) Patriarch and some of the leadership of the Latin Patriarchate, such as Bishop William Shomali and Fr. David Neuhaus, as well as leaders of the Greek Orthodox Church, especially Metropolitan Aristarchos, and the abbots and friars of the Dormition Abbey on Mount Zion, which I visited often, especially in solidarity visits with the Tag Meir forum following desecration of their church property by young Jewish fanatics. Just as I came to know them through my multiple involvements in dialogue and interreligious activism, they came to know me and they knew that they could call upon me when needed. Based on many years of working together, we tried to improve the lives of Christians and Christian institutions in Jerusalem and throughout Israel, while at the same time bringing Jews from Israel and abroad into meaningful encounters with Christians in Jerusalem, who often were invisible to the Jewish community, living as they do behind their walls in many Christian institutions in Jerusalem.

Within the West Bank ("Palestine")

Through my discussions with many Christian religious leaders, I have learned that Christians from communities in the West Bank (including East Jerusalem, where Palestinians perceive themselves to be part and parcel of the West Bank) experience a very different set of circumstances than those who are living in the state of Israel. In the West Bank, Palestinian Christians, as all other Palestinians, have lived under occupation for almost 50 years. They do not have the same freedoms of movement and of expression as do Palestinian Arab citizens of Israel.

In addition, within the West Bank (and Gaza),[82] they live in an area which is predominantly Muslim (the vast majority of Palestinians in the West Bank are Sunni Muslims) and they need to adjust to living in a Muslim majority which is not always easy, to say the least. Indeed, the growth of radical Islam—identified with Hamas, Islamic Jihad and other groups—has made conditions more precarious for Christians in the West Bank and Gaza, who often live in fear of extremist Muslim groups, even though they do not like to say this too openly and will only speak to journalists (both local and foreign) under condition of anonymity.

In Palestine (including East Jerusalem, where there are about 10,000 Christians), there are approximately 50,000 Christians (under 2% of the population).[83] The largest groups of Christians in the West Bank are Greek Orthodox and Latin Catholic, followed by smaller numbers of Melkite Greek Catholic, Anglican, Syrian, Lutheran and Armenian Christians. The Christians of all denominations place a high value on education, and therefore many of their young people have gone abroad to study. The Christians also have a relatively low rate of unemployment. Most of them (over 80%) work in services and commerce (e.g. banks, insurance, education, tourism, and medicine) and very few of them work in agriculture (less than 1%).[84]

According to some local Christians with whom I spoke (who prefer to remain anonymous), it is very difficult to get accurate data on the real number of Christians in the West Bank.[85] The data are scarce. The Palestinian Authority either does not collect data or does not broadly report information related to the Christian population. In addition, demographic data are often inconsistent in how they treat different cities and areas. Also, some data have been misreported in the past.[86]

What is clear is that the Christians in the West Bank are heavily influenced by three trends: 1) high level of education and high socio-economic status, which has led many to emigrate over the decades for economic reasons, i.e. better jobs and a higher standard of living, 2) the travails of living under military occupation, and 3) the growth of radical fundamentalist Islam which often persecutes Christians and makes their lives very uncomfortable.

All in all, it is not a comfortable situation, (neither is it a satisfactory situation for Muslims in the West Bank and East Jerusalem!) which is why, for the most part, Palestinian Christians in the West Bank keep a low profile and generally do not engage in political or anti-occupation "resistance", as do their Muslim counterparts. The one city that is an exception to this is Bethlehem, in which one finds not only major Christian sites and churches, but also a Christian-sponsored university, Bethlehem University. Bethlehem is still an important Christian city in the West Bank, even though most of its residents today are Muslim. On the other hand, Jerusalem, which is perceived by Palestinians as part of the West Bank, as discussed above, is very different since it is the home of so many important Christian churches and institutions which have a major physical and symbolic presence in the city (including in West Jerusalem).

For practical, as opposed to ideological reasons, most of my interreligious work was with Christians in Jerusalem but not in the West Bank. First of all, they were simply more accessible since there are no security restrictions preventing me from visiting the Christian Quarter in the Old City of Jerusalem most of the time as opposed to the West Bank (including the major Palestinian cities of Bethlehem, Hebron, Nablus, Ramallah and Jenin, which are all in "Area A" under Palestinian security control) which has been off-limits for Israeli Jews since the outbreak of the Second Intifada in the year 2000.

On the other hand, it has been possible to visit Christian institutions and meet with the Christians in Area C, under Israeli security control. Following the Interim Agreement between Israel and the PLO (1995) and more recent agreements, the West Bank has been divided into three administrative Areas: A, B and C. In Areas A and B, which together cover 40 percent of the West Bank, the Palestinian Authority has full control over physical planning and construction. In Area C, which covers 60 percent of the West Bank, planning authority rests exclusively with the Civil Administration. Consequently, in Area C, all construction and every planning scheme require the approval of the Israeli Civil Administration. The difference between A and B is that Palestinians have security control over A but not over B. [87]

So, for example, it has been feasible to meet Christians from Bethlehem and other parts of the West Bank at a Lutheran-run school and guesthouse called Talitakumi, in Beit Jala, just West of Bethlehem or at a little Christian-run hotel called Mount Everest in the same area. These two "oases" served as "neutral" meeting ground for many Palestinian-Israeli dialogue groups and organizations. I attended many conferences, workshops, and informal dialogues in both places over the years.

At one point in time, together with my staff, I reached out to a Christian organization in Bethlehem (whose name will not be mentioned here) which was working on interreligious dialogue with youth and young adults, and we initiated some cooperative programs. For about a year and a half, our dialogues were going well—even though they were often very emotional and difficult—and we were hopeful that we could continue to cooperate on dialogue and action projects for a long time. And then, all of a sudden, one day I received an email from my counterparts at this Palestinian organization in Bethlehem, with whom I had developed very cordial and collegial relationships, which explained that their Board of Directors had decided to break off all relationships with Israeli organizations until the occupation was over. This was part of a growing "anti-normalization" trend in Palestinian society, whereby heavy pressure was put on Palestinian organizations to disconnect, including with organizations committed to peace through dialogue such as mine. While I was very disappointed and frustrated, there was nothing that I could do about this. As a result, I went back to focusing my energies on the art of the possible, i.e. dialogue with Palestinian Christians within Jerusalem and within the state of Israel, where coexistence between Jewish Israeli citizens and Palestinian Arab Israeli citizens is still fraught with difficulties but is at least possible.

IMPLICATIONS OF CHRISTIAN DIVERSITY IN THE HOLY LAND FOR JEWISH-CHRISTIAN DIALOGUE AND INTERRELIGIOUS DIALOGUE

Since Christian diversity in Israel and the West Bank is a fact of life, I have discovered first hand that the art of entering into dialogue with Christians is complex and often requires careful planning and creativity. For most of the past twenty-five years, I have been engaged with Christians in Israel through dialogue in a variety of ways and through a number of very significant dialogue groups, and in so doing, I have come to know the commitments and concerns of local as well as visiting or expatriate Christians intimately, on a personal as well as communal and organizational basis.

In addition to my dialogue work with Bishop Younan, mentioned above, I have interacted with many of the local Christian leaders in Jerusalem, including the leadership of the local Catholic, Armenian and Anglican churches. For a long time, I have worked closely with these local Christian leaders in Jerusalem—as well as with Christian religious leaders in the Galilee—on issues of common concern, and in so doing, earned their trust as an honest partner in genuine dialogue. As a result, I appeared on countless panel discussions with them for local and visiting groups very often. Moreover, because of my close working relationships with these grass-roots leaders, they usually agreed to speak on panel discussions that I moderated. I would say that I facilitated literally hundreds of such panel discussions, both private and public, over the years in Israel and abroad, and I earned a reputation as a serious and sensitive moderator of such discussions.

I also engaged on a regular basis with some of the leading "expatriate" (long-term visitors from all over the world) Christians and Christian institutions in Jerusalem, including the Tantur Ecumenical Institute in Jerusalem (located in the Israeli-Jewish neighborhood of Gilo in southern Jerusalem, overlooking Bethlehem)[88], the Sisters of our Lady of Sion (in their beautiful convent in Ein Kerem, in western Jerusalem, and also in their famous convent and guesthouse known as "Ecce Homo" in the Muslim quarter of the Old City of Jerusalem),[89] the Swedish Theological Institute (located in an historic building on Prophets' Street in downtown Jerusalem),[90] the Focolare movement (based in Rome, but with volunteers in Jerusalem and a local chapter in Haifa), the Bat Kol Institute (located in central Jerusalem, which brings Christians from all over the world to study the Bible with Jewish teachers and Jewish sources in Jerusalem), Bridges for Peace (an international Christian evangelical organization whose headquarters are in central Jerusalem and who support Israel via good deeds), and others.

Many of the leaders of these organizations became not only trusted colleagues but also treasured friends, with whom I continue to be involved on many issues of common cause to this day. For example, I cooperated with the Sisters of our Lady of Sion and the Focolare movement in a major program called "Jerusalem Expo" in November 2015, which brought hundreds of Jews, Christians and Muslims together in the large auditorium of the Notre Dame Cultural Center in the heart of Jerusalem, for an evening that showcased the work of ICCI and other organizations in Jerusalem and the region.[91] These are people and institutions who devote their lives to the same ideals that I do—interreligious dialogue for the sake of peaceful coexistence. Their commitment and involvement to dialogue continues to inspire and to energize me, and their dedication to peace, tranquility and civility in Israel has been a blessing not only for me, but for so many other people and communities in Israel, who are enriched by their presence in this land.

NOTES

1. The "Green Line" represents the border between Israel and Jordan before the Six Day War of June 1967.

2. I use the term "Palestine" for the area which the Palestinians control and over which they have quasi-statehood, what is called officially the "Palestinian Authority" or the "Palestinian National Authority", i.e. the West Bank (and Gaza). Some Palestinians and the international community also refer to East Jerusalem as part of "Palestine" but this is not yet the case. "Palestine" is also referred to variously as the Territories or the disputed territories, or the Occupied Territories, "the West Bank and Gaza", and "Judea and Samaria."

3. The total population of Israel at the end of 2015 was 8,463,400 people. The Jewish population makes up 6,334,500 (74.9%); the Arabs (Muslims and Christians) make up 1,791000 (21%); and the remaining 4% are "other". Of the Arabs, 83% are Muslim, 9% are Christian and 7.6% are Druse. Muslims make up 17.5% of the total population of the citizens of Israel, and Christians make up 1.9%. (Central Bureau of Statistics, September 1, 2016.) In the official statistics, only people who are registered with Israel's Ministry of Interior are counted as citizens or permanent residents. In other words, all Jews living in the Territories are counted

because they are all citizens while only those Palestinians who are citizens or permanent residents are counted. Gaza and West Bank Palestinians are not accounted for.

4. For a full discussion of Palestinian Arab identity in Israel as outlined by a Palestinian Arab Muslim, see Issa Jaber, *Is Arab-Jewish Coexistence Still Possible?* in Ronald Kronish, ed. *Coexistence and Reconciliation in Israel—Voices for Interreligious Dialogue.* Paulist Press, 2015, pp. 160-168.

5. For a full discussion of the nature of Palestinian identity in Israel, see Ilan Peleg and Dov Waxman. *Israel's Palestinians. The Conflict Within*, Cambridge University Press, 2011.

6. Israel's Arab population are often referred to in official and public discourse as 'Israeli Arabs', 'Arab citizens of Israel', 'Palestinian Arabs' or as 'Palestinian citizens of Israel'. Identity is particularly complex for Arabs living within Israel, and they tend to identify by ethnicity and religion rather than nationality. Research conducted by Professor Sammy Smooha for the University of Haifa's Annual Index of Jewish-Arab Relations has shown that in 2009, 59.6% of the overall Arab population identified themselves in a form that incorporated the term Palestinian. While as recently as 2003, the majority (53%) defined themselves as Israeli Arabs without the Palestinian identifier. This shift is seen to be symptomatic of increasing tensions between the Jewish and Arab population groups in Israel. As quoted in "Israel's Arab Citizens: Key Facts and Current Realities, the UK Task Force on Issues Relating to Arab citizens of Israel", June 2013. http://soc.haifa.ac.il.

7. In the Israeli elections of 2015, Israeli Arab voter turnout was 63.5% compared to 56% in 2013, according to the Statnet research institute, which had predicted a 63.4% turnout prior to the election. Yousef Makladeh, CEO of Statnet.co.il, said that 82% of Israeli Arabs voted for the Joint (Arab) List compared to 77% who voted for Arab parties in 2013. The institute's polling had predicted 81.5% four days before the election. The rest vote for various Jewish parties.

8. The percentage of Arab university students in Israel has risen significantly in recent years, according to a Central Bureau of Statistics report. In the year 2015, 14.4 percent of bachelor degree students were Arabs, compared with 9.8 percent in 1999/2000. In that same period, the rate of Arab master degree candidates rose from only 3.6 percent to 10.5 percent, while Arab Ph.D. candidates doubled from 2.8 percent to 5.9 percent. The proportion of women among Arab higher education students has also risen. In 2000, 61.7 percent of Arab students were women, while in 2015 the figure was 67.2 percent. Yarden Skop, "More Arab Students in Israel Attending University in New Academic Year". *Ha'aretz*, Oct 15, 2015.

9. The growth rate of the Muslim population is in decline - from 3.8% in 2000 to 2.4% in 2014. Despite this, the Muslim population is still growing faster than any other in Israel - with the Jewish growth rate at 1.9%, Christian at 1.6%, and Druse at 1.5%. More than half of the Muslim population is concentrated in the North, with 36.2% of Israel's Muslims in the northern district and 14% in the Haifa metropolitan area. 21.6% of Israeli Muslims live in the greater Jerusalem area; 15.9% in the South; 11.1% in the Central District; and just 1.1% live in the Tel Aviv area. Large Muslim communities reside in Rahat (60,000; 98% of total residents); Nazareth (52,000); and Umm el-Fahm (51,000). http://www.israelnationalnews.com.

10. Interview with Dr. Aziz Haidar in Ronald Kronish, "Religious and Cultural Diversity among Muslims in Israel" in *Coexistence and Reconciliation in Israel*, p. 105.

11. The geographical terms relate to areas in the "Triangle" in central Israel which is a concentration of Israeli Arab towns and villages adjacent to the Green Line, located in the eastern Sharon plain in the Samarian foothills.

12. Interview with Dr. Aziz Haidar in Ronald Kronish, "Religious and Cultural Diversity among Muslims in Israel" in *Coexistence and Reconciliation in Israel*, p. 105.

13. Interview with Dr. Aziz Haidar, September 26, 2016.

14. Interview with Dr. Iyad Zahalka, a professor at Tel Aviv University and the Emek Yizrael College of Arab society in Israel, March 31, 2016.

15. Kronish, Ibid., p. 106.

16. Kronish, Ibid. p. 106, according to veteran educator, Dr. Marwan Darweish.

17. Interview with Masoud Ghanayem, a leader of the Southern branch of the Islamic Movement and chairperson of the Knesset faction for the Joint List (a coalition of 4 Israeli Arab political parties) on Galei Tzahal, Israeli Army Radio, April 11, 2016.

18. At the 58th commemoration in October 2014, President of Israel, Reuven Rivlin, attended and condemned the massacre in the village of Kafr Kassem. Rivlin, who became president in June 2014, has become a strong moral voice in the country.

19. See chapter 4 for a full description of one of my visits to Kafr Kassem with rabbis from Israel.

20. Interview with Sheikh Ibrahim Sarsur in his home in Kafr Kassem, May 22, 2016. Sheikh Sarsur served as a Member of Knesset (the Israeli parliament) from April 2006-March 2015.

21. Ibid.

22. A full history and analysis of the Kedem program can be found in chapter 4.

23. "Outlawing the Northern Branch of the Islamic Movement", the Van Leer Forum for Public Discussion, Jan. 13, 2016. http://www.vanleer.org.il.

24. Kronish, p. 107, quoting Dr. Aziz Haidar.

25. Interview with Aziz Haidar, September 26, 2016.

26. Iyad Zahalka. *Shari'a in the Modern Era: Muslim Minorities Jurisprudence.* Cambridge: Cambridge University Press, 2016.

27. A comprehensive interview article about Kadi Zahalka, which summarized his views on many topics for the Israeli public, appeared recently in an important Hebrew newspaper called *Makor Rishon*, which is widely read by modern orthodox Jews in Israel. *Makor Rishon*, January 13, 2017

28. Kronish, Ibid. p. 107, quoting Dr. Aziz Haidar.

29. Lauren Gelfond Feldinger, "Nazareth's Sufis Bullied by Fellow Muslims", *Ha'aretz.* Aug 10, 2012.

30. Ibid.

31. Ibid.

32. Al-Ghazali (*c.*1056–1111) was one of the most prominent and influential philosophers, theologians, jurists, and mystics of Sunni Islam. Stanford Encyclopedia of Philosophy, Sept. 22, 2014.

33. Kronish, Ibid., p. 108, quoting Howla Sadi.

34. Ibid.

35. Ibid.

36. Ibid, p. 109, quoting Dr. Mohammad Hourani.

37. Ibid., p.110.

38. Interview with Dr. Haidar, September 26, 2016.

39. For an in-depth discussion of the complexities of Palestinian Arab Israeli identity in general, see David Grossman's *Sleeping on a Wire: Conversations with Palestinians in Israel,* translated by Haim Watzman (New York, Farrar, Strauss, and Giroux, 1993).

40. Kronish, Ibid., p.112, based on interview with Dr. Marwan Darweish.

41. Interview with Dr. Aziz Haidar, September 16, 2016.

42. Ibid, interview with Dr. Aziz Haidar.

43. I read Sari Nusseibeh's autobiography, *Once Upon a Country: A Palestinian Life* (with Anthony David), Farrar, Straus and Giroux, New York, 2007, several years ago and heard him speak on a panel at the Jerusalem International YMCA with the Israeli author, Amos Oz, who had also written his autobiography, *A Tale of Love and Darkness,* the same year. I also had occasion to be with Prof. Nusseibeh at an interreligious conference for peace in Palermo, Sicily, where I was part of an encounter which I describe in chapter 5.

44. I relate a story about my encounter with Professor Sari Nusseibeh in Palermo in chapter 5.

45. Interview with Prof. Mohammed S. Dajani Daoudi by Lauren Gelfond Feldinger, *Ha'aretz*, reprinted with permission in *Wasatia: The Road to Reconciliation.* Published by Wasatia Press, Al-Bireh, Palestine.

46. http://www.wasatia.info/

47. Interview with Mohammed Dajani on September 18, 2016.

48. Ibid.

49. Ibid.

50. In 1876, the New York Society for Ethical Culture (NYSEC) was founded by Dr. Felix Adler, who was both a visionary and a revolutionary. Proposing a new movement which would work toward the advancement of social justice for all, Adler suggested that the movement should further the principles of ethics among adults and children through education, and members of the Society should express their religious consciences through moral and humane actions. http://www.nysec.org/history

51. Prof. Mohammed S. Dajani Doudi, Prof. Munther S. Dajani Daoudi, Prof. Martin Leiner, Dr. Zeina M. Barakat, Editors. "Teaching Empathy and Reconciliation in Midst of Conflict, Wasatia Press, El-Bireh, Palestine, 2016 and Nadine Epstein, "Mohammed Dajani Daoudi: Evolution of a Moderate", *Moment*, July 17, 2014, www.momentmag.com.

52. Introduction to booklet by Prof. Mohammed S. Dajani Doudi, Prof. Munther S. Dajani Daoudi, Prof. Martin Leiner, Dr. Zeina M. Barakat, Editors. "Teaching Empathy and Reconciliation in Midst of Conflict," Wasatia Press, El-Bireh, Palestine, 2016

53. Mohammed Dajani Daoudi and Robert Satloff, "Why Palestinians Should Learn about the Holocaust," *The New York Times,* March 29, 2011.

54. Central Bureau of Statistics, September 1, 2016.

55. Ethan Felson, JCPA Background paper on the The Palestinian Christian Population, spring 2012, p.12.

56. Ibid.

57. Central Bureau of Statistics, October 9, 2015.

58. Bernard Sabella, lecture at the Tantur Ecumenical Institute in Jerusalem, May 17, 2016.

59. Interview with Bishop Munib Younan, Bishop of the Evangelical Lutheran Church in Jordan and the Holy Land since 1998, in Jerusalem, May 18, 2016.

60. Bernard Sabella, Ibid.

61. Sabella, Ibid.

62. The number and percentage of Christians in Israel varies according to different researchers. In a study done in 2012, the figures are slightly different: Greek Catholic 40%, Greek Orthodox 32%, Roman Catholic 20%, Maronites 7%, Others (Protestant, Armenian, etc.) 1%. Johnny Mansour. Arab Christians in Israel—Facts, Figures and Trends, 2012, Diyar Publishing, p. 23.

63. Interview with Fr. David Neuhaus, June 22, 2016. David M. Neuhaus SJ is a Latin Patriarchal Vicar for the Latin Patriarchate of Jerusalem and the Saint James Vicariate for Hebrew Speaking Catholics in Israel.

64. Out of the 160,000 Christians in Israel, about 130,000 live in the Galilee. Interview with Fr. Hosam Naoum, November 22, 2016.

65. Ibid.

66. Two recent exceptions to this were the demonstrations and complaints about a major reduction in government funding for Christian schools in 2015, and frequent protests in recent years against the lack of enforcement of the law when it came to arresting Jewish perpetrators of hate crimes and vandalism against Christian institutions in Israel 2013-2016.

67. Ronald Kronish. "On Interreligious Dialogue: Lessons Learned." *The Jerusalem Post Magazine*, February 4, 2016.

68. See chapter 4 for more about the Kedem program.

69. www.pilgrimsofibillin.org.

70. Interview with Fr. Hosam Naoum, May 16, 2016. The 13 patriarchates and heads of churches in Jerusalem consist of: the Greek Orthodox Patriarchate, the Latin (Roman Catholic) Patriarchate, the Armenian Orthodox Patriarchate, the Custody of the Holy Land (Franciscans), the Coptic Orthodox Patriarchate, the Syrian Orthodox Patriarchate, the Ethiopian Orthodox Patriarchate, the Maronite Patriarchal Exarchate, Episcopal (Anglican), the Evangelical Lutheran Church in Jerusalem and Jordan, the Syrian Patriarchal Exarchate, the Greek-Melkite Catholic Patriarchate, the Armenian Catholic Patriarchal Exarchate.

71. The *status quo* as it is commonly called, in a broad sense, refers to the relations between the Christian communities of the Holy Land with the governments of the region. Specifically, *status quo* applies to the situation within the Holy Land in which the Christian communities find themselves regarding ownership and rights possessed by each within the Basilica of the

Holy Sepulcher, the Basilica of the Nativity in Bethlehem and the Tomb of the Virgin Mary in Jerusalem. http://www.custodia.org/default.asp?id=433

72. Most Palestinian Arab Christians in Jerusalem live in East Jerusalem, but there are some in West Jerusalem.

73. *Memorandum of Their Beatitudes the Patriarchs and of the Heads of the Christian Communities in Jerusalem on the Significance of Jerusalem for Christians,* Nov. 14, 1994, 4 pp, www.albushra.org.

74. Ibid.

75. Interview with Bishop Younan, Ibid.

76. The estimates of the number of Palestinian Christians in Jerusalem today run from 8,000 to 10,000. However, if you count Armenians, Ethiopians and Assyrians, the number gets closer to 15,000. Interviews with Fr. David Neuhaus, June 11, 2016 and Fr. Hosam Naoum on November 22, 2016.

77. The "Light Tag" Forum, or *Tag Meir,* as it is known in Hebrew, is a coalition of more than 50 Jewish and interreligious groups in Israeli society which combats religious extremism and hate crimes. I served on the Steering Committee of this coalition from 2013 to 2016, and in this capacity, I visited many churches and mosques which had been vandalized by Jewish extremists, and wrote about this in my blogs for *The Times of Israel* and *The Huffington Post.* Tag Meir works to bring light instead of darkness to Israeli society, in the context of a growing number of extremist hate crimes against peace workers, women, Christians and Muslims, by radical Jewish youth from Israel and the West Bank.

78. Bishop Munib Younan, Lecture at Van Leer Jerusalem Institute, Feb. 17, 2014.

79. Interview with Bishop Munib Younan, Oct. 18, 2016.

80. Ibid.

81. Ibid.

82. There are only about 2,000 Christians in Gaza, representing a tiny minority in an overwhelmingly Muslim enclave. Interview with Fr. Hosam Naoum, May 16, 2016.

83. Interview with David M. Neuhaus SJ, Latin Patriarchal Vicar, Saint James Vicariate for Hebrew Speaking Catholics in Israel, Pastoral Coordination for Migrants, July 23, 2016.

84. "The Sabeel Survey on Palestinian Christians in the West Bank and Israel, Historical Demographic Developments, Current Politics and Attitudes Towards Church, Society and Human Rights," Summer, 2006, p 17, as quoted in *JCPA Background Paper—the Palestinian Christian Population* by Ethan Felson and Marc Schlesinger, Spring 2012, p.4.

85. As of 2007, there were a total of 51,710, as opposed to 45, 855 in the 1961 Jordanian Census. Christians in the West Bank and Gaza Strip, including the Arab population in Jerusalem. Rania Al Qass Collings, Rifat Odeh Kassis, Mitri Raheb, Editors. *Palestinian Christians in the West Bank—Facts, Figures and Trends,* 2012, published by Diyar Publishing, p. 11

86. Ibid., p. 7.

87. Bimkom - Planners for Planning Rights, *The Prohibited Zone,* 2009. http://bimkom.org.

88. The Tantur Ecumenical Institute is situated on a hill in southern East Jerusalem, near Gilo, on the road to Bethlehem. It serves as a place in the Holy Land for groups and individuals including scholars from many disciplines, teachers, as well as university groups, church groups, and interreligious groups. http://tantur.org.

89. On the website of the Sisters of our Lady of Sion in Jerusalem they mention their involvement in my organization, the Interreligious Coordinating Council in Israel: "We have been active members of this council since its beginnings. This has brought a richness to our lives in the many friendships that have developed over the years as we work in solidarity with Jews, Muslims and Christians." http://www.notredamedesion.org/en/page.php?id=8&T=2

90. The Swedish Theological Institute in Jerusalem was established in 1951 by the Lutheran Church of Sweden. The stated goal is: "to enable Christians to deepen their knowledge of Judaism and Christianity in the land of the Bible... The institute offers study and interfaith programs for theology students, pastors and teachers from developing countries, short-term courses for Swedish clergy and laymen and international conferences and seminars." http://projects.jerusalemfoundation.org.

91. Interview with Sister Maureen Cusick of the Sisters of our Lady of Sion in Jerusalem, September 26, 2016.

Chapter Three

Engaging with the Vatican

As part of my career in interreligious dialogue in Israel—and international-ly—I was privileged to meet Pope John Paul II several times at conferences in the Vatican and in Assisi. Also, I was witness to the signing of the Funda-mental Agreement between the Holy See and the state of Israel in December 1993, and I have worked with all the nuncios (ambassadors) to the state of Israel since the signing of formal diplomatic relations with Israel until today.

During the Pope's historic week-long visit to Israel in March 2000, I wrote a special op-ed in the Jerusalem Post[1] welcoming the Pope to Israel and I was active in arranging briefings for the foreign press in advance of the visit. The visit of the Pope to Israel at that time changed the way that Jews in Israel and around the world related to Christianity, and especially to Catho-lics, and it opened up new opportunities for dialogue which were impossible before that. It also led to the production of a unique documentary film, *I am Joseph Your Brother* which has helped Jews and Christians around the world understand the changes that have taken place during the last 50 years, which I have called "the era of dialogue". The film and the accompanying study guide were originally produced in 2001, in cooperation with the Institute for Jewish Christian Studies in Baltimore. Since then the film has been translated into Hebrew and Italian and has been screened at film festivals, universities and international conferences around the world.

In this chapter, I will discuss the impact of the recognition by the Holy See of the state of Israel—and Pope John Paul II's visit to Israel—upon Jewish-Christian relations in particular and on interreligious dialogue in gen-eral. Interreligious dialogue was given a huge boost by this very special Pope, as was the commitment to peacebuilding. This was not only a great personal milestone for me, but a historical stepping-stone in cementing the partnership between the Jewish people, the state of Israel and the Catholic Church towards *tikkun olam*, repairing the world.

THE FUNDAMENTAL AGREEMENT
BETWEEN THE HOLY SEE AND THE STATE OF ISRAEL

As a result of the political peace process in 1993 (see chapter one), the Vatican decided to enter into negotiations with the state of Israel. They felt that a new political window of opportunity had been opened, which could now enable them to finally and officially recognize the state of Israel. The non-recognition of Israel had been a stumbling block in Catholic-Jewish dialogue for many years. It was a critical issue which the Jewish counterparts in the official dialogue process had brought up many times, usually to no avail. But now the time was ripe.

As a result of my increasing involvement in Jewish-Catholic dialogue, and the reputation I earned for being an honest dialogue partner, I was invited to the signing of the Fundamental Agreement between the state of Israel and the Holy See, at the end of December 1993, a few months after the signing of the Oslo Accords (September 13, 1993). This agreement was signed at the Foreign Ministry of Israel in Jerusalem, in the presence of the Deputy Foreign Minister Dr. Yossi Beilin. I was there to witness it. This was a new and very positive watershed in contemporary Jewish-Catholic relations. Not only did the political entity known as the Vatican, which represents more than a billion Catholics around the world, recognize the state of Israel, but the tiny Jewish state of Israel, which in some ways represents Jews all over the world, recognized the Vatican! This was the culmination of many years of persistent dialogue, which is why the preamble to this document sets this diplomatic achievement within the context of the unfolding dialogue between Catholics and Jews since the end of World War II. In addition, it is no accident that this agreement was concluded in December 1993, just three months after the signing of the Oslo Accords. Without this first development, the second would have been delayed interminably.

Since I was deeply involved in Jewish-Catholic dialogue for many years, I was also invited to give a paper at a seminar at the Vatican, chaired by Cardinal Edward Cassidy[2], who at that time (March 1998) was in charge of the Pontifical Commission on Religious Relations with the Jews, together with Gerhart Riegner, the legendary Jewish chairperson of the IJCIC (International Jewish Committee for Interreligious Consultations), the official Jewish umbrella organization which engaged in dialogue with the leaders of the Catholic Church (and other churches). During this seminar, the Vatican document on the Holocaust was published, and we were privileged to receive a special briefing on this ground-breaking document entitled *We Remember:*

A Reflection on the Shoah, published by the Pontifical Commission for Religious Relations with the Jews, March 1998. The briefing was given by Cardinal Cassidy and Dr. Riegner. Despite much criticism from some Jewish groups of some of the language of the document (for some Jews, it is never good enough!), I found this document to be an amazingly positive step forward in the constantly improving relations between the Catholic Church and the Jewish people. The explanations given to me by Cardinal Cassidy, both in the group briefing, and in private discussions, helped me greatly to understand the seminal significance of this document, in which the Catholic Church declared that it had been undergoing a process of *teshuvah,* repentance, vis-a-vis the Jewish people, since the Holocaust.

The theme of the seminar was "Educating About Each Other", specifically how Jews and Catholics changed the ways that they educate about each other since the famous Catholic proclamation known as *Nostra Aetate*[3] ("In our Time") in October 1965. *Nostra Aetate* is the Vatican's "Declaration on the Relationship of the Church to Non-Christian Religions" which was proclaimed by the Second Vatican Council on October 28, 1965. This declaration opened up the "Era of Dialogue", which is the era in which we still live today. In my paper on what we teach about Christians and Christianity in Israeli schools,[4] I candidly shared with all those at the seminar what was not being done to educate Jews about Christians and Christianity in the contemporary era. Most of my partners in dialogue—many of whom had been involved in dialogue for decades—were shocked and dismayed that pupils in Israel's Jewish schools learn practically nothing about Christians and Christianity beyond the Middle Ages!

I remained heavily involved in Jewish-Catholic dialogue for a number of years. In 1999, I participated in an amazing multi-religious conference at the Vatican which was sponsored by the Pontifical Commission on Interreligious Relations, the Vatican's arm for outreach to religions other than Judaism. On the eve of the new millennium I was invited to the Vatican City by Archbishop Michael Fitzgerald (who now lives in retirement in Israel and remains a good friend) to this important conference—which brought together hundreds of participants—to consider how we could all work together to make this world a more humane place.[5] In January 2003, Archbishop Fitzgerald invited me to participate in another important seminar on "Spiritual Resources of the Religions for Peace", at which I met leading Muslim, Hindu, Sikh and Buddhist scholars from all over the world to learn about sources on peace in each religion. I have stayed in touch with some of these scholars to this day and some of them have even visited me in Israel. While these historical documents—the recognition of the state of Israel by the Vatican (and vice versa) and the Vatican's statement on the Shoah—were of critical importance, they paled in significance compared with the powerful impact of the seven-day visit to Israel (including one day in Palestine, in the Bethlehem area) in

March 2000, which could have only occurred as a result of the progress both in the peace process and in Jewish-Catholic relations as well as Israel-Vatican relations during the 1990s.

THE HISTORIC PILGRIMAGE OF POPE JOHN PAUL II TO ISRAEL, MARCH 2000

During this period, the beginning of the new millennium, Pope John Paul II, whom I was privileged to have met three times (a photo of him with me hung in my office for many years), embarked on his historic eight-day pilgrimage to Israel and Palestine in March 2000. It was a ground-breaking visit, which completely changed the way Jews in Israel and around the world related to the Catholic Church and its leader. This pope was an extremely charismatic religious leader and did more to advance Jewish-Catholic relations than any pope in history.

I was privileged to be involved not only in the planning of parts of this historic pilgrimage but in covering the major events of the week by writing about them extensively and being interviewed all week long by the local and international media who covered this amazing journey in great detail. During that time, I was interviewed by CNN, BBC, and local radio and television stations, and I wrote a major op-ed in *HaAretz* about part of the visit.[6]

Despite predictions of impending gloom and doom—including a headline in a local Jerusalem Hebrew-language newspaper, just one week before the visit of the Pope to Israel in March 2000, which intimated that the Pope was entering *gehinnom*[7] (hell) because there was so much opposition to his visit here from so many people in the Jewish community—the visit of His Holiness Pope John Paul II was an extraordinary historical success. How did this happen? What were the factors that made his visit so successful? How did this particular Pope change the course of Jewish-Catholic relations - both in the years leading up to this pilgrimage to the Holy Land and during the pilgrimage itself, which was undoubtedly one of the spiritual highlights of his papacy? Why and how did this Pope focus on religious reconciliation with Judaism and the Jewish people in this official visit to the Jewish state as part of his overall pilgrimage to the Holy Land?

Background: Progress in Jewish-Christian Relations since Vatican II

The visit of Pope John Paul II to Israel was the culmination of systematic and substantive progress in Jewish-Catholic relations during the previous 35 years. In this period, we have witnessed a truly historic revolution in relations, evidenced primarily in the many documents and statements issued by the Catholic Church and other churches during these years, as well as by the many conferences and seminars devoted to improving relations between Jews and Christians. While these documents and statements are well known to the professionals involved with them, and with some elites, most Christians and Jews are largely unaware of these developments. According to Rabbi Harold Schulweis, a leading Conservative rabbi in Southern California and someone who was deeply involved in Catholic-Jewish dialogue over many years, "the war" with the Catholic Church is over. In a very powerful article in which he accuses the Jewish people of having slept through this revolution, he explains the changes—and the need for us to change accordingly—in graphic terms:

> It is understandable to want to fight yesterday's war and this time to give it a different ending. But to wage war with the wrong enemy, at the wrong time and on the wrong occasion is to fall into a trap of dangerous anachronism. Pope John Paul II is not John Chrysostom. The Church of Vatican II is not the Church of the middle ages. The new Catholic catechism is not the old Catholic catechism... There is something new under the sun and it requires a new statesmanship, a new politics, a new theology as we enter a new century.[8]

Indeed, so much has happened that is new during these past 50 years. The Catholic Church has totally revised its theology with regard to Jews and Judaism in ways that were simply inconceivable to previous generations.

In a paper prepared for the foreign press in advance of the visit of the Pope to Israel in March 2000 by Fr. Michael McGarry, rector of the Tantur Ecumenical Institute in Jerusalem and co-chairperson of the Interreligious Coordinating Council in Israel at the time, the major signposts along the new path of dialogue were highlighted:

> For forty years Catholics and Jews have walked a new path, the retracing of which reveals a number of significant steps towards a new understanding and a new relationship... while most of these signposts are official Church documents, all represent hours and years of consultations, often with our Jewish dialogue partners, and which represent a sea change of ways in which we Roman Catholics approach our Jewish brothers and sisters.[9]

In short, the Catholic Church has made enormous strides on the subject of relations to Jews and Judaism since Vatican II in the mid-60s. Even though the beginnings of this revolution in Catholic doctrine took place under Pope John XXIII, there is no question that Pope John Paul II encouraged and expanded these developments as a result of his personal history (having grown up in Poland among Jews) and of his own inclinations and theology.[10] Indeed, his very desire to come on a spiritual pilgrimage to the Land of Israel was very much a culmination of this process, a fact clearly expressed in many of his speeches and gestures during the visit. Despite his poor health, this was a dream that he fervently hoped to live to see. As became evident during the visit, this was as much a personal pilgrimage as an institutional visit on behalf of the universal Catholic Church.

After weeks of media hype and conferences speculating on what would happen during the Pope's visit, he finally arrived on Tuesday afternoon, March 21st at 5:30 p.m. at Ben Gurion Airport in the center of Israel. Like so many other moments in his visit, this was an amazing symbolic and emotional experience. The Pope and his entourage arrived on a Royal Jordanian Airline plane from Amman, where he had spent the previous day as part of his pilgrimage to the Holy Land, and on the front of the plane flew two flags—the blue and white flag of the state of Israel and the flag of the Holy See, a sovereign state as well as the capital of the universal Catholic Church.

This airplane signified the merging of the peace process with a new spirit of understanding and cooperation in Jewish-Christian relations that had been gestating since Vatican II. Just as the signing of the Fundamental Agreement between the state of Israel and the Holy See on December 30, 1993 was implemented three months after the signing of the Oslo peace agreements on the White House lawn in Washington D.C. on September 13th of the same year, so too this event was clearly a merging of political and diplomatic "normalization" processes with similar religious and interreligious processes of reconciliation that have become characteristic of Jewish-Catholic relations in recent decades.

Commentators on Israeli and international television networks confirmed this as the Pope landed at Ben Gurion airport, the national airport of the state of Israel, aptly named after Israel's first visionary Prime Minister, David Ben Gurion. "How different this visit is than the visit of the Pope to Israel in 1964," remarked Ya'acov Achimeir, the veteran anchorman on Israel's Channel One.[11] David Witztum, another commentator on the channel, added: "This visit is different because under this pope, there has been progress on three major fronts: between Catholics and Greek Orthodox, between Catholics and Jews/the state of Israel, and between Catholics and Palestinians."[12]

Thus began the unbelievable media love-fest for the Pope that continued throughout the visit. It seemed that the usually cynical foreign and Israeli media melted when the Pope's plane touched down at the airport. It was such an emotional moment. Indeed, the response of the Israeli media—and the foreign press - was so extraordinarily positive to the visit of this major world leader that it was probably unprecedented in Israeli journalistic history. It was an amazing phenomenon—somehow the media became mesmerized and enchanted with the rich combination of historical, diplomatic, religious and interreligious symbolism epitomized by this unprecedented papal visit to the Holy Land. Rather than striving to serve their own agendas, the media functioned as the major educator of the Israeli public—as well, of course, of the entire world community—in teaching about who this Pope was and what he represented and what the changes in the Catholic Church in the second half of the 20th century wrought.

After the plane came to a halt, Prime Minister Ehud Barak and President Ezer Weizmann went to the bottom of the stairs to receive the Pope. His Holiness received a state welcome, with all the protocol usually bestowed upon a leader on an official state visit. Thousands of security personnel surrounded the airport and a large receiving line of Jewish, Christian and Muslim public figures waited on the tarmac to receive the Pope. When the Pope emerged from the plane, and walked down the stairs by himself, showing the willpower that characterized his every move and speech throughout his visit, he was greeted symbolically by three children from Nazareth—a Jew, a Christian and a Muslim—who each gave him some earth from the Land of Israel, the Holy Land, which he promptly and emotionally kissed. In his speech at the airport, which was carefully crafted, as were all of the papal speeches throughout the visit, Pope John Paul II set the tone for the rest of the week:

> My visit is both a personal pilgrimage and the spiritual journey of the Bishop of Rome to the origins of our faith in 'the God of Abraham, of Isaac and of Jacob' (Exodus 3:15)... my journey is therefore a pilgrimage, in a spirit of humble gratitude and hope, to the origins of our religious history. It is a tribute to the three religious traditions which co-exist in this land . . . I pray that my visit will serve to encourage an increase of interreligious dialogue that will lead Jews, Christians and Muslims to seek in their respective beliefs, and in the universal brotherhood that unites all the members of the human family, the motivation and perseverance to work for the peace and justice which the peoples of the Holy Land do not yet have, and for which they yearn so deeply.[13]

Visit to the Chief Rabbis

Thursday, March 23rd, was the Pope's main Jewish day, with visits to the chief rabbis, the President of the state of Israel and *Yad Vashem*, Israel's official state memorial to the Holocaust. It was a day rich in symbolism and emotionalism, which undoubtedly left a deep impression on the people of Israel and on Jews all over the world. The Ashkenazi and Sephardi chief rabbis of Israel at that time—Rabbi Meir Israel Lau and Rabbi Eliahu Bakshi Doron respectively—welcomed the Pope at their offices in Heichal Shlomo, with the traditional Hebrew greeting *Baruch Ha'ba,"* Blessed be your coming to Israel". Their short speech, which was warm and conciliatory (and devoid of political references, unlike Rabbi Lau's provocative reference to Jerusalem later in the day at the Interfaith Meeting, see below), expressed appreciation for what this Pope had done for the Jewish people during his papacy:

We welcome one who saw fit to express remorse in the name of the Catholic Church for the terrible deeds committed against the Jewish people during the course of the past 2,000 years and even appointed a commission for requesting forgiveness from the Jewish nation with regard to the Holocaust. We remember and mention to his credit the decisive assistance he gave in the matter of moving the Carmelite convent out of the area of the Auschwitz concentration camp, a place where millions of our brothers and sisters were murdered for the Sanctification of the Name . . . We appreciate as well his recognition of our right to return and to live in the Holy Land in peace and brotherhood within safe borders recognized by the nations of the world and especially by our neighbors. All these things were given expression in the prayer he offered at Auschwitz [June 11, 1999] for the success of the Israeli people's efforts for peace.[14]

The Pope's remarks to the chief rabbis were equally conciliatory and uplifting, expressing the hope that this "uniquely significant meeting" would lead to increasing contact between Christians and Jews, "aimed at achieving an ever deeper understanding of the historical and theological relationship between our respective religious heritages". He also repeated what he had said on the occasion of his visit to the synagogue in Rome in 1986 that, "We Christians recognize that the Jewish religious heritage is intrinsic to our faith: you are our elder brothers."[15]

The Pope did inject one paragraph into his remarks to the chief rabbis which caused considerable speculation and discussion. In stressing the need for some reciprocity in the Catholic-Jewish relationship (without using the word 'reciprocity' specifically), he urged the chief rabbis, as Jewish leaders, to acknowledge that the Catholic Church repudiates anti-Semitism: "We hope that the Jewish people will acknowledge that the Church utterly condemns antisemitism and every form of racism as being altogether opposed to the principles of Christianity."[16]

The most specific call for reciprocity was in a sentence in this speech (which was repeated in his speech at Yad Vashem later in the day) that first appeared two years previous to this in the document called *We Remember: A Reflection on the Shoah:* "We must work together to build a future in which there will be no more anti-Judaism among Christians or anti-Christian sentiment among Jews." Given the long history of Christian virulent anti-Judaism, violence and anti-Semitism over many centuries (which was not paralleled by anything comparable by Jews against Christians), the symmetry of this sentence bothered most of the Jewish leaders who heard it for the first time at a seminar of the International Liaison Committee at the Vatican, March 1998, and it didn't sound any better with repetition during the visit of the Pope to Israel.

While there is undoubtedly a need to deal with some "anti-Christian sentiment" among Jews, this cannot be equated with the long history of anti-

Semitism against Jews by Christians. The equation just does not work, and it would be better if it had not been repeated twice on that day. Nevertheless, except for those who read each speech with a fine toothcomb, this point was generally overlooked by the media and did not serve to destroy or even inhibit the good atmosphere of the reconciliatory meeting between the Pope and the chief rabbis on this historic occasion. Indeed, the gestures and the geography (the location of the meetings), as on so many other symbolic occasions during the visit, were much more important than the words crafted by committees of speech writers, who often had to write things to please their own constituents.

These historic meetings with the chief rabbis of Israel and the Pope opened up new official channels of communication, which continue to this day. For many years, there has been an official dialogue between rabbis representing the Chief Rabbinate of Israel and religious leaders connected with the Vatican that has dealt with many important educational and ideological issues of common concern. I have found it interesting that although the chief rabbis would not discuss "theology" with Christian theologians, on account of their belief that there is nothing to learn theologically from them, they have decided to talk about fundamental ideas that are common to the two traditions. If this isn't theology, then I guess I don't know what it really is!

The Visit to Yad Vashem

Following the visits with the President and the chief rabbis of Israel, the Pope and his entourage attended a special ceremony at the Hall of Remembrance at Yad Vashem, Israel's memorial to the six million Jews who were annihilated during the Holocaust. The Pope began the ceremony by laying a wreath, with the help of Cardinal Etchegary, the then President of the Pontifical Commission for the Commemorations of the Year 2000, and Cardinal Cassidy, then President of the Pontifical Commission for Religious Relations with the Jews, both Catholic leaders who have played leading roles in the Jewish-Catholic dialogue of recent decades and in the fostering of good relations with Israel as part of this process. (I knew both of these cardinals personally and worked together with them in common cause.) As the cantor sang *El Maleh Rachamim* (God Full of Mercy), the traditional memorial prayer chanted for the dead and especially for martyrs of the Jewish people, we could see the Pope's face straining to take everything in at this highly personal and intensely emotional occasion. When it was over, the Pope, who is known as a master of the symbolic gesture, slowly got up from his seat and walked across the Hall of Remembrance to greet the Jewish Holocaust survivors who were standing there, one by one. As he shook each hand, the commentator on television revealed that many of these survivors had been saved by Righteous Gentiles, Christians in Europe who risked their lives to save Jews, including one woman who was saved by Pope John Paul II himself long before he became Pope, during the days when he was a young priest in Poland.

The Pope's speech at Yad Vashem had been distributed to all the journalists in the press room, so everyone there could read it as he spoke. On a cursory reading, I could not see that it contained anything new. But rereading it as the Pope delivered his speech—with such complete sincerity and in a mood of serene spirituality in this special place—I realized that it wasn't so much the words that mattered here as the spirit, symbolism and sensitivity he expressed through his gestures and expressions.

The Pope began and ended the speech with a quote from the Psalms. This was a carefully crafted symbolic gesture, to show the common spiritual patrimony between Jews and Christians that can be found in the Hebrew Bible, a theme that has characterized Jewish-Catholic dialogue since Vatican II in the 1960s. Indeed, the whole speech was more like a modern psalm than a typical speech. The words and the mood were poetic. His cry from the depths was reminiscent of that of the psalmist, which is what made the speech so evocative and so powerful. This was not your typical papal speech. Nor was it a "community relations" speech, which is why some Jewish community relations organizations—who had pumped the media for days prior to this with false expectations of some dramatic new announcement—were not satisfied. Rather, this was a deeply religious, spiritual declaration, expertly crafted for this very special moment in Jewish-Catholic history.

After quoting from Psalm 31:13-15, "I have come like a broken vessel, I hear the whispering of many, terror on every side, as they scheme together against me, as they plot to take my life, But I trust in you, O Lord; I say, You are my God," - the Pope captured the moment with a plea for silence suffused with his own personal memories.

> In this place of memories, the mind and the heart and soul feel an extreme need for silence. Silence in which to remember. Silence in which to try to make some sense of the memories, which come flooding back. Silence because there are no words strong enough to deplore the terrible tragedy of the Shoah. My own personal memories are of all that happened when the Nazis occupied Poland during the War. I remember my Jewish friends and neighbors, some of whom perished, while others survived. I have come to Yad Vashem to pay homage to the millions of Jewish people who, stripped of everything, especially of their human dignity, were murdered in the Holocaust. More than half a century has passed, but the memories remain.[17]

Beginning with silence and with the need to remember, the Pope also used this occasion to denounce anti-Semitism once again (as he had done so many times during his papacy):

> As Bishop of Rome and Successor of the Apostle Peter, I assure the Jewish
> people that the Catholic Church, motivated by the Gospel law of truth and love
> and by no political considerations, is deeply saddened by the hatred, acts of
> persecution and displays of antisemitism directed against the Jews by Chris-
> tians at any time and in any place. The Church rejects racism in any form as a
> denial of the image of the Creator inherent in every human being. [18]

This is clearly the point at which some Jewish organizational leaders were
expecting more. They wanted the Pope to accept responsibility on behalf of
the Catholic Church for the Church's failings during the Holocaust. But those
who know more about Catholic theology especially the doctrine of papal
infallibility—knew that this was not possible. In fact, the Pope went no
further in his words than he had done in the *We Remember: A Reflection on
the Shoah* document of March 1988, from which he quoted in this speech.
Yet, his gestures spoke much louder than his words, as did his very presence
at Yad Vashem.

Indeed, the picture of him standing, bent and broken-looking, next to
Prime Minister Ehud Barak, who stood straight and tall, spoke more than
words. It was the Pope's indomitable spirit on that day - and throughout the
trip - that moved Jewish people in Israel and all over the world to tears. It
was his spiritual presence that moved Prime Minister Barak to react so positively in his speech, which, like that of the Pope, was beautifully crafted for
this highly symbolic occasion. He welcomed the Pope, not only in the name
of the Jewish people, but also in the name of the state of Israel and all of its
citizens—Christians, Muslims, Druse and Jews—"in friendship, in brotherhood, and in peace, here in Jerusalem, the capital of Israel, the eternal city of
faith." [19] The Prime Minister also captured this special moment by acknowledging this Pope's special role in bringing about a historic change in the
relationship of the Church to the Jewish People and he saw this visit as the
apex of this process. Addressing the Pope personally and poignantly, he said:

> You have done more than anyone else to bring about the historic change in the
> attitude of the Church towards the Jewish people, initiated by the good Pope
> John the XXIII, and to dress the gaping wounds that festered over many bitter
> centuries. And I think I can say, Your Holiness, that your coming here today,
> to the Tent of Remembrance at Yad Yashem, is a climax of this historic
> journey of healing. Here, right now, time itself has come to a standstill . . . this
> very moment holds within it two thousand years of history. [20]

As if this was not enough, Prime Minister Barak also took two very bold
steps by expressing gratitude for the Pope's "Mea Culpa" (which was part of
the Pope's historic mass at St. Peter's on Sunday, March 12th, just nine days
before his coming to the region) and by enunciating the desire to continue to
work together to fight against racism and anti-Semitism: "Shortly before

setting out on your pilgrimage here, you raised the flag of fraternity to full mast, setting into church liturgy a request for forgiveness, for wrongs committed by members of your faith against others, especially against the Jewish people. We accept this noble act most profoundly."[21]

Here was the Prime Minister of Israel taking the Jewish-Catholic dialogue of the past several decades a few giant steps forward. In contrast to many Jewish organizational leaders outside of Israel who thought that the Pope had not gone far enough in his speech at Yad Vashem, the Prime Minister of Israel acknowledged the Pope's apology with great respect and profundity. I very much agreed with him!

A Failed Attempt at an "Interfaith Summit" in Jerusalem

Following his highly emotional and symbolic visit to Vad Vashem, the Pope journeyed across town to the Notre Dame Cultural Center, a major cultural institution in the center of Jerusalem, owned and operated by the Vatican, to attend the interfaith meeting, which was planned as a trialogue between the Pope, one of Israel's chief rabbis, and a leading Muslim cleric. Unfortunately, this event turned out to be an interfaith disaster, which some people, including myself, believe would have been better if it had not taken place at all. The planners of this event, especially the office of the Vatican nuncio to Israel, had been advised to drop the idea since we viewed the chances of its success as slight.There was no question that one of the Pope's main messages during his visit to Israel and Palestine during the week was the urgent need for more and better interfaith dialogue to build peaceful relations between the peoples of the Middle East. However, this message was only partially heeded at the interfaith meeting at Notre Dame.[22] Vatican officials who organized this meeting in the heart of Jerusalem originally had high hopes that it would be an historic interfaith summit. They had hoped that the Grand Mufti of Jerusalem would attend and would offer a message of peace and reconciliation similar to the one that the Pope and the chief rabbi would deliver. But attempts over many months to persuade the Mufti to participate in this meeting proved fruitless.

The Jewish speaker, Ashkenazi Chief Rabbi Meir Israel Lau, tried hard to demonstrate that he understood the symbolic significance of the moment by offering a warm reflection on *shalom* (peace) at the beginning of his talk. Not only did he warmly welcome the Pope, with whom he had clearly established a good rapport in his meeting earlier in the day (and in previous meetings in Rome) but he also injected a note of cordiality by referring to the Muslim speaker, Sheikh Taisir Tamimi, as "my colleague."[23]

After talking about the need for religious pluralism, by quoting the prophet Micah who said "Let all peoples walk in the name of their God and we will walk in the name of our God," and after emphasizing some of the basic values that followers of the monotheistic religions share—such as friendship, understanding, speaking and listening with mutual respect, and a yearning for peace—he then proceeded to make an extremely politically incorrect comment that clearly upset many people in the audience. Turning to the Pope and thanking him for his visit to Israel, Rabbi Lau also stated that his visit to Jerusalem signified that the Pope recognized the city as the eternal capital of the state of Israel. This was clearly a case of putting words into the Pope's mouth. And it injected an unnecessary political message into what was supposed to be an interfaith gathering for peace and reconciliation. It would certainly have been much better to have let the Pope's actions speak for themselves. There he was sitting in an auditorium in the center of Jerusalem, under Israeli sovereignty. The Chief Rabbi's ill-conceived political reference caused some Palestinians in the audience to yell out, "You know that this is not the case! This is not the position of the Vatican!"

It might not have been so bad if this incident had been the only one of the day. But when the Muslim cleric began to speak, things went from bad to worse. It was obvious from the first moment of Sheikh Tamimi's fiery speech that he had not come in the spirit of dialogue on this potentially historic occasion. Instead, it appeared that he came to deliver a diatribe meant to fan the flames of extremism. According to those who had seen his speech in advance, including one representative of the government of Israel whom I knew well and had worked with closely on this program, he had clearly come prepared to deliver an aggressive speech, regardless of Rabbi Lau's remarks. Most people in the room could see from the beginning of the Sheikh's remarks—which were made throughout in a loud screeching voice and were met with the somber facial expressions of the Pope—that this was not a religious leader who had come to enter into dialogue.

Pope John Paul II, in his wisdom, totally ignored the Sheikh's ranting by sticking to his prepared text which emphasized the need for more communication in what he called "the new era of interreligious dialogue."[24] In stark contrast to the Muslim speaker, he said, "We must find in each other's traditions the sources to ensure the triumph of mutual respect." Moreover, he urged that religion not become an excuse for violence. Instead, he said that religion and peace should go together.

The Pope reiterated his well-known position on the need for interreligious dialogue: "The Catholic Church wishes to pursue a genuine dialogue with members of the Jewish faith and members of Islam. We listen respectfully to one another and we should cooperate in everything that favors mutual understanding and peace."[25] Juxtaposed with the previous speech, the Pope's pronouncements sounded somewhat like a pious wish list. He and everyone else in the audience that day were presented with a bitter lesson on the gap between the ideal and the real in the Middle East. The Vatican organizers did not realize their goal for this interfaith meeting to be a symbol for the potential of interreligious dialogue in the cause of peace. This was to remain a vision and a challenge for the future.

This was unfortunate, especially since its failure was somewhat predictable. As far as I am concerned, this was the only event of the week that went off poorly. The rest of the week was unbelievably positive, with events and meetings which succeeded in changing the way that millions of Jewish people in Israel and the diaspora relate to the Catholic Church in our time. Its positive repercussions are felt to this day, both in Israel and all over the Jewish world.

At the Western Wall

One of the most moving events of the whole week, from the Jewish point of view, took place on the last day, March 26, 2000. This was the remarkable visit of the Pope to the Western Wall, the holiest site for many Jews and traditional Judaism in Israel. The image of this visit remains indelibly etched on the hearts and minds of Jews everywhere. There has never been anything quite like this in Jewish-Christian history.

On behalf of the government of Israel, Rabbi Michael Melchior, Israel's Minister for World Jewish Community and Israeli Society, welcomed the Pope at the Wall: "We welcome your coming here as the realization of a commitment of the Catholic Church to end the era of hatred, humiliation and persecution of the Jewish people."[26] Rejecting much of the past, especially the perversion of religion to justify war, Rabbi Melchior proclaimed that this was the beginning of a new period in world history. In addition, Rabbi Melchior responded positively to the Pope's call for religions to advance the cause of peace by announcing his intention to begin work towards the establishment of an interreligious forum to which representatives of the three great monotheistic faiths would be invited in order to promote peace among religions and believers in this sacred land.[27] The Pope made no formal speech at the Wall. Instead, he simply touched the stones of the Wall, prayed and placed a note in a crack, asking God for forgiveness. In the note, which was distributed throughout the world via the internet and television, the Pope offered the following short prayer: "God of our fathers, you chose Abraham and his descendants to bring your name to the nations. We are deeply saddened by the behavior of those who in the course of history have caused these children of yours to suffer, and asking your forgiveness, we wish to commit ourselves to genuine brotherhood with the people of the covenant. Amen."[28]

I remember vividly walking down the street in Jerusalem—on the way to an interview at a television station—when I received a phone call on my mobile phone from the BBC in London, asking me about what the Pope wrote in his note which he inserted into the Western Wall, before it had been announced via the internet. I told the BBC interviewer that I did not know the exact words, but I predicted that it would be an amazing statement, as it was. Many other people were interviewed for radio and television at that time. Internal Security Minister Shlomo Ben-Ami, a professor of European history, said in an interview on the radio, "For the first time, the Pope has explicitly said that he was sorry to the Jews."[29] And Rabbi Melchior was also quoted on the radio as saying, "He touched the Wall but the Wall also touched him."[30]

The Pope's visit to the Western Wall at that time was remarkable since as it was the first of its kind. Since then, Pope Benedict and Pope Francis have both visited Israel, and on each occasion, they went to the Western Wall and to Yad Vashem. Indeed, since the visit of Pope John Paul II to Israel in March 2000, and since the city-state known as the Vatican has diplomatic relations with Israel, these ceremonial visits are no longer "historic" but part of protocol for foreign leaders to Israel. This fact demonstrates how far we have come in such a short time. As a result of the political peace process of the 1990s, and against the backdrop of great progress in Jewish-Catholic relations of the past 50 years, it is now "normal" for popes to visit Israel regularly and for them to meet with the political and religious leadership of the state. This represents a profound change in relations between the Jewish state and the Vatican, and by extension it is an amazingly positive development in the history of relations between Jews and Christians in the contemporary world.

TOWARDS THE FUTURE: WHERE DO WE GO FROM HERE?

Never before in Israeli or Jewish history has so much education taken place—mostly through the electronic and print media—about Christianity and Catholic-Jewish relations in one week or in one month, especially relations between Jews and Christians in the contemporary era, since Vatican II in the 1960s. This was totally unprecedented in Israeli society and in Jewish society in the modern period. The people of Israel—and people around the world—were exposed to and educated about the progress in Jewish-Christian relations, which the Pope's visit to Israel came to symbolize, as never before.

Pope John Paul II's visit to Israel should thus be considered not only one of the hallmarks of his papacy but also the beginning of a new educational process. In a panel discussion for the foreign press on the last day of the papal visit to Israel, Brother Jack Driscoll—a member of the Congregation of Christian Brothers, former President of Iona College in New York, and for many years until his death in 2010 a student and teacher of Jewish-Christian relations in Jerusalem, and a good friend—reflected on some of the next steps that needed to be taken, from a Catholic perspective. In outlining a proposed action agenda for Catholics, he stressed the role of education as a major area of activity for the future.[31]

In the light of the unparalleled educational experience afforded to Israeli society—and Jewish communities throughout the world—by this historic healing journey of Pope John Paul II during the six days from March 21-26, 2000, more Jews than ever before are now aware of the revolutionary developments in Catholic-Jewish relations in the second half of the 20th century. Contemporary Jews will no longer be accused of sleeping through the revolution, as they had been previously by Rabbi Harold Schulweis.[32] I would add that since Pope John Paul II's clarion call in the year 2000 for more and better interreligious dialogue in the Holy City, it would seem appropriate for Jerusalem to play a more central role in interreligious dialogue, especially as a supplement to the political peace processes. As one interreligious activist in Jerusalem, with whom I worked closely for many years, succinctly put it, "If we are sincere in our prayers for the peace of Jerusalem, we must proclaim a ceasefire in our destructive wars of memory in which our memories and traditions often become prisoners of war. Rather, we must make Jerusalem the capital of dialogue between different memories, for dialogue is peace incarnate."[33]

Indeed, during my 25 years of active involvement in interreligious dialogue in Israel, Jerusalem has been and remains my home base of operations. Together with colleagues and counterparts from other organizations who were affiliated with my organization, we developed new methods and new models for making interreligious dialogue relevant to the real-life situations of Jews and Palestinians in our shared city, our shared society (the state of Israel) and our shared region (Israel and Palestine together). My organization, the Interreligious Coordinating Council in Israel (ICCI), was a coalition of 60-70 organizations and institutions within Israeli society, which worked separately and together to enhance Arab-Jewish coexistence within Israel and peaceful relations among Jews and Palestinians in the region. The next chapter will describe the work that we did over many years, which was our attempt to make Jerusalem a city of dialogue rather than conflict.

NOTES

1. Ronald Kronish, "Welcome, John Paul II, *Jerusalem Post*, March 17, 2000.

2. Cardinal Cassidy became a good friend for many years. I also hosted him for a seminar on Jewish-Catholic relations at the Van Leer Jerusalem Institute, and for a reception at my home with many of the leaders in the field of interreligious relations in Israel.

3. See the collection of essays by Rabbi Gilbert Rosenthal, *A Jubilee for All Time, The Copernican Revolution in Jewish-Christian Relations*, which contains 25 essays by prominent Christians and Jews in this field, including by this author, "The Implications of *Nostra Aetate* for Interreligious Dialogue in Israel", pp 207-218.

4. Ronald Kronish. *Teaching About Christianity in Israel,* unpublished paper presented at seminar of the International Jewish-Catholic Liaison Committee, at the Vatican, March 25, 1998.

5. The Pontifical Council for Interreligious Dialogue produced a book of the lessons presented at this seminar by its participants entitled *Spiritual Resources of the Religions for Peace. Exploring the Sacred Texts in Promotion of Peace,* Vatican City, 2003. I contributed a chapter to this book, which shared the same title as the seminar.

6. Ron Kronish. "The Pope and the pitfalls and potential of interfaith dialogue," *HaAretz,* March 26, 2000.

7. Eyal HaReuveni, et al. "Welcome to Hell," *Kol Ha'ir,* March 17, 2000, p. 23, in Hebrew.

8. Rabbi Harold Schulweis. "Sleeping Through a Revolution," *The Forward,* Oct. 11, 1999.

9. Fr. Michael McGarry. *Roman Catholic-Jewish Relations. . . Signposts along the New Path of Dialogue,* Jerusalem: Interreligious Coordinating Council in Israel, March 12, 2000.

10. For details on the Pope's life, see the excellent biography by Carl Bernstein and Marco Politi, *His Holiness, John Paul II and the History of Our Time,* Penguin Books, 1997, especially chapters 1-3 on his early childhood, adult development and beginnings as a priest in the Catholic Church.

11. Ya'acov Achimeir. Israel TV, Channel One, broadcast, March 21, 2000.

12. David Witztum. Israel TV, Channel One, broadcast March 21, 2000.

13. Pope John Paul II, address at Ben Gurion Airport, March 21, 2000.

14. Statement of the Chief Rabbinate of Israel, March 23, 2000.

15. Address of Pope John Paul II to the Chief Rabbinate of Israel, March 23, 2000.

16. *Ibid.*

17. Address of Pope John Paul II at Yad Vashem, March 23, 2000.

18. *Ibid.*

19. Address by Prime Minister Ehud Barak at Yad Vashem, March 23, 2000.

20. *Ibid.*

21. *Ibid.*

22. Ron Kronish. "The Pope and the pitfalls and potential of interfaith dialogue," *HaAretz,* March 26, 2000.

23. Remarks of Chief Rabbi Meir Israel Lau at Interfaith Meeting, March 23, 2000.

24. Address of Pope John Paul II at the interfaith meeting, March 23, 2000.

25. *Ibid.*

26. Speech by Rabbi Michael Melchior at the Western Wall, March 23, 2000.

27. Since his speech, Rabbi Melchior has helped to establish the First Alexandria Declaration of the Religious Leaders of the Holy Land, Alexandria, Egypt, January 21, 2002. In addition, he organized another Interreligious Summit for Peace in Spain in November 2016, and continues to pursue interreligious peace initiatives.

28. Prayer of Pope John Paul II at the Western Wall, as released by the Israel Government Press Office, March 26, 2000, and as published on the internet only minutes after the prayer was offered.

29. As reported in "Pope says `sorry' at Wall," *The Jerusalem Post,* Internet edition, March 26, 2000.

30. *Ibid.*

31. Br. Jack Driscoll. *What are the Next Steps? Reflections from This Catholic's Perspective,* briefing for Foreign Press at the International Press Center, Jerusalem, March 26, 2000.

32. Schulweis. *op cit.*

33. Daniel Rossing. *Mother Jerusalem: Memory, Symbols and the Between,* briefing for Foreign Press at the International Press Center, Jerusalem, March 22, 2000.

From l. to r.—Rabbi David Geffen, Malcolm Lowe, Rabbi Ron Kronish, Rabbi David Rosen, Mayor Teddy Kollek, Dr. Mithkal Natour, and Dr. Geert Cohen-Stuart. Members of ICCI Board of Directors meet with former Mayor Teddy Kollek.

From l. to r.—Rabbi Ron Kronish, former President of Israel Chaim Herzog, Sir Sigmund Sternberg, philanthropist, and Lady Hazel Sternberg. [Photo courtesy of President's Residence.]

From l. to r.—Sr. Kaye MacDonald of the Sisters of Sion, Rabbi Marc Rosenstein, former Director of Makom Ba'Galil, and Fr. Thomas Stransky, former Rector of Tantur Ecumenical Institute, Jerusalem.

From l. to r.—Former President of Israel Yitzhak Navon, Mr. Alan B. Slifka, philanthropist and founder of the Abraham Fund, Rabbi Ron Kronish.

Rabbi Ron Kronish and Cardinal Roger Etchegaray at Community of Sant'Egidio Annual Meeting of Peoples and Religions in Venice, 1997.

Dr. Geoffrey Wigoder, former editor of the Encyclopedia Judaica, and Archbishop Andrea di Montezemolo, Papal Nuncio in Israel, at a reception in the garden of the Institute of Holyland Studies on Mt. Zion in Jerusalem. [Photo courtesy of Debbi Cooper.]

Rabbi Ron Kronish and Issa Jabber, Mayor of Abu Ghosh, in conversation, February 1988. [Photo courtesy of Debbi Cooper.]

Bishop Munib Younan, Bishop of the Evangelical Lutheran Church in Jordan and the Holy Land, and Rabbi Ron Kronish, at the dedication of new ICCI Education Center, December 1999. [Photo courtesy of Debbi Cooper.]

Dr. Mithkal Natour and Rabbi Ron Kronish at opening of ICCI Education Center in Jerusalem, December 1999. [Photo courtesy of Debbi Cooper.]

From l. to r. – Msgr. Pietro Sambi, Apostolic Nuncio to Israel, Judge Mayer Gabay, former Civil Service Commissioner of Israel, and Rabbi Ron Kronish at ICCI Annual Meeting, 1999. [Photo courtesy of Debbi Cooper.]

His Holiness the Dalai Lama and Rabbi Ron Kronish at interreligious conference at the King David Hotel in Jerusalem, 1999. [Photo courtesy of Debbi Cooper.]

Japanese and Israeli-Palestinian young adult dialogue group in front of the Dome of the Rock in Jerusalem, cooperative program of Rissho Kosei-Kai and ICCI. [Photo courtesy of Rissho Kosei-Kai.]

From l. to r.—Rabbi Naftali Rothenberg, Senior Researcher at Van Leer Jerusalem Institute, Dr. Mohammed Hourani, Lecturer in Education at David Yellin College, Jerusalem, Rabbi Ron Kronish at an ICCI Jewish-Muslim dialogue, 2001.
[Photo courtesy of Debbi Cooper.]

Ambassador Daniel Kurtzer, former Ambassador of the United States to Israel, speaking at an ICCI event on the roof of the Museum on the Seam, Jerusalem, on September 11, 2001, immediately following the attacks on the Twin Towers.
[Photo courtesy of Debbi Cooper.]

Rabbi Levi Weiman-Kelman and Cardinal Edward Idris Cassidy, at ICCI Conference on Jewish-Catholic Relations, Jerusalem, 2001. [Photo courtesy of Debbi Cooper.]

Pope John Paul II and Rabbi Ron Kronish at the Vatican, 2001. [Photo courtesy of the Vatican.]

Prof. Sr. Maureena Fritz, President and Founder of Bat Kol Institute, and Rabbi Ron Kronish. [Photo courtesy of Debbi Cooper.]

Fr. Michael McGarry, former Rector of the Tantur Ecumenical Institute in Jerusalem, and Msgr. Giacinto-Boulos Marcuzzo, Roman Catholic Auxiliary Bishop of the Latin Patriarch of Jerusalem (located in Nazareth) at ICCI Conference on Jewish-Catholic Relations, Jerusalem, 2001. [Photo courtesy of Debbi Cooper.]

From l. to r. (front row)—Msgr. Michel Sabbah, former Archbishop and Latin Patriarch of Jerusalem, Ambassador Daniel Kurtzer, Rabbi Ron Kronish, Sheikh Abdel Salaam Manasra, head of the Qadiri Sufi Order in the Holy Land, and Prof. Alice Shalvi, former Head of Israel Women's Network, at ICCI September 11th commemoration, 2002. [Photo courtesy of Debbi Cooper.]

From l. to r.—Dr. Yitzhak Mendelsohn, psychologist and facilitator, Rabbi David Stav, Chief Rabbi of Shoham, Sheikh Ibrahim Sarsour, former Member of Knesset, and Sheikh Kamal Riyan, former Mayor of Kafr Bara, at an ICCI Kedem conference In Tel Aviv, 2005.

Prof. Mohammed Dajani, Founder and Chairman of Wasatia, and Rabbi Ron Kronish, October 2015.

Rabbi Ron Kronish speaking to interreligious conference in Binghampton, NY, November 2014.

Fr. Hosam Naoum, Dean of St. George's Cathedral in Jerusalem, and Kadi Iyad Zahalka, Judge of the Shari'a Court of the State of Israel in Jerusalem.

Chapter Four

Interreligious Dialogue in Israel as a Form of Peacebuilding— the Development of a New Model

INTRODUCTION

During the past twenty-six years, I have been actively engaged in the grass-roots work of interreligious dialogue and education.[1] While this work has had its share of ups and downs, successes and obstacles, challenges and setbacks, I can say that without a doubt, I have learned a great deal about the role of dialogue in peacebuilding in our part of the world by trial and error and by persistence and partnership with key organizations in the field.[2]

This chapter is divided into three parts:

1. A description of some of the most important peacebuilding programs that I have planned and implemented with some success in Israel and Palestine in recent years, with a special focus on programs for youth and young adults as well as programs for grassroots religious leaders.
2. The goals and the main components of interreligious dialogue.
3. A new model, which I developed with colleagues over the years, which is an outgrowth of best practices in this field as seen through the work of the Interreligious Coordinating Council in Israel (ICCI), which I founded and directed from 1991-2016.

DIALOGUE AND ACTION GROUPS AS A METHOD FOR PERSONAL AND COMMUNAL TRANSFORMATION

Dialogue and action groups can be a powerful method for transforming people into change agents for peaceful coexistence in their communities. When they are done well, participating in these groups can be a transformative experience in the lives of many people, some of whom go on to work in the field or become active in their communities. During my years as director of the ICCI, together with some of my key professional staff, we worked intensively on creating new dialogue opportunities for young people, with the awareness that young people are more open to dialogue than many of their elders who already hold fixed opinions, and with the consciousness that young people will be shaping the future for themselves, their communities, their societies and the region, in the years and decades ahead.

Through the implementation of programs for teens and college students together with my colleagues at ICCI, I learned first-hand the importance of careful planning of programs that include dialogue, intensive experiential encounters, and volunteerism or action projects.

Programs for Youth and Young Adults

In cooperation with Auburn Theological Seminary of New York, an institution that pioneered new programs which integrated conflict resolution methods together with interreligious dialogue, and originally with an organization out of Denver, Colorado, called "Building Bridges", we planned and implemented an annual program for high school youth. The program was called "Face to Face/ Faith to Faith" and it ran for 12 years (from 2001 to 2013), bringing together teenagers from four conflict Zones—Israel/Palestine, South Africa, Northern Ireland, and American cities to an intensive two-week summer experience at a Presbyterian camp in upstate New York (which was made kosher, halal and vegetarian, so that everyone could eat together). This was an amazing international effort which offered unique dialogue opportunities for youth from these regions. For us in Israel/Palestine, the program was developed over time into a year-long program which included several months of dialogical encounters in Jerusalem, which prepared the youth for the transformational experience abroad, and which culminated in action projects in the local communities. This year-long process was adopted by all four regions of the program.

As a result of a serious evaluation process of our program in Jerusalem undertaken several years ago,[3] we discovered that there are ten transformative ways in which participants were affected by this program:

1. Seeing that the conflict has two legitimate sides, and being able to accept people who have different opinions
2. Becoming better listeners
3. Realizing that not everything is solvable
4. Looking at the conflict in a more complex and realistic way
5. Realizing that people are similar in many ways yet still have strong differences
6. Allowing them to grow up and become more confident in their own abilities
7. Influencing them to become more active in society
8. Becoming stronger in their own opinions while simultaneously becoming more tolerant and accepting
9. Having more knowledge about other religions
10. Realizing that the 'other' is also a human being.

As part of the ongoing program, Auburn Seminary in New York also conducted a comprehensive evaluation process. Among the main insights gleaned from this process was that this experience was one of great personal transformation for many of the young people who participated in it. One participant expressed his own process of discovery, goal setting and growth through Face to Face particularly eloquently:

> I have to say that my Face to Face experience was a life changing one. It opened my eyes to things that I was blind to all my life. It took me out of my comfort zone and challenged me to question what I thought and why I thought it. The summer intensive was by far the part that worked best for me as it really was like nothing I had ever experienced before. The diversity of people and situations that I experienced in New York was something that could never and will never be simulated in the same way anywhere for the rest of my life.[4]

In addition to this program for high school students, we conducted an innovative program for four years for college students from both East and West Jerusalem, which sought to engage in interreligious dialogue together with action in order to change the tenor of public discourse and improve relations between Christian, Muslim, and Jewish students at their universities and in the city of Jerusalem as a whole. Jerusalem is divided by both physical and psychological barriers in such a way that young people growing up in the same city almost never visit the 'other' side. Participants in this program attended different universities/colleges, spoke different languages, and belonged to nations with opposing political objectives. In short, they lived in totally different realities.

During the course of the full-year program, participants discussed various topics dealing with the different holiday traditions and they visited each other's homes and celebrated each other's holidays in fulfillment of one of our central goals—to eliminate the psychological barriers that divide Jerusalem and expose the participants to the life of the 'other'. In order to get to know each other better, one group engaged in a photography project which involved their dividing up into pairs—one Israeli Jew with one Palestinian Christian or Muslim—and taking photos of themselves in places they love in Jerusalem. Even the simple task of visiting different neighborhoods in East and West Jerusalem was a challenging and eye-opening experience for the participants; many had to overcome fears about visiting the other side of the city.

Eventually this idea developed into a photo contest and exhibition, in which we solicited the best photos from Jewish Israeli and Palestinian Arab graduates of our dialogue programs, and, with the help of a special grant for innovation from Religions for Peace, published the best photos online, as well as exhibiting them in various venues in Jerusalem, including the Jerusalem Cinematheque, the coffee house at the Khan Theatre, and a new center for young adults in Jerusalem called Beta, in the trendy area of the 'shuk' (the open air central market in downtown West Jerusalem).

In addition, under the leadership of Avigail Moshe, who directed our Youth and Young Adult department with much energy, expertise, and efficiency for 6 ½ years, we embarked on an unusually poignant and powerful set of programs for four years, which we called "Collective Memory and its Implications for Conflict Transformation—Youth Exchange Program for Japanese and Israeli Jewish and Arab Students". These programs were planned and implemented in cooperation with a Japanese Buddhist cultural and educational organization called "Risho Kosei-Kai", whose leadership we were introduced to by Rev. Kyochi Sugino, the Associate Secretary-General of Religions for Peace, who has been representing Risho Kosei-Kai on the professional leadership team of Religions for Peace for many years, and who became a trusted friend and colleague over many years.

We first met the leadership of RKK's youth department when they came to a special seminar for Palestinian Arabs of Israeli citizenship in dialogue with Jewish Israelis at the Ramat Rachel conference center in July 2006, at the beginning of the Second Lebanon war. This seminar was billed as a "Pre-Assembly Seminar" before the World Assembly of the World Council of Religions for Peace, which took place in Japan in August 2006, attended by Ms. Moshe and other ICCI staff. Our positive personal encounter with the Buddhist leaders from Japan during that summer led to the development of constructive cooperation through which RKK funded and helped us plan some of the most amazing dialogue programs I have ever witnessed.

During the years 2006 to 2010, two groups of Palestinian Arabs of Israeli citizenship and Jews of Israeli citizenship went through a carefully planned process, which included dialogue in Israel for several months, a journey to Japan for 10 days, including to Hiroshima, and the implementation of action projects in the months immediately after returning from Japan. This was the only youth and young adult project we did which included only Israeli citizens. Most of the time, we included Palestinian youth and young adults from East Jerusalem (as well as from Palestinian Arab towns within Israel) in our dialogue groups.

One of the most impressive action projects of this group was the preparation and implementation of an arts fair, held at the Jerusalem Intercultural Center on Mount Scopus, for which all the participants prepared beautiful and meaningful projects, including the use of film and plastic arts, through which they demonstrated their profound identification with the issues of memory and reconciliation. As a result of the powerful emotional and intellectual experiences that they had in Japan, and through the excellent facilitation of Avigail Moshe and the Palestinian co-facilitators, I am convinced that the participants in these groups underwent transformational experiences that will influence their identities for many years to come.

There were several reasons why this intensive encounter with Japan was so meaningful to the participants. First, in dealing with memory it related to a major component of the identity of both Jewish and Palestinian Israelis. Second, the presence of outside observers—Buddhist students from Japan—was a positive influence, on account of their shared interest in the topic of memory and reconciliation. Third, the fact that this project included only Palestinian citizens of Israel made it more relevant for Israeli Jews, who had to think through issues that deeply affect the lives of their fellow citizens.[5]

One of the Palestinian Israeli Arabs in the group eloquently expressed the profound impact that her participation in this group had on her. She attributed this to the thorough recruitment process, which brought excellent and committed people to participate in this group, and to the excellent facilitation of both the Jewish and Palestinian facilitators. Also, she felt that the experiences in Hiroshima and other parts of Japan acted as catalysts for the group to engage in serious reflection on issues of reconciliation and non-violence. "If the Japanese can pursue the path of reconciliation, maybe we can do that too, in our conflict," she said.[6]

One year of dialogue activities stands out strongly in my memory. In the year 2008-9, all of our dialogue groups experienced difficulties during the war in Gaza (Operation "Cast Lead"). Our college student group met twice during this period: once during the Jewish holiday of Hanukah, on the first day of the war, at the home of one of the Jewish participants. During this meeting, participants decided that despite the war, and the difficulties of the time, it was important for them to continue meeting. As a result, they met again during the height of the war, and the participants had a difficult discussion about how they felt about the war, and what it meant for them to engage in interreligious dialogue at such a time of conflict—demonstrating their commitment to dialogue, even when the going gets rough.

In fact, one of my greatest surprises was that most of our dialogue groups, especially the ones with youth and young adults, continued to meet during times of crisis (such as sporadic violence or even mini-wars). I had expected the groups to dissolve during these difficult periods. On the contrary, the young people in these groups saw these dialogue groups as a rare and unique opportunity to hear first-hand about the pain and suffering—as well as hopes and aspirations—of people from 'the other side' with whom they had developed friendships and relationships built on trust and openness. Also, their desire to continue to meet in dialogue during very difficult times was due to the persistence of very dedicated professional staff, who knew how to work with young people, as well as to the high quality of the participants who found great personal meaning in dialogue—often for the first time in their lives—and therefore simply did not want to give up.

As a result of these programs, a number of our graduates went on to attend peace camps or to work as counselors in interreligious camps during the summers. One participated in a "Building an Interfaith Community" seminar in Bossey, Switzerland, through the World Council of Churches, where she was given a wonderful opportunity to meet new people, encounter new points of views, and learn new perspectives on religions, peace and community-building. A number of our graduates have served as counselors in the Face To Face/ Faith to Faith Summer Intensive Experience (mentioned above); and another traveled to Walberberg, Germany, and participated in "Breaking Barriers", an Israeli-Palestinian solidarity project founded in 2002, an initiative by Israelis and Palestinians which aims to end the vicious cycle of violence in Israel-Palestine by building mutual interest, solidarity, and trust between peoples.

In subsequent years, several of the young adults who graduated from our dialogue programs not only went on to attend other similar programs and to participate in important conferences, but also went on for advanced degrees in coexistence and conflict resolution. The fact that many of our young adult graduates continue to be involved in other peace and interreligious initiatives is the true measure of success of our informal educational programs for peace. Indeed, some of these young adults, both Jewish Israelis and Palestinian Arabs, came to work as facilitators and organizers for ICCI under the supervision by Ms. Moshe, which they did with all their heart and soul.

A Strategic Decision

Subsequently, my staff and I made a strategic decision to focus more on young adults than on high school students. In 2011, with the help of a grant from Religions for Peace—the leading international interreligious organization for peace in the world, with which I worked closely for many years—we established our Jewish and Palestinian Young Adult Community for Peaceful

Coexistence, which drew upon a database of hundreds of young adults who had been participants in our Dialogue and Action programs over 10-12 years. At one point, we had about 250 youth and young adult graduates of our programs in our database.

At the end of August, 2014, we sent 16 of these alumni—8 Jewish and 8 Palestinian—to a special seminar in Northern Ireland, at the residential center of the Corrymeela Community in Ballycastle. I had met the educational and spiritual leadership of this unique peace community several times, both at their famous center and in Israel, where in both places we worked together on staff training seminars and on a beautiful multi-color guidebook on best practices in group facilitation[7]. These principles reflect the outcome of a collaboration between three organizations in London, Israel and Northern Ireland, who work with interreligious and intercultural encounters. The list of best practices emerged through our reflective practice and through exploring what our different approaches share in common. During my years as director of ICCI, I visited the Corrymeela Community twice in Northern Ireland, and I spoke in the famous tent of the St. Ethelburga's Center for Reconciliation and Peace several times. Through these visits, I got to know the professional leadership of both institutions well, and I hosted them for staff training of my staff and the staff of other organizations in Jerusalem. These personal relationships, which were developed and which thrived for several years, led to the preparation and publication of these principles.

At this exceptionally beautiful retreat center, our graduates spent an intensive week in deep dialogue with Protestant and Catholic young adults from Northern Ireland. Following this experience, many of the participants returned with renewed energy and ideas to engage in action projects in Israel and Palestine, for the betterment of both communities.

Later, this alumni community became branded with Face to Face/Faith to Faith of Auburn Seminary in New York, which also made a strategic decision at that time (2013) to focus on young adults. While I believed that these participants were potentially able to become leaders in their communities, I discovered that as time went on, and these young people grew up and became young professionals, often with families of their own, that we were not able to sustain their involvement in interreligious dialogue and action projects in the same way. On the other hand, many of these young adult graduates of our programs agreed to speak on panel discussions for visiting groups from abroad, and they always told positive stories of their experiences in dialogue with programs of my organization. I was always gratified to hear them speak so powerfully and poignantly about how dialogue had transformed their lives. In addition, several of them accompanied me to international conferences where they were also given opportunities to share their insights and experiences with people from around the world.

One major problem that I encountered was that young professional staff brought in to work with these young people were not always able to develop the kinds of relationships with them that would motivate them to action. Nor did they have the requisite community organizing skills or the necessary motivation to plan and implement successful action projects with these young people. In fact, some of the professional facilitators argued that they were not trained to lead people in action projects and that the best that they could do was the dialogue, which in itself was an action project. In contrast, I felt that this circular and dichotomous thinking limited the scope of what these young informal educators could do and prevented them from catalyzing the participants in their groups to integrate action and dialogue.

Nevertheless, I continued to believe in the powerful potential of bringing young adults together. In July of 2014, I brought together 75 young adults from all over Jerusalem for an *iftar* supper (meal ending the fast during Ramadan) and seminar in a special arts center in the market area of West Jerusalem. In addition to learning texts about fasting from a rabbi and a sheikh, the group enjoyed listening to the music of a Sufi band from Nazareth. This unique encounter led many of the group to express their interest in continuing to be involved in interreligious cultural and educational programs.

Kedem—Voices for Religious Reconciliation

The most ambitious and most important program that I ever planned and implemented was a unique interreligious dialogue and action program entitled Kedem (a Hebrew acronym for "Voices for Religious Reconciliation") which lasted for six years (from 2003-2008). Over these years, together with an experienced facilitator of dialogue groups in situations of conflict, Dr. Yitzhak Mendelson, we carefully developed creative and consistent dialogue and learning programs, which we constantly evaluated and improved with the help of professional evaluators. Over time, this project developed a new model for interreligious reconciliation and peacebuilding (more on this new model later in this chapter) which had a major impact on its participants. In fact, one of the leading Jewish participants in the group expressed in a candid way how this experience impacted his life:

> The Kedem dialogues were productive and have had a major lasting impact. The Kedem activity enabled me and my rabbinical colleagues to get to know Israel's Palestinian Arab minority—its problems, the hardships it faces, its needs—in a firsthand way that cannot be rivaled by academic articles, newspaper stories or books. I came to realize that life is not easy for Israel's Arab minority and that it is indeed affected by mistakes, injustices and discrimination on our part, on the part of the Jews who are the majority in the state of Israel.[8]

Kedem was the longest-lasting systematic and substantive interreligious encounter ever undertaken in Israeli society to bring grassroots religious leaders of Israel's Jewish, Christian and Muslim communities together to get to know one another and to learn to work together.[9] Influential Jewish, Christian and Muslim religious leaders from all over Israel met in intensive dialogue encounters through which they searched together for new and innovative ways of bringing about interreligious and inter-communal reconciliation.

Over six years, the main programs of the Kedem process were:

- *Ongoing monthly encounters,* bringing religious leaders together from communities within Israel to meet one another, build mutual understanding and trust, and to plan action projects which catalyze Jews and Arabs to work together to constructively address societal issues of mutual concern. Each dialogue session included both study of each other's sacred texts on themes of common interest, as well as discussions of core issues of the conflict that were of mutual concern to the participants.
- *Historical Narrative Curriculum*—In 2006, the Kedem group published a booklet for the classroom entitled: *I'm from… Stories from Biram Village and Kfar Etzion from 1948,* which is based on two incidents from Israeli/ Palestinian history: the uprooting of Palestinian Christians from Biram in the northern Galilee and the massacre of Jews at Kfar Etzion.
- *Expanding the impact of Kedem via outreach to the media*—In order to increase the impact of the religious message of coexistence and reconciliation, members of Kedem were involved in reaching out to the Israeli public via radio and television interviews, and op-eds in the Hebrew, Arabic and English media.
- *Educating about the 'Other' in Israeli High Schools*—Many of these religious leaders gave lectures in a high school in the community of one of his colleagues of another religion, on subjects such as "relating to the Other," "basic concepts in Judaism/Christianity/Islam," "common values—different sources."
- *Summer Seminar*—Each summer for the first four years, Kedem participants spent five or six days in an intensive summer seminar abroad, in which they learned about how other countries dealt with their intergroup conflicts. In addition, they continued their learning, coalesced more tightly as a group and planned joint action projects. During these summer seminars, Kedem members traveled together to Ireland (Northern Ireland and the Republic of Ireland), Bosnia-Herzegovina, Cyprus and Spain, to engage each other in dialogue and learning, which led to some very powerful personal transformational experiences, some of which I describe below.

The Story of Personal Transformation
during One Summer Seminar

The first Kedem summer seminar was particularly dramatic and ground-breaking. It was probably the most amazing interreligious experience in which I participated during my entire career. In July, 2003, I took the first group of religious leaders to Ireland (Northern Ireland and also the Republic of Ireland in the south) for an intensive week-long seminar on the theme of reconciliation. At that time, the group was comprised of seven modern Orthodox rabbis and seven Palestinian Arab religious leaders—five Muslim and two Christian (reflecting the percentages within Israeli society). All of these religious leaders were citizens of the state of Israel, and all were men. Together with my staff at that time, I decided that this would be an all male program, the first and only one that I ever did. There were a few reasons for this: first, there are no women imams or kadis or Christian religious clergy in Israel. Second, we wanted to try to influence mainstream Jewish religious leaders, which meant reaching out to Orthodox rabbis who were modern Orthodox and Zionist, and none of these are women. Third, we felt that bringing Reform or Conservative rabbis into this program would only complicate things and get us involved in other issues, which were not central to this program. All other dialogue projects that I did over all the years were pluralistic and gender inclusive.

The 14 local religious leaders were all carefully chosen and invited to participate in this unique, groundbreaking dialogue process. Never before within Israeli society had Muslim, Christian and Jewish grassroots religious leaders met over a sustained period of time to learn about each other and each other's history, tradition, and contemporary concerns, and also to see what could be done together in the area of reconciliation between Palestinian Arabs and Israeli Jews within Israeli society. Each person was selected because of his openness to the process of sustained dialogue on this theme and because he represented a local community in Israel, where the lessons of this dialogue process could be applied in a practical, concrete way in the years ahead. In other words, the participants came to this process willing to undergo both personal as well as communal transformation and to eventually become voices for religious reconciliation within Israeli society.

On the Jewish side, the list of rabbis included one rabbi who later went on to become the Minister of Education of the state of Israel and one rabbi who was on the short list for selection as one of the chief rabbis of Israel. And on the Muslim side the list included two leading kadis (Muslim judges) and one influential former mayor of an Israeli Arab town in the center of Israel. It was a remarkable group of intelligent, committed and sincere religious leaders, and for most of them, this was their first experience in real dialogue with the 'Other'.

The first stage of this program—which included two study days in a conference center outside of Tel Aviv in the spring of 2003—as well as a week together in Northern Ireland and the Republic of Ireland in July of that same year—focused systematically on getting-to-know-one-another on a personal basis and building relationships of trust and respect. Through active listening to each other's personal stories—which were all particularly poignant and meaningful since they were shared in an atmosphere of genuine openness and intense curiosity—these 14 religious leaders came to know each other as persons, rather than as media stereotypes.

More than this, however, was achieved during the week in Ireland. In addition to getting to know each other well on a personal basis—a process which took place over coffee breaks and meals and on the field trips, as well as in the formal group discussions—some rather special moments occurred.

After focusing during the first two days of the seminar both on personal stories and on the conflict in Northern Ireland, the group decided on the third day to focus more on itself and less on the Irish experience of reconciliation. By the third night of the seminar, a group decision was reached to cancel all additional discussions with outside experts on the Irish problem, and to focus the discussion on internal issues among the rabbis and the Arab religious leaders. This was the turning point that led to some rather remarkable results in the days ahead.

By the end of the third morning of dialogue—in which each person in the group had had a chance to share his personal story with the others in the group—it was clear that the group was beginning to coalesce. Two remarkable and surprising developments occurred on that day.

One of the imams told his story about the massacre of Palestinian Arabs in his Galilee town of Kafr Kassem in 1956 (a well-known tragic episode, which has been well documented in Israeli history, in which Palestinian women and children in the Galilee, who were outdoors after curfew, were shot and killed by Israeli soldiers). He told the story of the massacre as he had heard it in his family from his aunt. It was a very gripping telling of the story. Very personal. Very sincere. Very human. Not in any way recounted as the one true version of history, but simply his own story, his own narrative as he had learned it from his family and community. I remember vividly the active listening going on in the room—you could hear a pin drop. Following the telling of this story, a very interesting development occurred.

Another of the Arab religious leaders, Sheikh Kamal Riyan, who was the leader of the Palestinian group in this dialogue process, told the group that each year a memorial service was held in the town of Kafr Kassem to commemorate this massacre and he invited one of the rabbis to come that year, on a specific date at the end of October. The rabbi thought about it for a moment—and consulted with one of his colleagues—and then said that he would come if the event was solely to commemorate their pain and suffering and to express solidarity on the religious and human level,if the Arab religious leader could guarantee that the event would not be manipulated for political purposes. The sheikh fully understood what his friend the rabbi was saying, and responded sincerely by saying that he would invite all of the rabbis to attend a special memorial ceremony on the day after the communal one, so as to guarantee that there would be no misunderstanding or media manipulations. The response was immediate, sincere and to the point: "If that is the case, we'll be there," the rabbis said. This was the clearest indication so far that the religious leaders were carefully listening to each other and at the same time seeking genuine opportunities for religious reconciliation and active peacebuilding.

Later that day, a second opportunity manifested itself in a surprising way.

The plan was to go to Dublin for the weekend, where the group would be hosted by local religious leaders for a meal, for study and to attend worship services together in a mosque on Friday, in a synagogue on Friday night and Saturday morning, and then in a church on Sunday morning. It had all been worked out carefully in advance, with the help of a Catholic woman who was a member of the Sisters of Sion in Dublin and who was deeply involved in interreligious dialogue in the Republic of Ireland. However, that Thursday morning I received a fax at my hotel in Belfast that indicated that there was going to be a serious problem with our visit to the mosque in Dublin the next day—the rabbis would be required to remove their *kippot* (head-coverings) and the Christian religious leaders would need to remove their crosses before entering the mosque. This was a sensitive matter, one that I and the main facilitator of Kedem felt we needed to discuss together as a group. Therefore, we brought the matter up over lunch. At first, one rabbi suggested that the rabbis could wear hats instead of *kippot* and asked if this might solve the problem; another rabbi said that he was not prepared to do this, that the *kippah* was too central to his identity.

And then, all of a sudden, something very dramatic and unexpected happened: one of the Palestinian Muslim religious leaders rose to his feet and said: "We will not go to the mosque. If our brothers and friends, the rabbis, will not be welcome as they are, we are not going. Our solidarity is with them. They are our partners in this dialogue—our destiny is with them in Israel, more than with the Muslims in Dublin or in other place in the world." This was a startling and moving response to a real dilemma, which left its mark on the group in a profound and lasting way. Indeed, one of the rabbis, Rabbi Shai Piron, co-head of the Hesder *yeshiva* (seminary) in Petah Tikva, who later became Minister of Education for the state of Israel, who had to leave to go back to Israel after lunch, said to the Muslim religious leaders: "You have given me a wonderful gift to take home to Israel for Shabbat."

After this occurred, one of the other Muslims in the group pointed out the difficulty that would arise since they would need to attend Friday prayers in

Dublin. During the brief discussion which followed, it was quickly decided that the group as a whole would not go to the mosque for the Friday meal and hospitality as originally planned, but the Muslim members of the group would go as individuals to attend prayers.

But things are never so simple! The next day, another crisis arose when the synagogue leadership requested that the Muslim and Christian leaders wear head-coverings in the synagogue. This led to a Muslim boycott of the worship service and of the Shabbat dinner on Friday night (the Christians, however, did join the rabbis for the Shabbat dinner at the synagogue, and one of them even joined for the worship service and donned a *kippah* for the occasion!). On Friday night, and for the worship services on Saturday morning at the synagogue, the Muslims stayed away.

Finally, after intensive negotiations by our facilitator, Yitzhak Mendelson, with the Muslim leaders in the group, a group decision was reached for the Muslims to join the rabbis for the Shabbat lunch, which followed the Shabbat morning worship service. And at noon on that Saturday, the Muslim and Christian religious leaders joined the rabbis and the members of the Jewish community of Dublin for *kiddush* (the reception following the morning prayers) and lunch, where they were warmly welcomed by the chief rabbi of Ireland. It was a moment of great reconciliation and it reminded me a bit, with all the differences entailed, of the reconciliation between Joseph and his brothers in the Bible. It was apparent from the way that the group came together again that some real bonding and some genuine relationships had developed over the previous days.

The group then enjoyed its first and only Sabbath meal together. It was a moving spiritual occasion, not only because the religious leaders were able to break bread together and share a religious meal, but also because of the act of coming together in religious fellowship. Moreover, one of the Muslims, Kadi Abdelhakeem Samara, who later became the head of the Shari'a courts of the state of Israel and later the president of the courts, spoke eloquently on behalf of the group to the chief rabbi of Ireland and indicated how much he and his colleagues appreciated this rare opportunity to share these special moments in the synagogue in Dublin. He also spoke positively about Kedem's dialogue process, expressing the hope that this would lead to further dialogue and genuine acts of reconciliation in the future. This coming together over a simple Shabbat meal was unquestionably one of the highlights of this journey on the path towards reconciliation.

At the concluding summary and feedback session on Sunday morning, all participants spoke about the need to continue the process of dialogue, reconciliation and peacebuilding that had begun in a very deep and meaningful fashion in the intensive week together in Ireland. While some crises, large and small, were encountered during the week as part of the process, the high level of motivation of most of the members of the group to continue the process carried the day. This intensive encounter was important to them. It was a good beginning, and even though many obstacles had to be overcome, they were dealt with in a positive and constructive manner throughout the week under Dr. Yitzhak Mendelson's leadership. By engaging the group in uni-national and bi-national group processes and decision-making, he managed to involve the participants in determining how the group would proceed. In so doing, the participants felt that they were partners in a developing process of interreligious reconciliation.

Following the seminar in Ireland in July 2003, plans were developed to continue the process in Israel. The group continued to meet at each other's homes. The October meeting took place at the home of Rabbi David Stav, rabbi of Shoham (who later ran in elections to become Ashkenazi chief rabbi of Israel) in his family *sukkah* (booth) during the holiday of *Sukkot* (this was the first time that the Arabs in the group had ever been invited to sit in a *sukkah*). And in November, the group shared a Ramadan dinner (perhaps the first kosher Ramadan dinner in Israeli history) in the home of one of the Muslim leaders in the Israeli Arab village of Baka Al-Gharbiyah. Moreover, in December, the rabbis visited the village of Kafr Kassem—as a follow-up to the discussion that had taken place in July in Ireland—and in solidarity with their brothers in dialogue stood at the memorial to the massacre in the center of the town, a poignant gesture of reconciliation which was deeply appreciated by the Arab members of the group.

The Kedem program was expanded in its second year to include 14 more religious leaders, bringing the group to 28 participants after two years. At the same time, we developed a plan to enlarge the group by 14 people each year, so that after five years the program would have comprised 70 religious leaders from all over Israel. This would have helped us to achieve a "critical mass" in Israeli society of religious leaders who could have become the vanguard for peace and reconciliation. But the plan was not brought to fruition, mostly due to the inability to secure enough funding and because of the ongoing escalation in violence between Palestinians and Israelis, which always made dialogue more fraught and more complicated.

Following a terrible terror attack by some extremist Palestinians which killed eight Jewish students in a famous *yeshiva* in Jerusalem known as *Mercaz HaRav* in March 2008, some of the leading members of the group—among the rabbis and among the Muslim leaders—could not reach agreement on a common statement. Some of the rabbis wanted a clear-cut denunciation of the massacre, but some of the Muslims insisted on linking their statement to criticism of violence by the Israeli army against Palestinians in Gaza during the previous week. Unfortunately, the attempts that were made to bridge this gap did not succeed in bringing about agreement. After this, the group never met again. Personally, I found this quite troubling since after almost six years of dialogue, I would have expected the leaders of the group to have been more forthcoming and more willing to reach an agreement, but apparently, some of the leaders of the group were burnt out by then, which was another factor that led to the demise of the process at that time.

Nevertheless, the Kedem program continued for six years, from 2003-2008, and many of the religious leaders who were involved in it—who were transformed in major ways—continued to be involved in interreligious and intercultural dialogue in Israeli society for many years thereafter. Many of them have responded to my invitations to share their reflections and experiences with groups from abroad and from within Israel on the importance of substantive and serious interreligious dialogue. And many of them have remained friends and colleagues to this day.

THE GOALS OF INTERRELIGIOUS DIALOGUE FOR PEACEFUL COEXISTENCE AND THE MAIN COMPONENTS OF THE DIALOGUE PROCESS

Before I describe the details of my model for dialogue, which I developed over many years in consultation with colleagues and researchers, I feel that it is important for me to say a few words about the goals of interreligious dialogue as a method of peacebuilding.

In my view, interreligious dialogue is not an end in itself. I have found that some people love dialogue because they like to talk and like the idea of group therapy. Rather, dialogue ought to be a means to an end. Genuine dialogue—which requires active listening, caring, and compassion—should not only lead to deeper understanding of each other, but to constructive social change for the mutual benefit of both sides in the conflict.

Similarly, for me, dialogue is not simply discussion or intellectual debate. When I am involved in a dialogue process, I am not interested in learning about the other's religion or culture just to be smarter or more knowledgeable. Rather, I am interested in learning about the other's religion or culture so that I can find better ways and means to live together in peaceful coexistence in the same community or country or region.

According to scholars who study interreligious dialogue, the process has some very well-defined objectives:

> Within the context of peacebuilding, most dialogue aims to facilitate a change from narrow, exclusionist, antagonistic, prejudiced attitudes and perceptions, to more tolerant and open-minded attitudes... Based on the contention that violent conflict is often a consequence of mutual ignorance and the absence of meaningful interaction between the parties, interreligious dialogue aims to foster mutual learning, clarify misconceptions, and provide opportunities for constructive contact with the 'other'... Interreligious dialogue may bring diverse groups together to break down stereotypes and images; inspire hope;

build trust for dealing with tough issues; create a sense of social inclusivity; develop models of constructive engagement; transform the conflict; or solve a specific issue facing the faith communities involved. Interreligious dialogue can be organized to share grievances, facilitate transformation of relationships, highlight similarities and differences, encourage apology and/or forgiveness, and encourage mediation. [10]

In my experience, each dialogue group must set its own achievable goals and not all dialogue groups should be expected to achieve the same things, especially when it comes to trying to solve or deal with macro-national issues. The dialogues that I have planned and implemented with professional staff and consultants over the years, set out to achieve most of the objectives described above, with the exceptions of encouraging apologies or forgiveness, or encouraging mediation. I am not convinced that these would have been reasonable goals for our groups, nor is it reasonable to request that any one group be expected to achieve all of these goals.

One other point is important to stress here. When engaging in dialogue between Palestinian Arabs and Israeli Jews, our goal was not to solve the political problems of the Israeli-Palestinian conflict. This is a job for other people—mainly politicians and diplomats. For us, the political issues were the context, the backdrop to our discussions. Our main goal, if I had to put it succinctly, was peaceful coexistence—will we be able to find ways to live together—Palestinian Arabs and Israeli Jews—in the same country or the same region? Dialogue, education and action were our methods of peace-building to accomplish this goal.

The Main Components of the Dialogue Process

At this point it is worthwhile describing some of the main components of our dialogue work:

- *Two nationalities/Three Religions*: My dialogue work brought together people from two nationalities—Zionism (Jewish nationalism) and Palestinian nationalism—and three religions—Judaism, Christianity and Islam. The Zionists were the Jews, even if they did not all define themselves as 'religious'; and the Palestinians were mostly Muslim with some Christians. In this way, our dialogue was actually a 'trialogue', which made it unique in Israeli society, especially since most people and organizations in Israel which do peace and reconciliation work are secular and avoid religions like the plague.
- *Target Audiences*: My target audiences were key groups in Israeli civil society: grassroots religious leaders, educators, youth and young adults. I generally did not work with politicians or academics, since most of them would have failed the listening test—their specialty is monologue rather

than dialogue. Without some patience and minimal openness to listening to the other, one cannot effectively engage in meaningful dialogue.

- *Recruitment*: We actively recruited people for dialogue groups through interviews and workshops. In the recruitment process, we tried to ascertain the commitment to dialogue of the potential participant and to explain to him or her the nature of the dialogue, especially some of the potential pitfalls. In pre-dialogue workshops, we were often able to weed out mono-loguers or people who did not understand our goals and methods. The recruitment process always helped to make the dialogue group a success. As a result, there was a very low drop-out rate and we found that most people stayed for the entire course of the dialogue group, even during very difficult times.

- *Small groups*: most of our dialogue groups consisted of 12-18 individuals, usually mixing gender, nationality and religion. This enabled the partici-pants to really get to know one another and to have substantive and sensi-tive discussions on complex issues in a frank and open environment.

- *Facilitation*: The main method that my colleagues and I used was careful facilitation. Facilitation of dialogue groups is very different than giving frontal lectures at academic conferences. It is an acquired skill that helps the participants in the dialogue group engage effectively with one another. It fosters active listening and genuine inquiry, which can lead to mutual understanding and empathetic learning. I was fortunate to have worked with some excellent facilitators, and I garnered much experience in group facilitation and supervision.

- *Two Languages—Hebrew and Arabic*: The dialogue groups that I planned and implemented took place in the two main local languages—Hebrew and Arabic—with a translator. This had several benefits. First, it was not a dialogue of the elites who only knew English. Second, it respected the language and culture of the participants. Third, it slowed the discussion down, creating an atmosphere of more careful listening. At the beginning, the translator was generally a Palestinian Arab, but over time more and more young Jews, who had learned and spoke Arabic, also served as translators, which I viewed as a very positive development. (In fact, hun-dreds of young Jews now study spoken Arabic in a variety of institutions in Jerusalem, which is a very important development in general and for the field of interreligious dialogue for peace in particular.)

- *Co-facilitation*: Co-facilitation in the two main local languages became an ideological and practical mainstay of all the dialogue groups under my direction for many years. Over time, more and more Israeli-Palestinian groups also adopted this method, for similar reasons. In addition to the two facilitators—one Palestinian Arab and one Israeli Jew—there was always a third professional person in the room, a translator, who could be

Palestinian or Jewish, and who tried to remain as neutral as possible, leaving the facilitation to the facilitators.

• *Long-term Dialogue*: The dialogue groups that I arranged were all long-time processes. Not a 'one-off' event on a weekend morning or a weekday evening. Not just a meeting at which platitudes were spoken and photos were taken (too much of that goes on in the name of 'dialogue' it is really just a superficial show). Rather, my dialogue groups would last anywhere from 10 months to 1 year to 3 or 4 or even 6 years. The longer the investment of time, money, energy and commitment, the higher the returns (as in the Kedem program described above). It was always a long process, with ups and downs, crises and challenges, as well as achievements and successes. Below I describe the process in some detail.

As a result of our work on the ground, I developed a model for successful interreligious dialogue, which emerged after many years of trial and error, especially during the many difficult years of violence and counter-violence which prevailed in Israel during the first decade of the twentieth century. This model was developed in consultation with many excellent professional colleagues who worked with me in designing and implementing unique dialogue programs. However, the development of the model is essentially my own, based on observation and evaluation of dialogue programs and based on my own research and reading.

A NEW MODEL FOR INTERRELIGIOUS DIALOGUE

My model is comprised of four major elements:

• Personal interaction–getting to know each other as individual human beings
• Interreligious, text-based learning
• Discussing core issues of the conflict
• Taking action, separately and together

1. The Personal Element

All of our dialogue groups brought together people from various religious (Judaism, Islam and Christianity) and national groups (Palestinian Arab and Jewish Israeli). Each person came to the dialogue with his or her own personal identity, which he or she shared with the group. The group learned to understand and respect the identity and narrative of each of its members by listening carefully and genuinely seeking to come to know as much as possible about each participant. Through this process, people in the group came to recognize the human dignity and integrity of the others.

I have come to call this process *de-demonizing the other*. As a result of the ongoing violent struggle known as the Israeli-Palestinian conflict, Palestinian Arabs and Israeli Jews who had never met each other before coming to the dialogue group tended to see the other only through the prisms of the conflict and the negative media stereotypes which dominate our print and electronic media. Jews tended to have a preconceived notion that all Palestinians were terrorists or suicide bombers or simply people out to kill them. On the other side, Palestinians usually thought that Jews were occupiers, soldiers or settlers. In other words, both sides were deeply influenced by media and societal stereotypes. In our dialogue groups, these stereotypes were shattered by the facilitators who asked each person to explain their identities and share their life stories with the others. When this is done over time—at least a few months and sometimes even up to a year—I have found that people are actually quite shocked to discover that the other, who is supposed to be *the enemy*, is actually a human being!

This first layer of our dialogue process built an important foundation of mutual trust, which was essential for the rest of the dialogue process. It often created lasting friendships or at the very least much collegiality, which was critical for constructive, honest, and fruitful dialogue as the year progressed.

Changing behaviors and attitudes is an important aspect of peacebuilding. According to one scholar, "In deep-rooted conflicts, the parties are not disputing over material interests but are suffering from deeply damaged social relationships... Building trust requires clarifying misunderstandings, removing negative perceptions and transforming enemy images."[11] According to another scholar:

> Dialogue is a powerful tool that deepens individuals' understanding of the other's perspectives and worldviews. One transformative phase occurs when members of conflicting groups mutually acknowledge their side's collective wrongdoing against the other. Such acknowledgement takes place when there is enough security and trust in the group to walk through the parties' history and critically examine each side's responsibility in creating this history.[12]

I found in our dialogue groups over and over again that the personal element was crucial for the whole process. It was an essential building-block that could not be skipped or eliminated since it helped to develop personal relationships which were critical for the steps ahead.

2. Interreligious Learning

To my shock and dismay, I have discovered over many years that individuals often know very little about the cultural practices and beliefs of members of other religions in Israel and Palestine. Accordingly, Israeli Jews know almost nothing about Islam or Christianity. And, what they do know is usually negative and was learned in courses in Jewish history in which they learned that Muslims or Christians oppressed or massacred Jews throughout the centuries. In a paper which I presented at a seminar at the Vatican in March 1998, I shared with Jewish and Catholic partners in dialogue my research on what Jewish young people learn about Christianity. My findings were a shock to my colleagues, especially the Catholics among them.[13] Nor do Muslims or Christians who live in Israel or Palestine know much about Judaism. Much of what they do know is negative, as they learned it mostly from their print and electronic media and from the street and the family, which passes down negative ideas about the 'other' from generation to generation.

After bringing in interreligious text study, I discovered that even a little formal education—properly and sensitively taught by good teachers—can go a long way in a short time to breaking down ingrained negative stereotypes of each other's religions. These teachers—especially many of the religious leaders who were involved in the Kedem program discussed above—chose good texts with a positive message from the sacred canons of each religion, such as the Bible and later commentaries (Midrash and Talmud), the Koran and the Hadith (Sayings of the Prophet), the New Testament and the Church Fathers. They taught them in a way that can be readily understood and appreciated by 'the other side'. This educational component to our dialogue process was especially important in our work with religious leaders in our Kedem program. Muslim, Jewish and Christian religious leaders not only shared texts with positive messages in text study sessions, but they also re-interpreted problematic texts in creative and beneficial ways in the spirit of reconciliation. When this was done well, I discovered that another very important level of trust was developed, what I like to call 'interreligious trust'. Participants who went through this process in our dialogue groups could talk about common humanistic values shared by the three major monotheistic religions, and they could sense a spirit of religious partnership which motivated them to continue the dialogue and to seek meaningful paths of action together.

For example, in one group, a rabbi was teaching about the value of the sanctity of human life. Afterwards he quoted a source from the Talmud, which said "He who saves a single life is as if he has saved the whole world." As soon as he said this, one of the imams said, "We have this verse too!" This was a moment of great recognition of a value shared among Muslims and Jews, a moment of consciousness which could not have happened without the dialogue process.

Using religious texts as a tool for dialogue has been documented by several scholars as a critical tool in the process. Shared study of each other's sacred texts has proven to be very useful. According to one scholar in the field, "several Israeli interfaith organizations have moved in this direction, sharing numerous study sessions on one another's religion... Study appears to be a rather natural activity for Jews and Arabs trying to get to know each other and may, in fact, create much deeper bonds than Western styles of dialogue about 'problems'."[14] Another scholar goes even further when she writes:

> Religious texts and scriptures often richly articulate values central to reconciliation and peacebuilding, including compassion, forgiveness, and accountability, among others. Rooting these values within the parameters of sacred texts provides legitimacy. Participants of interreligious dialogue often introduce verses and passages on the designated theme or topic from their religious texts and invite other participants to have a conversation about that text. These values and texts inspire and provide guidance to the participants, especially when difficult issues are being discussed, and provide a level of 'certainty' and 'truth'. As such, they facilitate the transformation of perceptions and help to rebuild relationships.[15]

In my own work over many years, I have found that use of religious texts as a basis for dialogue can often be very helpful. But it can also be confusing and unconstructive, especially when there are radically divergent approaches to texts, from fundamentalist to liberal. Nevertheless, in some circumstances, especially with religious leaders or religious groups, their religious texts are so much a part of their national narrative that using them is inescapable and usually extremely important to developing a mutual understanding of each other's worldviews.

3. Discussing Core Issues of the Conflict

Since our dialogue process took place in Israel and Palestine, in the midst of an ongoing and often violent conflict, my colleagues and I felt that we could not ignore the contemporary context in which we live and function. More accurately, we chose not to ignore the conflict—whereas other organizations in our country and region actively sought to prevent 'politics' or 'the conflict' from entering into the discussion.

Participants in these dialogue groups were always asked by their facilitators to make "I" statements, rather than to tell each other what they thought that their political or religious leaders had to say about the issues of the day. People were asked to bring up issues related to the conflict that bothered them personally and to share with the group how these issues affected their personal and communal lives. In this way, participants were able to hear the diverse narratives of each group relating to the ongoing unresolved political and security conflict in the region. As a result, Palestinians were exposed to both the meta Jewish narrative underlying the conflict—as well as many diverse personal narratives—and Jews were exposed to both the meta Palestinian narrative of the history and contemporary nature of the conflict, as well as to Palestinians' personal stories. For most of the people in these dialogue groups, this was the first time in their lives that they heard—through careful and compassionate listening—the narratives of 'the other', which undoubtedly shaped their consciousness throughout the dialogue process and for a long time afterwards.

I have come to believe that in a genuine dialogue process, after mutual trust has been established, the core issues of the conflict can be discussed in an open, honest, and sensitive fashion, guided by careful and consistent professional facilitation, without animosity or acrimony. In fact, I have found that participants in our dialogue groups told me many times that they continued to participate in the group for the duration of the process precisely because the discussion was frank and forthright. This meant that the discussions in this part of the dialogue process were often very painful and difficult. But when significant levels of trust have been developed, most of the participants in the process found this phase particularly meaningful and enriching as a way to genuinely get to know the other. It led to deep mutual understanding of the other's religious, cultural, and political realities, even if it also delineated where people fundamentally did not—and often could not—agree with the other. Indeed, the purpose of the dialogue was not to reach agreement but to understand each other deeply and to then seek ways to cooperate with each other.

4. Taking Action, Separately and Together

Many years ago, one of my Muslim colleagues said to me when we were preparing to convene a dialogue group: *Dialogue is not enough!* It is not enough for us to learn and undergo personal transformation. As responsible members of society, we must take our learning to heart and create change. We are obligated to work for peace, to influence others, and to cause a ripple effect. As a result, I strove for our groups to engage in both dialogue and action. In other words, all of our participants—religious leaders, women, youth, young adults, educators—were asked to take some action—separately or together—as a result of the personal transformational processes that they went through within this intensive experience.

Action can take many forms—personal, social, educational, and/or political—but I always felt that every person who is moved by the dialogue process should have been obligated and committed to share their experiences with others in whatever ways possible, even through gestures of reconciliation. From my experience, I have found that often simple human gestures of reconciliation, such as visiting the sick or the bereaved, can go a long way towards cementing personal relationships and creating genuine trust and profound relationships among friends and colleagues (former 'enemies') who are involved in long-term dialogue processes. Moreover, each person—through personal and professional networks and associations—should seek to act in such a way as to bring the insights and lessons of their dialogue processes to the attention of people in their own communities. In this way, each participant becomes a multiplier who can spread the message of the possibilities and benefits of peaceful coexistence, and the method of dialogue and education, to many other people in his or her society.

I could give many examples of actions that were meaningful and impactful. For example, at the end of the first summer session of dialogue with the Kedem group, we returned to Israel from Ireland and I discovered that the brother of one of the leading Muslim members of the group had died suddenly. After I received the phone call about this, I shared the news with the rabbis in the group, and there was an immediate consensus that we should go to pay a condolence call to the home of the bereaved man since it was the right thing to do for a friend and colleague. Two days later, a group of rabbis—most of whom had never before been in an Arab home or in an Arab village in Israel—went to the home of their Muslim colleague to offer personal condolences on the death of his brother, just as they would have done for a fellow Jew. The Muslim man was overwhelmed with the genuineness of this gesture of solidarity on the part of his new friends and colleagues, and this simple religious act of offering condolences to the bereaved went a long way to furthering and developing trust and friendship between him and this group of rabbis for years to come.

Another example of a gesture of reconciliation was a similar condolence visit but under very different circumstances. During the second year of the project, a Jewish man killed four Palestinian Arabs of Israeli citizenship in the Israeli Palestinian town of Shfaram, not far from Haifa. Two of the people who were killed were members of the Greek Catholic community in the town. It just so happened that the Greek Catholic minister of their church in this town, Rev. Nadeem Shakour, was a member of our dialogue group. When the rabbis heard about it, they immediately decided to pay a condolence call to the tent of mourning of one of the Christian families in the town, and one of the rabbis in the group spoke briefly in the tent of mourning to all the Christians in attendance. His remarks were very warmly received. The next day this story made a front-page headline in one of the main newspapers in Israel (which was an extremely rare event since we did not often get much publicity for our programs from the mainstream media in Israel). While we did not do this for the publicity, we were gratified that many people in Israel and beyond could learn about our gesture of reconciliation through the media.

Another excellent example of action occurred in the area of education. One of the rabbis in the group, Rabbi Shlomo Brinn, was so moved and inspired by what he had learned and experienced in our dialogue group after

the first two years that he decided to plan and implement a course for religious women on humanistic values in Judaism and reaching out to the Palestinian minority in our midst. He called the course "Israel and the Nations". In
this course, he prepared texts on attitudes toward the non-Jew in Jewish
sources. He taught this new course at two religious Israeli teacher-training
colleges over a three-year period. In addition to covering the relevant *hala-
chot* (Jewish religious rulings) and sources, one course session included an
encounter with an Israeli Muslim Palestinian Arab from the town of Abu
Ghosh, just west of Jerusalem, who shared his unique perspective with the
students. The encounter was tense and several young women refused to even
attend the session. They argued that an encounter with an Arab who does not
identify with Zionism (they would not have found too many in Israel!) con-
stitutes a legitimization of the enemy.[16] They were clearly not aware that the
Israeli Arab whom they were supposed to meet is a loyal Israeli citizen who
comes from a village which supported the Haganah (the pre-state Israeli
army) during the 1948 War of Independence.

According to Rabbi Brinn, this was a very important educational experience:

> A world of Jewish thought with which the students had never been acquainted
> was opened up to them, and it aroused both curiosity and criticism on their part
> (i.e. they asked why, if what they were learning was really true, they had never
> heard of it before). I also found it gratifying to transmit important basic knowl-
> edge rooted in an educational approach that added yet another layer to their
> religious Jewish perspective on the non-Jew. Many of the young women who
> attended the course emerged with a sense of responsibility towards the minor-
> ities who live in our country.[17]

I attended one of the concluding classes with Rabbi Brinn and his outstanding students. In the summary discussion, I too was surprised to learn
that not only was this the first time that these students had ever learned these
materials in all the years of their intensive Orthodox Jewish education, but
that many of them felt that all Orthodox young women who are training to be
teachers should learn these sources and the proper attitudes towards non-
Jews that are expressed within them. Indeed, I had developed a plan to get
this course into all religious teacher-training schools in Israel but the money
for the project ran out and we could not expand it as we had hoped. However,
the potential was there for educational action that could have created major
changes in Jewish teacher training.

In sum, the action component of the dialogue programs that I planned and
implemented with colleagues over many years was always meant to be an
integral part of the process. However, I must admit that it did not always
work out well. Graduates of our dialogue programs did not always follow
through with action projects as I had hoped. Why not?

In retrospect, I think that there are three main reasons: 1) Many of them were genuinely afraid of taking what they had learned in the dialogue group back to their homes and communities for fear of rejection by their family or peers, or for fear of failure. They had felt comfortable in "the bubble" of the warm and cozy and well-facilitated dialogue group, and they felt that their friends and colleagues would not appreciate or understand the insights that they had gained through sustained dialogue with 'the other'. 2) Graduates of dialogue programs often did not have the educational or organizational skills to implement new projects. They were good at talking but not trained in planning and implementing action projects. 3) Some of the educators/facilitators with whom I worked over the years felt that dialogue is itself action and they did not feel a responsibility to motivate their participants to other action. They said that they were educators, not activists, and they felt that a commitment to activism was an individual decision, not a mandatory one.

I will have more to say about this in the next chapter when I discuss "Lessons Learned" and analyze the various reasons why dialogue did not lead to enough action and what I believe can be done to remedy this in the future.

One of the ways that I took action was to hold public lectures and symposia with prestigious conference centers and institutions in Jerusalem, for the benefit of the general public. This was a way for me to share our method (dialogue) and our message (peaceful coexistence) with people from all walks of life in Jerusalem, including journalists who frequently attended these programs (but rarely wrote about them). For example, for most of my 25 years as director of ICCI, I worked closely with the leadership of the Konrad Adenauer Foundation in Jerusalem, which co-hosted many symposia with my organization at their beautiful conference center in Mishkenot Sha'ananim (a guesthouse in the heart of the historic Yemin Moshe neighborhood, the first Jewish neighborhood built outside the walls of the Old City of Jerusalem), and also at other major venues, such as the King David hotel in central Jerusalem. In addition to regular symposia on topics of contemporary interest a few times a year, and hosting off-the-record seminars and workshops, we also co-sponsored important seminars, some of which were open to the public.

One of the most important ongoing programs which we co-sponsored was a three-year project of seminars between Palestinians and Israelis in the years immediately following the Oslo Accords in 1993, which took place in both Jerusalem and Ramallah. In addition, for four years we co-hosted an *iftar* (end of Ramadan) supper and seminar for leading Muslim religious leaders and Jewish clergy and educators. This was a special opportunity for us to break bread together with our Muslim counterparts, as well as to share the spiritual and social meaning of fasting in our respective religious traditions with audiences in Jerusalem.

I also worked closely for many years with the professional leadership of the Van Leer Jerusalem Institute, where I moderated symposia and held important conferences. A few years ago, I moderated a series of three public lectures with Christian leaders, which were well attended by the general public. This was a unique opportunity for the Jewish public in West Jerusalem to meet and hear from Christian leaders whom they have never met or heard speak before, in order to come to know something about what Christians in Jerusalem really think about contemporary issues. During that year, I hosted important lectures by Bishop Munib Younan, bishop of the Evangelical Lutheran Church in Jordan and the Holy Land, Fr. David Neuhauss of the Latin Patriarchate in Jerusalem, and Fr. Hosam Naoum, dean of St. George's Cathedral in East Jerusalem. These Christian leaders whom I came to befriend and respect during my career, were only too happy to give public lectures to Jewish audiences in Jerusalem (see chapter three for more about these Christian leaders).

I also hosted important conferences with the Catholic Church at the Van Leer Jerusalem Institute and at the Jerusalem Center for Israel Studies on the revolutionary changes in the Catholic Church towards Jews and Judaism, with leading personalities from the Vatican, such as Cardinal Cassidy and Cardinal Walter Kasper, and leading rabbis from Israel, such as Rabbi David Rosen, Rabbi Shear Yeshuv Cohen, and others. This was a way in which I could share with the public in Jerusalem some of the highlights of how the Catholic Church—and other churches—had changed their attitudes to the Jewish people in recent decades, a fact that is still hardly known to most Jews in Israel (and beyond).

In addition, I was privileged to host the Dalai Lama twice in Israel in one year. The first event, held in June of 1999, was initiated by a San Francisco group called the "Interreligious Friendship Group", which was an amazing group of people from the USA led by Bishop William Swing, and a Jewish businessman, Richard Blum, both from Northern California. They organized a special group of people whose purpose was to encourage interreligious and intercultural dialogue and friendship between religious leaders in different parts of the world. This led to an amazing three-day seminar held at the King David hotel in central Jerusalem, which culminated in a large public reception in which Mr. Blum was honored for his interreligious leadership and I was honored for my leadership in the field of interreligious dialogue in Israel during the past 8 years. I was fortunate to receive this honor on behalf of the organization that I founded and directed, in the presence of His Holiness the Dalai Lama and many other distinguished religious personalities in a crowded ballroom of friends and guests from all over Israel.

In my remarks upon accepting this honor, I thanked all those present, including and especially the Dalai Lama by saying, "Your being here with us is the greatest honor. It inspires us to continue our efforts, with your help, to promote peace between people, not just between governments, in our part of the world."[18] I also was blessed by a very special encounter during my brief remarks. When I turned to address His Holiness the Dalai Lama to thank him, I looked to my right and then to my left, and then he suddenly came up from behind and tapped me on the shoulder and smiled! Everyone had a good laugh, including the Dalai Lama himself. This was typical of him, expressing his mindful presence with a smile. I turned to him and said: "Your Holiness. We are deeply inspired by your message of kindness and compassion, and by your efforts to spread your message around the world and to come together with other religious seekers in pursuit of peace here and everywhere."

The Dalai Lama had come to Jerusalem as a pilgrim. This was actually his second visit to our city. Previously in 1994, we also hosted him for a public lecture. But this time was different. On this occasion, he also visited the holy sites of Judaism, Christianity and Islam in the Old City of Jerusalem. I was fortunate to accompany him on this part of his pilgrimage. It was remarkable to see the deep respect he accorded each site and each religious tradition and the people of each religious group. The public pilgrimage to the holy sites and the public ceremony very much helped spread our message of peaceful coexistence.

In November, also in 1999, we hosted the Dalia Lama again for a very special three-day seminar with local and international religious leaders at a beautiful retreat center, Bet Gavriel, on the shores of the Sea of Galilee. During the course of the entire seminar, he listened very carefully to everything that everyone said, radiating the kind of compassion which is the essence of his religious worldview and Buddhist practice. Without doubt, this seminar inspired me and many of my colleagues to become interreligious activists for peace in the years ahead. These were among the most profound interreligious experiences of my life which have continually made me mindful of the inseparable link between dialogue and activism.

I also had the privilege of hosting the famous Vietnamese Buddhist monk, Thich Nhat Hanh, for a "dharma talk" in Jerusalem one year. And I participated in a wonderful workshop with him which included walking in silence back and forth across a lawn on a kibbutz outside of Jerusalem and saying "Yes, yes, yes... thanks, thanks, thanks..." over and over again, in gratitude for my life, the blessings that I share with others, and the historical opportunity of making my contribution to this world through my work in interreligious activism in the land of Israel. I learned from Thich Nhat Hanh then, and later from reading one of his books[19], that the kind of meditation that he was involved with was called "Engaged Buddhism". One doesn't go up to the mountain to meditate and just stay there in a monastery. One must come down from the mountain and become engaged in healing the world. This was a Buddhist way of saying that prayer or dialogue is not enough. Rather, meditation, prayer and dialogue ought to be catalysts for improving the world.

CONCLUSION

In this chapter, I have described both the goals and the methods of interreligious dialogue as a form of peacebuilding. In so doing, I have tried to provide a sense of how the dialogue was unique in the special context of the ongoing Palestinian-Israeli conflict. Moreover, I have discussed the new model that I and my colleagues developed over many years, which I believe has implications for interreligious dialogue everywhere, especially in areas of conflict. An essential ingredient of this new model is to connect dialogue to action, so that our work for peace is not just "talk" but engages us in concrete action for change on the ground.

In the next and concluding chapter of this book, I will share the major lessons that I have learned from my engagement in dialogue in Israel for more than a quarter of a century, and will make some recommendations for the future. In addition, I will share some of my favorite stories and anecdotes, which shed light on both the message and the method of dialogue amidst conflict.

NOTES

1. This chapter has been adapted in part from my article *Interreligious Dialogue in Israel, Lessons Learned* (pp. 183-200), which appeared in a book of essays which I edited entitled *Coexistence and Reconciliation—Voices for Interreligious Dialogue in Israel,* Paulist Press, 2015. I have expanded and revised this material greatly, based on hundreds of lectures that I have given in Israel and abroad on this topic, and based on discussions with colleagues and graduates of my dialogue programs over many years.

2. Over the years, the Interreligious Coordinating Council in Israel (ICCI) partnered with the World Conference of Religions for Peace (now known as Religions for Peace), the Auburn Theological Seminary in New York, the St. Ethelburga's Centre for Reconciliation and Peace in London, the Corrymeela Community in Northern Ireland, the International Council of Christians and Jews (ICCJ), The Abraham Fund, The Cordoba Iniative, Risho Kosei-Kai in Japan, FAITH—the Foundation for the Advancement of Interfaith Harmony of the UK and the USA, the Focolare Movement in Jerusalem, The Sisters of Sion in Jerusalem, the Tantur Ecumenical Institute in Jerusalem, the Swedish Theological Institute in Jerusalem, the Konrad Adenauer Foundation's Jerusalem office, the Van Leer Jerusalem Institute, the Jerusalem Institute for Israel Studies, and others.

3. Rebecca Russo, *Face to Face Evaluation Report,* Jerusalem: Interreligious Coordinating Council in Israel, 2009. Rebecca Russo was a Dorot Fellow in Israel who served as an intern with ICCI during 2008-2009.

4. *Evaluation report of Face to Face/Faith to Faith* by Jay Rothman, 2011, p. 20

5. Interview with Avigail Moshe, December 4, 2016.

6. Interview with Haneen Majadleh, December 6, 2016.

7. This guidebook entitled *Principles of Group Facilitation*, which was a joint project of ICCI, the Corrymeela Community and the St. Ethelburga's Center for Reconciliation and Peace

in London, is available in print from St. Ethelburga's and also on their website www.stethelburgas.org/.

8. Shlomo Brinn, "Teaching about the Other in Religious Zionist Education—a Pilot Program," in *Coexistence and Reconciliation: Palestinian and Jewish Voices for Interreligious Dialogue,* Ron Kronish, ed., Paulist Press, 2015, p. 241.

9. This project was made possible by support from the Embassy of the Federal Republic of Germany in Tel Aviv, a Spanish NGO, Tres Culturas, the Conflict Mediation and Management (CMM) program of USAID via Religions for Peace, and the Konrad Adenauer Foundation.

10. S. Ayse Kadayifci-Orellana. "Interreligious Dialogue and Peacebuilding", in *The Wiley-Blackwell Companion to Interreligious Dialogue.* Edited by Catherine Cornille. John Wiley and Sons, West Sussex, UK, 2013, pp. 154-155.

11. S. Ayse Kadayifci-Orellana, *Ibid.,* p. 151.

12. Mohammed Abu-Nimer. "The Miracles of Transformation through Interfaith Dialogue", p. 25, in *Interfaith Dialogue and Peacebuilding.* Edited by David R. Smock. Wash DC: United States Institute for Peace, 2002.

13. Ronald Kronish, *Teaching About Christianity in Israel,* unpublished paper presented at a seminar at the Vatican of the International Jewish-Catholic Liaison Committee, March 25, 1998.

14. Marc Gopin. "The Use of the Word and Its Limits", in *Interfaith Dialogue and Peacebuilding*, David Smock, ed., p. 39.

15. S. Ayse Kadayifci-Orellanna, *Ibid.,* p. 154.

16. Shlomo Brinn. *Ibid.,* pp 241-242.

17. *Ibid,* p. 242.

18. Ron Kronish. *Insight Israel*, Jerusalem: an ongoing publication of the ICCI. July 1, 1999.

19. Thich Nhat Hanh. *Peace is Every Step. The Path of Mindfulness in Everyday Life.* New York: Bantam Books, 1991.

Chapter Five

On Interreligious Dialogue in Israel — Lessons Learned and Thoughts for the Future

I will divide my reflections in this chapter into three parts:

1. Lessons learned from my experience and reflections on practice during the past 25 years in Israel and internationally.
2. Thoughts for the future—challenges and hopes for future practitioners and for all those concerned about the future of peace for Israelis and Palestinians in the land that is perceived as holy to them, the land that they must somehow figure out a way to share and to live in peacefully together.
3. Some final thoughts about "The Other Peace Process"

LESSONS LEARNED [1]

During the past quarter century, I have been actively engaged in the grass-roots work of interreligious dialogue and education in Israel and internationally. During this period, I served as the founding director of the Interreligious Coordinating Council in Israel (ICCI), which was founded on January 16, 1991. While this work has had its share of ups and downs, successes and obstacles, challenges and setbacks, I can say that without a doubt, I have learned a great deal about the role of dialogue in peace-building in our part of the world by trial and error and by persistence and partnership with key people and organizations.

A few years ago, when I began thinking about "retirement", or what I prefer to call "transitioning" (from management of an organization to writing, teaching and mentoring), I decided to edit a book of essays which would bring together some of the best thinking, as well as reflections on practice by Jews, Christians and Muslims with whom I have labored in the vineyards of dialogue for the past quarter century. This led to the publication of *Coexistence and Reconciliation: Voices for Interreligious Dialogue* (published by Paulist Press, 2015), which was the first book of its kind in many years[2], and much of the information in it is virtually unknown and certainly unappreciated in much of Israel and in the rest of the world.

The 22 essays that appeared in this book—many by authors who were writing articles for the first time in their lives—were meant to inform readers about significant projects and programs that had been going on for decades in Israel and Palestine, mostly under the radar, usually without much fanfare or publicity. In addition, many people who have read selections from this book of essays told me that they were inspired by the idea that interreligious dialogue, education and action could be a substantial force for reconciliation and peacebuilding in this part of the world. This is one of the reasons that motivated me to write this current book.

This reminds me of an incident from many years ago. I was speaking at an international conference in Bucharest, sponsored by the Community of Sant'Egidio, a wonderful Catholic organization based in Rome that works for peace and reconciliation around the world, with whom I have cooperated for many years. The Community of Sant 'Egidio is a worldwide movement of lay people, based on prayer, solidarity, ecumenism, and dialogue. Among other things, they organized an annual gathering of Peoples and Religions in cities in Europe (Venice, Padua, Rome, Assisi, Barcelona, and Bucharest) which I had the good fortune to attend, which always included a magnificent concluding prayer ceremony, candle-lighting, and reflections for peace, usually in the central town square, with beautiful music in the background. At the Bucharest conference I spoke about the work I had been doing for peace and reconciliation through dialogue in Israel. During the question period, an archbishop from Mozambique (where the Community of Sant'Egidio had been helping resolve a conflict) stood up and said: "You are the first person whom I have ever heard talk about efforts for peace in Israel. I had no idea that anyone on the ground was doing anything about this." In other words, he had never read anything about this in his newspapers or emails, nor had he seen anything about it on television. Apparently, like so many other people in the West, he had only read and heard about the daily violence and counter-violence in our region that dominates the news.

One of the reasons for writing this book is the hope that I never hear this comment again. I want it to be well known in the world that there are people who are working at many levels in Israel and Palestine to promote mutual underotanding, cooperation and coexistence, peace and reconciliation, even if we don't make the mainstream news very much. In fact, thousands of people in civil society are working on a daily basis to mitigate conflicts and to bring hope to their people, but not much is reported about that.

What are the main lessons that I learned from engaging in interreligious dialogue in Israel and Palestine during the past 25 years?

Firstly, I learned that interreligious dialogue, when it is done with good facilitation, careful planning, and persistent implementation, can be very helpful in building trust among people on the grassroots level of our ongoing conflict, including religious leaders, educators, youth and young adults. (I will have more to say about the vital importance of good facilitation for effective dialogue later on in this chapter.)

Secondly, I discovered over and over again that there are in fact people to talk with on "the other side". Many Palestinians—especially those who live in Israel and are citizens here—are eager to encounter their Jewish neighbors and to understand them better, towards the goal of learning to live in peaceful coexistence within our country and within the region.[3]

In encounters with Palestinians of good will in East Jerusalem and in the West Bank, I have learned that they are also interested in dialogue and the concrete resolution of our conflict. In contrast to the conventional wisdom, too often perpetuated by government leaders and other propagandists, not all Palestinians are terrorists! The opposite is the case: most Palestinians— whether they be Christians or Muslims—are interested in getting on with life and learning to live together in peaceful relations, rather than prolonging the conflict which is harmful to them as well as to us. It is the minority of rejectionists on their side—as well as on the Israeli side—who prevent the peace process from going forward and diminish all attempts to bring peace to our region due to their incitement to hatred and exclusionist ideologies. Unfortunately, this minority on both sides appears to be growing as a result of the political despair that set in after the political peace process failed to produce any significant results. Indeed, the lack of progress on the diplomatic front for a very long time, has led many people to feel apathy and despair, since they see no political solution to the conflict in sight.

Third, I have encountered moderate Muslims, both in Israel and around the world, who preach and teach a version of Islam that is vastly different than the one represented in the mainstream media and on the internet.

Four of these Muslims presented their views of Islam in eye-opening essays in the book mentioned above. They are: Professor Mohammed Dajani—the founder and director of Wasatia, a Palestinian Muslim movement which actively promotes the idea of moderation in Palestine; Kadi Dr. Iyad Zahalka—the Muslim judge of the Shari'a court in Jerusalem of the state of Israel, who also teaches at Tel Aviv University, Bar Ilan University, and Emek Yizrael College; Mr. Issa Jaber, a veteran Israeli Arab educator, who now serves as the mayor of the town of Abu Ghosh, just west of Jerusalem; and Sheikh Ghassan Manasra, a Sufi educator and activist from Nazareth, who is currently living in the USA. These Muslims, whom I have described and discussed in chapter two, became my principal partners in dialogue over many years, and continue to be trusted friends and colleagues. I appeared with them in many public dialogues, both in Israel and abroad, and we continue to cooperate on projects and programs of mutual interest. They taught me that true Islam is not the one portrayed by the radical Islamic groups, who with the help of the Western media have hijacked Islam from its fundamental ethical and just principles.

In my view, much more needs to be known about Islam in Israel and the region, as it is lived and practiced here, rather than as it is practiced in some parts of the Arab world, especially by ISIS and Al Qaeda and their friends, where it is much more extreme and fundamentalist in its outlook and behavior.

Fourth, I learned over and over again that Christians are no longer our enemy.

The crusades are over! We are no longer at war with Christians or Christianity. On the contrary, we in our generation are in dialogue with Christians in more ways than was ever possible previously.[4] For the past 50 years— since the promulgation of the famous Vatican document known as *Nostra Aetate* ("In our Time") in October 1965, Jews and Christians at the highest levels, and at the grassroots, have been engaged in an unprecedented ongoing dialogue which has totally changed the relationships between Christians and Jews around the world. This dialogue has taken place in Israel and Palestine as well.

Fifth, I have seen how interreligious and intercultural dialogue can be part of the solution, as opposed to part of the problem.

Dialogue that remains only ephemeral, intellectual, theological or abstract is not the kind that we need in our region. Too much of this goes on in many forums in Israel and abroad, where I often feel that I have listened to too many monologues about the importance of dialogue, rather than actually engaging in genuine dialogue. Rather, I have felt for a long time that we need a dialogue that is connected to real life, one which will change the hearts and minds of the people to be aware of the benefits and opportunities inherent in genuine peace.

Sixth, throughout this book I have argued that we need peacebuilding as a supplement to peacemaking.

In addition to peacemaking—the work of the politicians, diplomats and lawyers—that results in peace treaties, what I like to call "pieces of paper", we urgently need peacebuilding—the work of rabbis, imams, priests, educators, psychologists, social workers, architects and more—to bring people to encounter one another and to act for peace, not just to talk about it.

Rabbi Michael Melchior, a former minister in Israel's governments (especially ones that furthered the Oslo Peace Process in the 1990s) and now chairman (and founder) of the Mosaica Center for Religious Conflict Transformation, and a friend and co-worker in the vineyards of interreligious dialogue for peace in Israel and the region for many years—discussed this eloquently in his essay "Establishing Religious Peace"[5] and I know that he has been actively working towards this goal for a long time. Indeed, in 2016, he organized a historic interreligious summit in Spain, which brought together leading orthodox rabbis, along with Muslim and Christian religious leaders from the Holy Land, which led to the publication of an amazing declaration that stated that religion should no longer be a barrier to peace.[6] Among other things, this statement declared:

> In the name of God, We, people of the Holy Land and leaders of its religious communities are gathered to take upon ourselves to relentlessly seek peace in the Land. We emphasize that our two peoples are responsible for their common fate, that the three religions are responsible for creating peaceful existence, and that we, as religious leaders are responsible for promoting a life of mutual respect based upon justice and safety, in the spirit of the word of God as conveyed by His prophets. We live in the Holy Land by the grace of God, and wish to subject ourselves to His will. We recognize the holiness of the Land for all three religions.
>
> All three religions value the principle of the sanctity of life, and we call for its practice in daily life in our Land. The violence that is conducted, supposedly in the name of God, is a desecration of His name, a crime against those who are created in His image, and a debasement of faith. The proper means of solving conflict and disagreement is by negotiation and deliberation only.

Just a few days later, at the end of November 2016, at another conference which I attended in Seville, Spain, hosted by the Tres Culturas Foundation (with which I have cooperated for many years), I met a diplomat from the Spanish Ministry of Foreign Affairs, who told me that her government was very proud to host this conference and other conferences of this nature. This same woman chaired a panel on which I spoke about the role of interreligious dialogue in combating "religious" extremism. I subsequently wrote a blog post about this.[7]

While the statement issued in Spain is beautifully crafted and well-intentioned, I am nevertheless skeptical that many of these religious leaders will do anything meaningful about it on the ground, in their communities in Israel and Palestine. My skepticism comes from two places: First, most of the Orthodox rabbis who signed the statement have never done anything real for peace, except to pay lip service to the ideal of peace on very rare occasions. Second, I sat as an observer on behalf of Religions for Peace on the "permanent implementation of the Alexandria Declaration"[8] in 2002 for a full year, during the height of the Second Intifada, and to my sorrow, nothing was implemented on the ground following that declaration. Due to the ongoing violence and counter-violence that prevailed in the region at that time, all I heard for a full year were arguments and squabbling and each side blaming the other for the demise of peace and the rise in violence in the region.

Moreover, many of my colleagues and I have been doing this work for many years, mostly at the grassroots level, rather than at the national leadership level, which I call the "photo-op" level, at which religious "leaders" smile and say nice things, usually at the urging of their political establishments, to make them look good. During my two and a half decades of involvement in interreligious dialogue on intermediate and grassroots levels, we have created a successful model of dialogue[9], which I believe has the potential for creating a lasting impact on the participants of carefully constructed dialogue groups. If there was more funding for such dialogue groups, and many more could be organized and conducted in a professionally responsible manner, there would be much more impact on both Palestinian and Jewish society, which could help transform the conflict from a violent one to one that could embark on a new path of reconciliation.

While I am on the subject of funding, I want to say that lack of funding for interreligious and intercultural dialogue in Israel/ Palestine is a severe handicap for making significant progress and developing projects and programs with long-term impact. This is a major obstacle. I spent a great deal of time in fundraising during my 25 years as director of a non-profit organization, especially from foundations and governments, which was not an easy task. Many of the large foundations and government bodies which funded this kind of peace work made the applications for funding so complicated and cumbersome that procuring a grant was extremely difficult. Their guidelines were developed by social scientists, who seemed to have very little understanding of the realities on the ground in Israel and Palestine, or the ability to accomplish projected goals and objectives in real time.

My favorite story about this concerns a 50-page application I once wrote to the "Partnership for Peace" grant-making program of the European Union. After working for months on the proposal, I found an interesting question on page 51 (or thereabouts): "What might cause your projected program from not going according to timetable?" The answer, of course, is real life in the Middle East! Everything can and does happen to prevent programs from going according to timetable! Every time I tell this story, people break out laughing. Maybe it was the work of two jokers in a cubicle in Brussels wanting to give us a good laugh.

I was once asked by a researcher of peacebuilding programs in Israel and Palestine, many years ago, what I thought was the impact of all of these programs. My response was: "what had been the investment?" The answer is obvious: very little! And I wonder why. Is it because major funders are still people for whom only politics is important? Or is it that they don't understand the power of peacebuilding programs from the ground up to effect change over time? Or is it that the peace groups in Israel have simply not come up with good enough projects that could lead to real change? Or, is it all of these reasons?

THOUGHTS FOR THE FUTURE

As I think about the future, I want to share some of my practical recommendations and at the same time discuss some of the main obstacles and challenges facing interreligious dialogue, as well as sharing some anecdotes which guide me as I look forward. Let me begin with some practical suggestions.

At a conference on the future of rabbinic training in Israel in 2015, I offered "10 tips for succeeding in interreligious dialogue" to young Jewish Israelis who were studying to be Reform/Liberal/ Progressive rabbis in Israel. This was especially important since many of these students will most likely go on to be involved in interreligious dialogue and education over the course of their careers in Israel. I offer these 10 tips or suggestions here for any and all people preparing to lead interreligious or intercultural or intergroup dialogue workshops in the future, with the hope that they will enhance good practice in the field of dialogue in Israel and Palestine or anywhere else in the world.

1. Learn spoken Arabic

I did not take the time to learn Arabic. This was a mistake which I often regret. Fortunately, there is a new trend—especially among younger Jewish professionals involved in Arab-Jewish coexistence education, peacebuilding, interreligious dialogue and related activities—toward learning conversational Arabic for the sake of communicating directly with our Palestinian Arab neighbors in East Jerusalem, Israel and the region. For example, at the Intercultural Center on Mount Zion in Jerusalem, hundreds of Jews have been learning conversational Arabic, with much success during the past several years. Indeed, there is now a long waiting list of people who want to study spoken Arabic. Moreover, there are at least four other places in Jerusalem where one can do this, and the number grows every year. I certainly hope that this trend continues. In particular, I advise all Jews who are getting involved with Palestinians in interreligious and intercultural dialogue on a professional or volunteer basis to learn spoken Arabic. (In addition, Palestinians who want to engage in meaningful dialogue with Israeli Jews should learn conversational Hebrew.)

2. Get acquainted with Christianity as it is lived and practiced in Israel, in all its diversity

Unfortunately, most Jews in Israel know very little about Christianity. They do not study it in their public schools or anywhere else, except for a select few who study it at universities as part of "Comparative Religion" programs. On the other hand, many Jews know something about Christianity from their study of history, which is usually negative, i.e., they learn mostly about the history of Christian anti-Semitism [10]. Also, some Jews in Israel learn something about Christianity in the West, mostly from their frequent visits to Europe where they visit museums and churches and therefore imbibe something about the history of Christianity. However, almost nobody in Israel learns much about how Christianity is lived and practiced in its fascinating diversity within the state of Israel. This has to change. If we want to understand our Christian neighbors, we must come to know them as they understand their own religion. Going to the library, or taking courses about the history of Christianity at universities, will help a little but is not enough. In order to understand Christianity in Israel, one has to encounter the Christians who practice it and learn from them. (Similarly, Christians in Israel should do much more to learn about Judaism and Islam.)

3. The same for Islam. It is important to get acquainted with Islam as it is lived here, and not rely only on biased media reports

Contrary to conventional wisdom, Islam, like Christianity and Judaism, is also diverse. Not all Muslims think or practice the same brand of Islam. This is true in Israel as well, where we find ultra-religious, modern Orthodox, traditional and secular Muslims. We can only learn about the varieties of Muslim identity among Muslims in Israel by encountering them and talking with them [11].

4. One must learn how to do "dialogue" as opposed to "monologue" or "Q &A"

Many people use the term "dialogue" when it is totally inappropriate. For example, a "question and answer" session after a lecture is not dialogue. It is simply an attempt by people in the audience to understand the lecturer better. Neither is a meeting of "high level" religious leaders—which could include chief rabbis, patriarchs and Muslim religious leaders, where they pose for a good photo-op and smile for the cameras—a dialogue, especially when these so-called "leaders" have hardly talked about anything meaningful, or God forbid, controversial.

Also, a series of lectures or panel after panel at a conference is not a "dialogue". I am not sure what to call it. It is often the way "academics" present their Ideas—the results of their research or their learning—to each other or to audiences who are interested in their topics. But it is all too often very boring, with people in the audience either falling asleep or fiddling with their smart phones or laptops, if they are not in the hallway actually having a meaningful encounter with another human being over coffee or tea. I have attended too many international conferences after which, when asked "How was the conference?" I all too often responded "the coffee breaks and conversations over meals were the best part" (and I was not joking!).

Dialogue is something very different. It requires active and even compassionate listening, is usually done in small groups, and it is a systematic way to encounter the other. Furthermore, it is done in order to learn what the other person is actually feeling or thinking about a variety of core issues which are central to our mutual concerns and our real lives in the world. It is a method or an art form that needs to be learned, practiced and experienced by more and more people, so that it can have more impact upon "multipliers" in our communities.

5. Recruitment of people to the dialogue is a critical phase and must be done well

This is a vital first step which should not be overlooked. There are various ways to do this, via interviews and workshops. One must make a real effort to bring people to a dialogue who are not soloists or lecturers who engage in monologue. Careful recruitment will bring people to the dialogue process who really want to be there and who are genuinely motivated to learn about the other, and to see how one can live with the other in the same community or country or region.

6. Good dialogue is a process

It takes time, sometimes months or even years. One needs to have a long-term vision of where one wants to go with dialogue, including overall goals, and some specific objectives.

In my experience, effective dialogue takes a long time, at least a year, to have any results. There are many ups and downs, deep valleys and high mountains to climb. It is definitely not a one-off event, like a Sunday morning breakfast with speakers, where everyone concludes by singing a song together. This is "Kumbaya" dialogue, and while it may work for some people, I have always felt that it is simplistic, superficial and sometimes even silly.

7. Dialogue is not the goal. It is the method
and requires careful and committed facilitation

In my case, I have often said that dialogue is the method, and peace is the goal. Once, however, when I put this on my organization's website, I was criticized for not bringing peace to Israel! (as if this were something that I or my small organization could singlehandedly accomplish.) So, I changed the "branding" to say: "Peaceful coexistence is our goal. Dialogue, education and action are our methods." Dialogue for dialogue's sake is not useful, although some people find it helpful as group therapy. Rather, I believe that dialogue needs to lead to action, to social change, to healing the world. Otherwise, it is self-serving and even narcissistic.

Over the years, I have found consistently that for dialogue to succeed, it needs excellent professional facilitation. When this major component is not there, dialogue groups often flounder and fail, and can cause more harm than good. Excellent facilitators need to be recruited and trained and supervised to make dialogue groups meaningful and life-changing for their participants.

Since I have for a long time believed in the centrality of good facilitation for dialogue groups, I worked with some experts in London and Northern Ireland several years ago, and together we produced an important (and colorful) booklet on "Principles of Good Facilitation" which contained 10 principles:

- Preparation
- Hospitality
- Safe Space
- Creativity
- Embracing Different Perspectives
- Modeling
- Presence and Commitment
- Empowering
- Being responsive and flexible
- Taking it further.[12]

8. The context and the place where dialogue takes place
are important

Dialogue in America or Italy or Switzerland is much easier than in conflict zones like the Middle East or many parts of Africa! I once brought a group of Christians and Jews who were visiting Israel to the Knesset (Israel's parliament) to meet with a right-wing politician named Benny Begin (who became famous in his own right but is also known as the son of the first Likud Prime Minister of Israel, Menachem Begin). He began his remarks by welcoming the group and by telling them that, "This is the Middle East, not the Mid-west". In other words, he was trying to say that context really matters. In the American Midwest people are normally very polite and courteous and the pace is slow. This is not the case in the Middle East, nor in Israel/Palestine, where there is lots of yelling and screaming and very little listening.

Doing dialogue in the context of the ongoing, unresolved, not-likely-to-be-resolved-soon conflict is complicated, confusing and complex. It requires knowing a lot about what is going on around you. It means that one cannot ignore "politics" or what I have called "the core issues of the conflict", even if the purpose of the dialogue is not to reach a political solution to the macro problems confronting the state of Israel and the Palestinian Authority but to find ways and means of managing the conflict, or mitigating the violence, or creating hope for a better future.

9. Becoming well acquainted with the culture and the mentality of "the other" with whom you are in dialogue is essential

In my many years of leading and observing dialogue groups, I often found that cultural misunderstandings were a great barrier to dialogue. For exam-ple, the concept of time differed greatly from group to group. I often wit-nessed that the Christians came early to seminars or workshops or confer-ences, the Jews came more or less on time, and the Muslims came later. Also, hospitality varied from group to group. I remember vividly attending a meet-ing with my staff in Nazareth, the largest Arab city in Israel, in which we visited a well-known Muslim journalist in town to get an idea of what was really going on at the time concerning conflict between Muslims and Chris-tians relating to the building of a new mosque next door to one of the major churches in the city. We arrived one hour late to the meeting and when I took out my yellow pad to begin the meeting, my host said "*Shweiya, shweiya*, slowly, slowly, first drink your juice and then your coffee, and then we will get to your agenda!"

Another major cultural obstacle was food. It was often a great barrier to communication and informal encounters. In my religious leaders' groups called Kedem, when we traveled to seminars abroad, we obviously had to have kosher food for the Orthodox rabbis, and, as a result, they would eat every meal separately from the Palestinian Muslims and Christians in the group. Or, if the hosts abroad served too much fish and too little meat and rice, the Muslims in the group were personally offended. This negatively affected their mood and their sense of honor and led to several boycotts of meals and much unhappiness during some of our seminars.

10. Dialogue is not enough. Action is also imperative

Over time I found that when dialogue was done well, it was often like good group therapy and the participants actually liked it and found it personally beneficial to them. But when they had to leave the cozy bubble of the group and go back to their religious, educational or social settings to try to effect some change, this was quite another thing. As a result, I learned that much more attention must be paid to the action component of dialogue groups from the very beginning, if any meaningful and impactful actions were to come from the group.

Moving from dialogue to action was very difficult for most dialogue groups that I observed. This hampered the ability of the participants in dialogue groups to have significant impact in their communities when the dialogue group ended. After much reflection, I have come to the conclusion that an important element was missing in our dialogue programs which I would call "community organizing" or "project planning, implementation and evaluation". For the future, I would recommend to people who organize dialogue groups that they want to lead to action, to do so with the relevant professional personnel—in order to provide the participants in the dialogue group with the requisite consciousness and skills to help them create significant impact via projects that can be monitored, mentored and evaluated.

With regard to action, I would add that we have not figured out how to mobilize social media effectively enough to help us get our message out into the world in big ways, in order to lead to real change. One encounter that I had a few years ago in Vienna illustrates this clearly.

I attended an international conference on Educating about the 'Other', sponsored by KAICID, the King Abdullah Bin Abdulaziz International Centre for Dialogue, a new venture financed by Saudi Arabia for interreligious and intercultural dialogue. At this conference, I attended a workshop on social media at which a representative of Google for the Arab world told us that we peaceniks are much too timid, too slow, and too far behind in the use of social media for peace. The extremists are far ahead of you, he said, and he was right. They know how to rally people to their cause using social media and they do it, unfortunately, all too well.

What is needed in the future is a systematic, sophisticated and well-coordinated plan for getting our messages of peace and coexistence out into the world via social media. The professionals who will do this in the years ahead will need to get serious funding and recruit the best and the brightest from this field of endeavor, which is shaping the hearts and minds of millions of people on a daily basis, including political and religious leaders. Without it, we will simply not be keeping up with the major informational and opinion-molding methods of the 21st century!

OBSTACLES AND CHALLENGES

At this point, I want to focus on three major issues concerning the future:

1. What are the main issues and challenges facing interreligious dialogue as a method to counter radicalization of religious groups in the years and decades ahead?
2. Why is the dialogue with Islam so important—and yet so neglected—and what needs to be done?
3. How can we connect our dialogue to reality, especially to the critical issues of peacebuilding in Israel/Palestine and other parts of the world?

1. The main issues and challenges facing us

The main problem that we face in Israel and Palestine—and around the world—is ignorance. After all these years, we still don't know very much about each other. Accordingly, we still need multi-faceted, sustained and systematic educational programs in many and diverse settings: schools, seminaries, teacher-training schools and universities, in the curricula of Jewish, Muslim, and Christian schools, in newspapers and magazines, in scholarly journals, at conferences and workshops, in formal and informal education, in dialogues and seminars, and through the media.

For a long time, I have felt that "the dialogue" was more about community relations than about actually learning from each other. In my view, this too has to change. We need to develop a genuine interreligious dialogue; a dialogue based on mutuality, and the existential need to learn about each other and from each other towards the practical end of finding better ways to live together in communities, countries, regions and in the world. This is not learning for learning's sake. Rather, it is a set of programs that should be designed to build trust among people of different religions, who must then develop this into ways and means of living peacefully together.

Our dialogue with people of other religions and cultures in the future needs to be more reciprocal, with both sides taking responsibility for improving relations with members of other religious groups within their own communities. This new era of reciprocity will inevitably lead us into theological territory. We need not be afraid of this. On the contrary, we need to learn about each other's basic beliefs—as is increasingly being done in new dialogues and seminars and conferences in recent years—if we really intend to understand one another and be able to live together in peaceful relations with each other.

We need to study each other's central ideas, such as: creation, revelation, redemption, justice and peace, salvation and messianism, sacred space and sacred time, universalism and particularism, and much more. And we need to study each other's texts and systems of interpretation, the way each tradition has learned to live by its sacred texts. We cannot rely on the mainstream media or the social media to learn about each other's religions and cultures. We have to do it face to face, with serious and sensitive teachers who are committed to dialogue and not just spewing propaganda. These teachers exist in every society—they must be found and recruited and trained to join our cause of fighting extremist doctrines by teaching the true universal ideas and values which are essential to the basic fabric of our religions.

In so doing, we will learn what unites us as well as what divides us. We don't have to agree on everything. This would be superficial and simply wrong. Indeed, this is too often one of the pitfalls of interreligious dialogue. Rather, it is essential that all parties discover what makes them distinctive and unique and what they have in common, such as the reverence for human life, and the pursuit of a just society.

2. Why is the dialogue with Islam so important— and yet so neglected—and what needs to be done

Why are so many people where I live (in Israel) and around the world, especially in the West, not yet engaging with moderate Muslims (who are the overwhelming majority) in a systematic, substantive and sensitive way?

• Because we are all afraid. We have become somewhat Islamophobic. Some of our fear is rational. Yet, much of it is a "phobia", an irrational fear, fed by rumors and stereotyping of a whole community and a whole religion and all of its followers.
• Because we and our communities have largely been influenced by the media—who only portray the work of fundamentalist extremist radical Muslims—ISIS, Al Qaeda, and all the rest. The media is constantly indoctrinating us that this is who Muslims are! This is their religion. This is how they think and act. And we—most of our leaders and our communities—go along with it.
• Because we don't really make the effort to come to know Islam. We don't study the sacred texts of Muslims and their holy teachings. Rather, we rely on the internet and the tabloids to "teach" us the basic tenets of Islam. Fostering hatred of another's religion—due to the fanatical acts of certain extremist groups who claim to be inspired by this religion but actually distort it unrecognizably—is not a good prescription for building a better world for all of God's children.

Accordingly, I would argue that developing a genuine dialogue with Muslims around the world—beginning in our own local communities—is one of the highest religious and ethical imperatives for those who are involved in interreligious and intercultural dialogue now and for the future. We can no longer engage in denial and apathy on this issue. We cannot continue to bury our heads in the sand and ignore this topic. It is vital for our common future.

I have been engaged in this for much of the past 25 years, and in so doing, I have come to know well another kind of Islam, not the one in the news every day and not the one on the internet every minute. I have encountered many kadis, imams, sheikhs and ordinary Muslims—both in Israel and internationally—who preach and teach a moderate and rational brand of Islam, one that is generally not reported in the mainstream media (because it does not sell newspapers!), one that espouses ethical and righteous ideals, which are very similar to the basic humanistic values that are shared by normative Judaism and Christianity.

We have begun to engage in substantive dialogue with Muslims in Israel. It is just a first step. And some of this is beginning to take place in other parts of the world, although it is very limited so far. Much more needs to be done. But I believe that we need to place this high on our interreligious agenda, because it is imperative for our future! Moreover, from my experience it is clear that this is not only possible, but that there are ready and willing Muslim partners with whom we can engage in fruitful dialogue and cooperative actions.

3. How can dialogue be connected to reality, especially to the critical issues of peace-building in Israel/Palestine and in other parts of the world

People engaged in interreligious dialogue will remain irrelevant and out-of-date if they do not address themselves to the critical issues of peace and justice in the world. Just as it should no longer be limited to Christians and Jews, it should no longer be ephemeral and abstract, focusing on the past, rather than the future. It must be related to peacebuilding efforts—and efforts to ensure social justice—all over the world.

In the future, therefore, interreligious dialogue, education and common action for healing the world will be needed more than ever before. This will be a time not to divest of the possibilities of peace—as some Christian churches have suggested in recent years—but to invest in peace—building programs in Israel and Palestine, and in many other places in the world, across borders and within societies, for the sake of all of God's children in the region.

Furthermore, I feel confident that the model I described (in chapter 4) can be adapted in other countries where people involved in the dialogue are seeking to have more of an impact on the social and political problems which they and their colleagues face together.

THE OTHER PEACE PROCESS

As I draw near to the conclusion of this book, I want to share with you, my readers, several special stories from encounters that have inspired me and helped me keep hope alive, amidst much despair, over many years.[13] I have shared these stories orally at conferences, seminars and lectures all over the world during the past few decades.

In a recent talk that I gave at a synagogue in England in December 2016, on the eve of the Jewish festival of Hanukkah (the Jewish festival of light), I linked these anecdotes to 3 major themes of Hanukkah that have guided me in my work: 1) the need for "miracles", and our human role in helping to bring them about, 2) the importance of spreading light, especially in the context of so much darkness seemingly consuming our world lately, and 3) the need to rededicate ourselves to the values we cherish and believe in, foremost among them the search for peace.

One of the most meaningful encounters in my career relates to the theme of miracles. It took place several years ago, at an interreligious conference in Palermo, the capital of Sicily. It was the annual meeting of People and Religions, sponsored by the Community of Sant' Egidio. At this conference, there was a morning plenum on "Religions and Peace" which offered wonderful presentations by Jewish, Christian and Muslim leaders from Israel and elsewhere. I thought that it was a challenging and uplifting symposium.

But over lunch I was engaged in a discussion with an American journalist and with Prof. Sari Nusseibeh, a distinguished scholar of Islamic thought and culture, and at that time president of Al Quds University in Jerusalem. Prof. Nusseibeh is a well-known cultural figure, who, among other things is known for his secular/cultural outlook on life, but he is not a "religious" person, at least not in the sense of religious observance.

At lunch, the journalist asked Professor Nusseibeh what he thought about the lectures by religious leaders that morning. He surprised the journalist by responding negatively and saying that he did not like their speeches and went on to ask—what have they really done for peace in our region? The journalist, who was a bit taken aback, nevertheless persisted and asked, "So, what do you think is the solution for peace in the Middle East?" Prof. Nusseibeh thought for a moment, then gave a wink and a smile and responded ironically: "We need a miracle!"

What did he mean by a miracle? Certainly not a supernatural event! Rather, I think that he was talking about something of extraordinary human dimensions that would radically surprise us.

When Sadat came to Jerusalem, this was perceived by most Jews in Israel and around the world to be a miracle. It was a great surprise. No one would have predicted it, even days or weeks before it happened. Who could imagine this man of war, the architect of the war in October 1973 which shook Israel to its foundations, coming to Israel to announce that he wanted to make peace? That visit led to the peace treaty with Egypt which has lasted more than 30 years!

Another great example of a political "miracle" took place in 1993. When Prime Minister Yitzhak Rabin shook hands with Yasser Arafat on the White House lawn on September 13, 1993, giving one of the most inspiring speeches of his life, sharing hopes and dreams for peace for the Jewish people in Israel and worldwide—this too was a miracle since it was totally unexpected, and heralded the beginning of the peace process in our region. Here were two men of war who decided to change course, to embark on a peace track, in a courageous attempt to create a new reality for their peoples.

I have often said and I say it again here that I agree with Prof. Nusseibeh. It is time for a miracle! It is time for our leaders on both sides to summon the courage and creativity to make peace, for us and our grandchildren and for the future. Not just a "piece of paper," i.e. a formal treaty between us and the Palestinian people, but a sustainable peace, which will include ways and means of learning to live together in peace, now and for the decades to come.

One should not read the daily news to find this miracle. Rather, one must believe in the creative power of human beings to make miracles, as has been done in the past. If another peace agreement is achieved, it will probably be via back channel secret talks, like the ones that led to the Oslo Accords. In my view, this is the only way that a substantive peace agreement can be reached.

No one in Northern Ireland ever believed that their conflict would be resolved; nor in South Africa, nor in Bosnia Herzegovina. But conflicts do get resolved, and not always in predicable ways. I believe that our conflict too can be solved. As Theodor Herzl, "the father of Zionism" said a long time ago: "If you will it, it is not a dream".

One of my consistent goals during all my work in interreligious dialogue was to keep the dream of peace alive, not to let it be buried by the rejection-ists. I have always felt and said that we are on the long and bumpy road to peace. We have had many ups and downs, and have climbed many moun-tains, and gone down into many valleys. Sometimes the drivers of the pro-cess have been excellent, careful, consistent and determined; other times, they have driven too fast or too slow, and lately it seems that they have forgotten how to drive at all or have fallen off the road. Nevertheless, our job as religious leaders is to keep the vision of peace alive, to always remind people of its benefits and opportunities.

The second theme—the existential need of spreading the light in the world, especially in the context of very dark scary trends towards the funda-mentalist radical extremist right in many countries, including Israel—is an-other one that has dominated my consciousness and my activism in recent years. That is why I joined the *Tag Meir* (Light Tag) forum [14] five years ago, at Hanukkah, and became a member of its steering committee. In so doing, I was involved personally and directly in many solidarity visits to Christian and Muslim institutions and communities and homes inside Israel and the West Bank which had been vandalized by Jewish "religious" extremists, who distorted Judaism beyond belief, so that they could burn and attack innocent people without any moral qualms.

The most significant solidarity visit in which I was involved was in the summer of 2015, when I went with two busloads of Jewish Israelis from organizations affiliated with the Tag Meir forum, to the home of a Palestinian family in the village of Duma in the West Bank. Their home had been burned to the ground during the night, killing a mother, father and child in that family. We went to pay a condolence call, which was coordinated in advance with members of the family and leaders of the village. After this I wrote some reflections on my blog for *The Times of Israel*:

> I am worried, very worried, at this point in our history. It is time for the silent majority in Israel to wake up! A few thousand people of good will attended demonstrations against racism and violence last night in Jerusalem, Tel Aviv and other parts of the country. We need hundreds of thousands of people to take to the streets and say *Maspik !* (Enough). [15]

I am still worried. But I am an optimist and an activist at heart. I feel the pressing need to constantly re-dedicate myself to action, to healing the world, to taking whatever steps are possible to mitigate violence and hatred in our country and region arising from the ongoing unresolved, not-likely-to-be-resolved very soon, conflict in which we continue to live.

The third theme concerns the need to constantly resist despair and to continually re-dedicate oneself to the value of peace, the pursuit of political peace and peaceful coexistence among the peoples of the region. The constant delays in seriously pursuing the diplomatic path to peace has led to a lack of belief in the peace process during the past several years among both Israelis and Palestinians, leading to what I have called "political despair", i.e. the belief that our particular conflict is irresolvable and that we are somehow destined to live with it forever.

I was invited, several years ago, to give a talk at a "Rector's Forum" at St. Bartholomew's Anglican Church on Park Avenue in New York City. When I arrived, about 15 minutes early, I greeted the rector who was busy greeting some of his congregants at the end of the Sunday morning worship services. As I said hello, he introduced me to Senator George Mitchell, the former senator from Maine who had successfully mediated the famous "Good Friday Agreement" between Protestants and Catholics in April 1998. [16] The rector and I then adjourned to a special room, where my lecture on interreligious dialogue as a form of peacebuilding in Israel and Palestine would take place

In the form of an interview. Toward the end of the interview, when I was discussing the problematics of political despair in Israel and Palestine, Senator Mitchell, who was in attendance for the whole presentation, raised his hand to make a very important comment. He told us that when he went to Northern Ireland for the final time to negotiate an agreement with the Protestants and the Catholics who had been in conflict for so many decades, a poll was released on the day he arrived which said that 84% of the Protestants and the same number of Catholics believed there would never be a peace agreement! And five days later, they were all proven wrong when the agreement, mediated by Mitchell, was actually signed!

I have told this story dozens of times to audiences around the world. I tell the story here because I do not accept the notion that we will live by the sword forever (as the Prime Minister of Israel said in an interview in 2015!) and that our conflict will never end. This is the notion of the pessimists who have given up on peace. I do not share their view, and I never will. It is not divinely ordained that this conflict will go on forever. The one hundred-year-old conflict between the Jewish national movement and the Palestinian national movement can and will someday be resolved.

I am often accused of being too optimistic or too hopeful. I accept the accusation. I prefer to see our cup half full than half empty.

Fortunately, I am not completely alone in this effort to keep hope alive.

At a demonstration in Tel Aviv in November 2015, in memory of the assassination of Israel's Prime Minister Yitzhak Rabin, the first and probably most important speaker was the current President of Israel, Reuven (Ruby) Rivlin. In his first year and a half in office, he had already become the moral conscience of the state, saying all the right things at the right times. He did it again when he reminded us of the need to sustain a vision of a better future and to keep hope alive in Israel. These were his words:

> Without vision, without hope, without a dream, the people will be left desolate... Two decades have gone by, and still we remain overly focused on the wounds of the past, and not enough on building the future . . . Too much are we focused on fear and not enough on hope.

President Rivlin is correct, and I could not agree with him more.

All too often, it seems—by reading the mainstream media and much of the social media—that the leaders of Israel and Palestine (who don't spend nearly enough time trying to come up with realistic and constructive ideas for peace) have given up on offering genuine visions of a better future for both peoples in our region. They prefer to spin the narrative—each in his own way—trying to score *hasbara* (propaganda) victories. Indeed, it appears that they are more focused on the past than on the future.

What is wrong with focusing on the past? And why is it more important to envision the future?

Many years ago, I attended workshops in Jerusalem on conflict resolution and transformation methods with Professor Jay Rothman, who is now a professor in this field at Bar Ilan University in Israel. At these workshops, we learned that when one starts with history—with the origins of the Palestinian-Israeli conflict—one often remains mired in the past, the result being an ongoing argument over the two main narratives, without the option of transcending or integrating them into one synthetic narrative. One learns, for example, about the creation of the state of Israel in 1948, which for Israeli Jews was a great miracle and a religious event, and for Palestinians was the *nakba* (catastrophe), in which 750,000 Palestinians became refugees and 450 Palestinian villages were destroyed. This often leaves participants in dialogue groups duly depressed, and their despair can lead to paralysis rather than action.

Instead, Professor Rothman suggests that we begin our dialogue groups with envisioning the future. What would we like to see for our people? For the Palestinians? For all of us? What are our overarching goals, as well as some specific objectives? What processes—political, psychological, religious, spiritual, and educational—can help us bring the real closer to the ideal? And, what is our role—each and every one of us in civil society (and not just our political leaders) in designing programs and processes that can help us achieve our goals of peaceful coexistence over time?

What then is a good vision for the future?

Can we imagine two states, living side by side in peaceful coexistence, with new and improved economic and educational opportunities for all? Can we conceive of a long-term truce (what the Palestinians call a *hudna*) which might bring an end to so many wars (in recent years alone, we have lived through 3 mini-wars in Gaza, and the Second Lebanon War!) and considerable violence. We have already suffered through two intifadas (uprisings) and some say that we are now at the beginning of the third one. Can we imagine how "normal relations" might look, with open borders, educational exchanges, economic development and much more?

This has been particularly difficult in recent years. Nevertheless, I have always written, preached and taught that we must do all we can to resist despair and depression, and keep a flicker of hope alive in what all-too-often appears to be a desperate situation.

As I think about the future, I am mindful that my father, Rabbi Leon Kronish (about whom I wrote in the introduction to this book), who for 54 years was a rabbi at Temple Beth Sholom in Miami Beach, always responded to the simple question of "how are you?" with a typically Jewish/Israeli response: "*Yiheyeh tov*—It will be good". The future will be better than the past.

In that spirit, I still believe that despite the current difficulties and obstacles in the political peace process—and there are many—the process will work itself out, i.e., there will be a political solution sooner or later between Israel and the Palestinians (and all of the Arab states) and it will undoubtedly be a two-state solution—Israel and Palestine will coexist side-by-side. This is the unfolding reality of the past 25 years, since the Madrid peace process began in 1991, followed by the Oslo Accords two years later, even if it is coming about much too slowly and painfully and rejectionists on both sides repeatedly delay it. This is the solution supported by the international community as well as by the political leaderships of Israel and Palestine, at least officially, although this may be changing as both governments become more intransigent and less forward-thinking. There is an agreement in principle that we need two states for two peoples in the region, but the devil is in the details and the lawyers and diplomats still have to work this out. Yet, where there is a will, there is a way, and with the help of the many creative and constructive ideas coming out of think tanks that have been designing solutions for this seemingly intractable conflict, the issues can be resolved.

And then what? What if another peace treaty—another piece of paper—is signed next year or the year after, or whenever? What will we do then? Will we be prepared for the next steps? What will be needed in the future?

What will be needed is what I have called "The Other Peace Process"— the educational, religious, psychological and spiritual one, to supplement the political process. There will be a desperate need for a massive educational campaign, to change the hearts and minds of the people on both sides to understand the benefits of living in peaceful coexistence. This campaign will include sets of programs which will educate the next generations about the values and methods of learning to live together in the years ahead.

This will not be simple, nor will it be quick. But there is no time like the present to begin paving the way, as I have tried to do in my work during this past quarter century. I believe that the "Other Peace Process" will require many human and physical resources. But it will eventually become the historic imperative of the new era, just as it did when other conflicts were resolved politically (Northern Ireland, South Africa, Bosnia-Herzegovina) and moved to the post-conflict phase of reconciliation and learning to live together. Ultimately, once we are sick and tired of ongoing violence—living by the sword—we will have no other choice but to bring people together to learn to live in peace.

Who will be involved in this campaign?

- Religious leaders—rabbis, kadis, sheikhs, imams, priests, ministers—at the grassroots level (as we did in our Kedem project) and also at the highest levels

- Educators—principals, teachers, teacher-trainers, curriculum writers—at every level of the educational system, on both sides
- Informal educators—youth movement leaders, camp directors and staffs, youth counselors—as we did for 12 years via our Face to Face/Faith to Faith and other youth/young adult programs
- Women—professionals, as well as laypersons, educators and activists, housewives and mothers, community leaders and community participants—as is being done through the Women Wage Peace movement in Israel in recent years.[17]

And many more people and groups in civil society, including social workers, psychologists, community organizers, architects and grassroots activists of all kinds.

I believe that the next generation of professionals and volunteers involved in interreligious and intercultural dialogue in Israel and the region will have a major role to play in this essential and long-range people-to-people peacebuilding process. In addition, religious leaders—and their followers—from abroad will be called upon to help support this campaign, especially those that believe deeply in the benefits of peace for all people in our region.

In the long run, interreligious dialogue will become part of the solution, rather than part of the problem, as together people from different religious and cultural backgrounds confront the challenges and crises of the present and the future.

NOTES

1. The beginning of this chapter is based on an article which I wrote for the *Jerusalem Post* magazine on April 2, 2016, entitled "On Interreligious Dialogue: Lessons Learned". http://www.jpost.com/Opinion/On-interreligious-dialogue-lessons-learned-443860.
2. In 1992, a similar book of essays was published by my friends, David B. Burrell and Yehezkel Landau: *Voices from Jerusalem: Jews and Christians Reflect on the Holy Land,* Paulist Press, Mahwah, New Jersey. In those days, Muslims were not involved in "the dialogue", which was dominated by Jews and Christians (mostly from abroad).
3. In chapter two of this book, I discussed and described many of my Palestinian dialogue partners.
4. I have described this in chapter 3 of this book.
5. Michael Melchior. "Establishing a Religious Peace." in Ronald Kronish, ed. *Coexistence and Reconciliation in Israel*, pp.117-129.
6. A statement by religious leaders from Israel and Palestine was published at a special conference in Spain on November 16, 2016, which was hosted by the Ministry of Foreign Affairs and the Ministry of Justice. www.ccjr.us/.
7. Ronald Kronish "Interreligious Dialogue as an Antidote to Radical Religious Violence", The Huffington Post, December 6, 2016.
8. The first Middle East Interfaith Summit with the participation of the leaders of the three monotheistic faiths, held in Alexandria, Egypt, issued a statement on January 21, 2002. www.mfa.gov.il/.
9. I discussed both the goals and methods of my new model for interreligious dialogue in some detail in chapter 4 of this book.

10. See my unpublished paper on teaching about Christianity in Israeli schools. *Teaching About Christianity in Israel,* academic paper presented at a seminar of the International Jewish-Catholic Liaison Committee, at the Vatican, March 25, 1998.

11. In chapter two of this book, I describe Muslim diversity within Israel in some detail.

12. www.stethelburgas.org/.

13. "Time for a Miracle", *Times of Israel,* Dec. 15, 2012.

14. See chapter 2, footnote 77, for information about Tag Meir.

15. Ronald Kronish. "An Emergency Situation – It is Time for Action", blog post for *The Times of Israel,* August 2, 2015.

16. The Belfast Agreement, also known as the Good Friday Agreement because it was reached on Good Friday, April 10, 1998, was an agreement between the British and the Irish governments and most of the political parties in Northern Ireland, about how Northern Ireland should be governed.

17. The "Women Wage Peace" movement is a non-political, broad-based, and rapidly growing movement of thousands of women taking action to influence the public and political arena. They want to restore hope and work towards a peaceful existence for themselves, their children and future generations.

Bibliography

Abraham, S. Daniel. *Peace is Possible: Conversations with Arab and Israeli Leaders from 1988 to the Present.* New York: Newmarket Press, 2006.

Abu-Nimer, Mohammed. "The Miracles of Transformation through Interfaith Dialogue: Are You a Believer?" in *Interfaith Dialogue and Peacebuilding,* edited by David R. Smock, 15-33. Washington, DC: United States Institute of Peace, 2002.

Bardin, Hillel. *A Zionist among Palestinians.* Bloomington, IN: Indiana University Press, 2012.

Bernstein, Carl and Marco Politi. *His Holiness, John Paul II and the History of Our Time.* New York: Penguin Books, 1997.

Boys, Mary C. *Has God Only One Blessing? Judaism as a Source of Christian Self-Understanding.* Mahwah, NJ: Paulist Press, 2000.

Brinn, Shlomo. "Teaching about the Other in Religious Zionist Education: A Pilot Program." In *Coexistence and Reconciliation in Israel: Voices for Interreligious Dialogue,* edited by Ronald Kronish, 236-42. Mahwah, NJ: Paulist Press, 2015.

Buber, Martin. *I and Thou.* New York: Charles Scribner's Sons, 1958.

———. *Israel and the World: Essays in a Time of Crisis.* New York: Schocken Books, 1963.

———. *Pointing the Way: Collected Essays by Martin Buber,* edited and translated by Maurice S. Friedman. Freeport, NY: Books for Libraries Press, 1971.

Burg, Avraham. *The Holocaust is Over; We Must Rise From its Ashes.* New York: Palgrave Macmillan, 2008.

Burrell David B. and Yehezkel Landau. *Voices from Jerusalem: Jews and Christians Reflect on the Holy Land.* Mahwah, NJ: Paulist Press, 1992.

Carroll, James. *Jerusalem, Jerusalem: How the Ancient City Ignited Our Modern World.* Boston, MA: Houghton Mifflin Harcourt, 2011.

Cassidy, Edward Idris Cardinal. *Ecumenism and Interreligious Dialogue.* Mahwah, NJ: Paulist Press, 2005.

Chazan, Barry, ed. *Studies in Jewish Education I: Theory and Research.* Jerusalem: Magnes Press, 1983.

Cohen, Hillel. *Good Arabs: The Israeli Security Agencies and the Israeli Arabs, 1949-1967.* Berkeley, CA: University of California Press, 2010.

———. *Year Zero of the Arab Israeli Conflict: 1929.* Waltham, MA: Brandeis University Press, 2015.

Collings, Rania Al Qass, Rifat Odeh Kassis, and Mitri Raheb, eds. *Palestinian Christians in the West Bank: Facts, Figures and Trends.* Bethlehem: Diyar, 2012.

Cornille, Catherine, ed. *The Wiley-Blackwell Companion to Inter-Religious Dialogue.* Hoboken, NJ: Wiley, 2013.

Covey, Stephen R., with England, Breck. *The 3ʳᵈ Alternative: Solving Life's Most Difficult Problems.* New York: Free Press, 2011.

Dajani Daoudi, Mohammed S. *Big Dream/Small Hope. Peace and Reconciliation Vision.* Al Bireh, Palestine: Wasatia Press, 2014.

Dajani Daoudi, Mohammed and Robert Satloff. "Why Palestinians Should Learn about the Holocaust." *The New York Times,* March 29, 2011.

Dajani Daoudi, Mohammed. S., Munther S. Dajani Daoudi, Martin Leiner, and Zeina Barakat, comps. *Teaching Empathy and Reconciliation in the Midst of Conflict.* Al Bireh, Palestine: Wasatia Press, 2016.

Driscoll, Jack. *What are the Next Steps? Reflections from this Catholic's Perspective.* Monograph for the Foreign Press presented at the International Press Center, Jerusalem, March 26, 2000.

Eilberg, Amy. *From Enemy to Friend: Jewish Wisdom and the Pursuit of Peace.* Maryknoll, New York: Orbis Books, 2014.

Epstein, Nadine. "Mohammed Dajani Daoudi: Evolution of a Moderate," *Moment,* July 17, 2014.

Feldinger, Lauren Gelfond. "Nazareth's Sufis Bullied by Fellow Muslims," *Ha'aretz.* August 10, 2012.

———. *Wasatia: The Road to Reconciliation.* Al Bireh, Palestine: Wasatia Press, 2014.

Fitzduff, Mari. *Beyond Violence. Conflict Resolution Process in Northern Ireland.* New York: United Nations University Press, 2002.

Galtung, Johan. *50 Years: 100 Peace & Conflict Perspectives.* Bergen, Norway: Transcend University Press, 2008.

Golan, Galia. *Israeli Peacemaking since 1967: Factors behind the Breakthroughs and Failures.* London: Routledge, 2015.

Goodman, Hirsh. *The Anatomy of Israel's Survival.* New York: PublicAffairs, 2011.

Gopin, Marc. *Holy War, Holy Peace: How Religions Can Bring Peace to the Middle East.* New York: Oxford University Press, 2002.

Gopin, Marc. "The Use of the World and Its Limits: A Critical Evaluation of Religious Dialogue as Peacemaking," in *Interfaith Dialogue and Peacebuilding,* edited by David R. Smock, 33-47.Washington, DC: United States Institute of Peace, 2002.

Green, Henry. *Gesher Vakesher, Bridges and Bonds: The Life of Leon Kronish.* Atlanta, GA: Scholars Press, 1995.

Greenberg, Irving. *For the Sake of Heaven and Earth: The New Encounter between Judaism and Christianity.* Lincoln, NB: University of Nebraska Press, 2004.

Grossman, David. *Sleeping on a Wire: Conversations with Palestinians in Israel.* New York: Farrar, Straus and Giroux, 1993.

Hareuveni, Eyal et al, "Welcome to Hell," *Kol Ha'ir,* March 17, 2000, p. 23 (Hebrew).

Henderson, Katharine Rhodes. *God's Troublemakers: How Women of Faith are Changing the World.* New York: Continuum, 2006.

Heschel, Abraham Joshua. *Israel: An Echo of Eternity.* New York: Farrar, Straus and Giroux, 1969.

———. "No Religion is an Island", in *No Religion is an Island: Abraham Joshua Heschel and Interreligious Dialogue,* edited by Harold Kasimow, and Byron L. Sherwin, 3-22. Maryknoll, NY: Orbis Books, 1991.

Hoffman, Charles. *The Smoke Screen. Israel, Philanthropy and American Jews.* Silver Spring, MD: Eshel Books, 1989.

Isaacs, Alick. *A Prophetic Peace: Judaism, Religion and Politics.* Bloomington, IN: Indiana University Press, 2011.

Jaber, Issa. "Is Arab-Jewish Coexistence in Israel Still Possible," in Ronald Kronish, ed, *Coexistence and Reconciliation in Israel,* edited by Ronald Kronish, 160-68. Mahweh, NJ: Paulist Press, 2015.

Kadayifci-Orellana, S. Ayse. "*Interreligious Dialogue and Peacebuilding.*" In *The Wiley-Blackwell Companion to Interreligious Dialogue,* edited by Catherine Cornille, 149-67. New York: Wiley, 2013.

Kasimow, Harold and Byron Sherwin, eds. *No Religion is an Island: Abraham Joshua Heschel and Interreligious Dialogue*. Maryknoll, New York: Orbis Books, 1991.

Kaufman, Edy; Walid Salem and Juliette Verhoeven, eds. *Bridging the Divide: Peacebuilding in the Israeli-Palestinian Conflict*. Boulder, CO: Lynne Rienner, 2006.

Khalidi, Rashid. *Palestinian Identity: The Construction of Modern National Consciousness*. New York: Columbia University Press, 2010.

Kimmerling, Baruch and Joel S. Migdal. *Palestinians: The Making of a People*, Cambridge, MA: Harvard University Press, 1993.

Klein, Menachem. *Lives in Common: Arabs and Jews in Jerusalem, Jaffa and Hebron*. New York: Oxford University Press, 2014.

Kreisberg, Louis. "Nature, Dynamics and Phases of Intractability." In *Grasping the Nettle*, edited by Chester Crocker, Fen Osler Hampson, and Pamela Aall, 65-8.Washington, DC: United States Institute for Peace, 2005, pp. 65-68.

Kreisberg, Louis and Bruce Dayton, *Constructive Conflicts: From Escalation to Resolutions*. Lanham, MD: Rowman and Littlefield, 2011.

Kronish, Ronald. "The Conflicts of Jewish Youth," *Congress Bi-Weekly*, June 15, 1973: 10-12.

———. *The Influence of John Dewey upon Jewish Education in America*. Doctoral dissertation, Cambridge, MA: Harvard Graduate School of Education, 1979.

———. "Educating for Jewish-Zionist Identity in Israel." *The Melton Journal* 16 (spring-summer 1983): 7, 12. Reprinted in *Forum on the Jewish people, Zionism and Israel* 54/55 (sprint 1985): 125-29.

———. "Bridging the Gap. Israel and the Diaspora: Problems and Possibilities." In *Towards the Twenty-First Century: Judaism and the Jewish People in Israel and America*, edited by Ronald Kronish, 137-9. New York, Ktav. 1988.

———. "Understanding One Another: Jewish Identity in Israel and America," *Jewish Education News*, winter/spring 1988: 1, 10-11.

———, ed. *Towards the Twenty-First Century: Judaism and the Jewish People in Israel and America, Essays in Honor of Rabbi Leon Kronish on the Occasion of His Seventieth Birthday*, New York: Ktav, 1988.

———. "All the Problems Can be Solved," *The Jerusalem Post*, Feb. 5, 1989, p. 4.

———. "On the Road to Becoming Israeli," *Davar*, July 21, 1989 (Hebrew).

———. "Getting Absorption on the Right Track," *The Jerusalem Post*, Aug. 1, 1989.

———. "Going Beyond Philanthropy," *The Jerusalem Post*, Oct. 28, 1990.

———. "The Jewish 'Intra-fada': One Year Later," *The Jerusalem Post*, Jan. 23, 1990.

———. "Common Destiny," *The Jerusalem Post*, February 20, 1990.

———. "Understanding the Differences," *The Jerusalem Post*, June 26, 1990.

———. "Going Beyond Philanthropy," *The Jerusalem Post*, October 28, 1990.

———. "Cautious But Real Pursuit of Peace," *The Jerusalem Post*, December 3, 1991.

———. "Cautious Optimism Among Soviet Jews," *The Jerusalem Post*, October 8, 1991.

———. "The Reasons Behind the Rhetoric," *The Jerusalem Post*, February 9, 1992.

———. "The New Peace Atmosphere in Israel," *Palm Beach Jewish Journal South*, September 14, 1993: 5A, also appeared in the *Dade Jewish Journal*, September 16-22, 1993: 5.

———. *Teaching About Christianity in Israel*, unpublished paper presented at seminar of the International Jewish-Catholic Liaison Committee, at the Vatican, March 25, 1998.

———. "The Pope and the pitfalls and potential of interfaith dialogue," *Ha'aretz*, March 26, 2000.

———. "Welcome, John Paul II, *Jerusalem Post*, March 17, 2000.

———. "The Historic Visit of the Pope to Israel in March 2000: Jewish Israeli Memories and Hopes," *Ecumenical Trends*, Graymoor Ecumenical and Interreligious Institute 33, no. 2, (February 2004).

———. "The Role of Interreligious Dialogue in Peace-building in Israel," *Ecumenical Trends*, Graymoor Ecumenical and Interreligious Institute 33, no. 8 (September 2004).

———. "Forty Years Since the Second Vatican Council: Central Challenges Facing Jewish-Christian Dialogue Today: A Jewish Point of View," *Ecumenical Trends*, Graymoor Ecumenical and Interreligious Institute 34, no. 6 (June 2005).

————. "The Implications of *Nostra Aetate* for Interreligious Dialogue in Israel." In *A Jubilee for All Time, The Copernican Revolution in Jewish-Christian Relations*, edited by Gilbert Rosenthal, 207-18. Eugene, OR: Pickwick, 2014.

————. "Interreligious Dialogue in Israel: Lessons Learned." In *Coexistence and Reconciliation in Israel: Voices for Interreligious Dialogue*. edited by Ronald Kronish, 183-99. Mahwah, NJ: Paulist Press, 2015.

————. "Religious and Cultural Diversity among Muslims in Israel." In *Coexistence and Reconciliation in Israel: Voices for Interreligious Dialogue*. edited by Ronald Kronish, 103-16. Mahwah, NJ: Paulist Press, 2015.

————. "Time for a Miracle", *Times of Israel*, December 15, 2012. Available at: http://blogs.timesofisrael.com/time-for-a-miracle/

————. "An Emergency Situation--It is Time for Action", *The Times of Israel*, August 2, 2015. Available at: http://blogs.timesofisrael.com/an-emergency-situation-it-is-time-for-action-2/

————. "On Interreligious Dialogue: Lessons Learned." *The Jerusalem Post Magazine*, February 4, 2016.

————, ed. *Coexistence and Reconciliation in Israel: Voices for Interreligious Dialogue*. Mahwah, NJ: Paulist Press, 2015.

Landau, Jon. "The Brandeis Questionnaire (Interview)", *Brandeis Magazine*, summer 2013. Available at: http://www.brandeis.edu/magazine/2013/summer/featured-stories/bq-landau.html

Lederach, John Paul. *Building Peace: Sustainable Reconciliation in Divided Societies*, Washington, DC: United States Institute of Peace Press, 1997.

Lewis, Sheldon. *Torah of Reconciliation*. Jerusalem: Gefen, 2012.

Lippman, Thomas W. *Understanding Islam. An Introduction to the Muslim World*. New York: Penguin Books, 1990.

McGarry, Michael. *Roman Catholic-Jewish Relations... Signposts along the New Path of Dialogue*, Jerusalem: Interreligious Coordinating Council in Israel, March 12, 2000.

Makovsky, David. *Making Peace with the PLO: The Rabin Government's Road to the Oslo Accord*. Boulder, CO, Westview, 1996.

Mansour, Johnny, ed. *Arab Christians in Israel: Facts, Figures and Trends*. Bethlehem: Diyar, 2012.

Maslow, Abraham H. *Towards a Psychology of Being*. New York: Van Nostrand Reinhold, 1968.

Melchior, Michael. "Establishing a Religious Peace." In *Coexistence and Reconciliation in Israel: Voices for Interreligious Dialogue*, edited by Ronald Kronish, 117-29. Mahwah, NJ: Paulist Press, 2015.

Memorandum of Their Beatitudes the Patriarchs and of the Heads of the Christian Communities in Jerusalem on the Significance of Jerusalem for Christians, November. 14, 1994. Available at: http://www.al-bushra.org/hedchrch/memorandum.htm

Moore, Deborah Dash. *To the Golden Cities: Pursuing the American Dream in Miami and L.A.*, NY: Free Press, 1994.

Nusseibeh, Sari with Anthony David. *Once Upon a Country: a Palestinian Life*. New York: Farrar, Straus and Giroux, 2007.

Oz, Amos. *A Tale of Love and Darkness*. London: Vintage Books, 2005.

Peleg, Ilan and Dov Waxman. *Israel's Palestinians: The Conflict Within*. New York: Cambridge University Press, 2011.

Rauf, Imam Feisal Abdul. *Moving the Mountain. Beyond Ground Zero to a New Vision for Islam in America*. New York: Free Press, 2012.

Romano, Bethany. "Neuroscience for Peace," *Heller: A Magazine for the Heller School for Social Policy and Management*, Brandeis University, summer 2016. Available at: https://issuu.com/brandeis/docs/heller-magazine-summer-2016/9

Rosenthal, Gilbert S. *A Jubilee for All Time: The Copernican Revolution in Jewish-Christian Relations*. Eugene, OR: Pickwick, 2014.

Rossing, Daniel. *Mother Jerusalem: Memory, Symbols and the Between*. Monograph presented to Foreign Press at the International Press Center, Jerusalem, March 22, 2000.

Rothman, Jay. *Evaluation Report of Face to Face/Faith to Faith.* Jerusalem: Interreligious Coordinating Council in Israel, 2011.

Russo, Rebecca. *Evaluation Report of Face to Face/Faith to Faith.* Jerusalem: Interreligious Coordinating Council in Israel, 2009.

Sacks, Jonathan. *Not in God's Name: Confronting Religious Violence.* London: Hodder and Stoughton, 2015.

Schulweis. Harold. "Sleeping Through a Revolution," *The Forward,* October 11, 1999.

Skop, Yarden. "More Arab Students in Israel Attending University in New Academic Year." *Ha'aretz,* October 15, 2015.

Savir, Uri. *The Process: 1,100 Days that Changed the Middle East.* NY: Random House, 1998.

Shalev, Nir, and Alon Cohen-Lifshitz. *The Prohibited Zone: Israeli planning policy in the Palestinian villages in Area C.* Jerusalem: Bimkom - Planners for Planning Rights, 2009. Available at: http://bimkom.org/eng/wp-content/uploads/ProhibitedZone.pdf

Smock, David R., ed. *Interfaith Dialogue and Peacebuilding.* Washington, DC: United States Institute of Peace, 2002.

Smooha, Sammy. "Israel's Arab Citizens: Key Facts and Current Realities, the UK Task Force on Issues Relating to Arab citizens of Israel," for the University of Haifa's Annual Index of Jewish-Arab Relations, June 2013. Available at: http://soc.haifa.ac.il.

Spiritual Resources of the Religions for Peace. Exploring the Sacred Texts in Promotion of Peace, Vatican City, Pontifical Council for Interreligious Dialogue, 2003.

Thich Nhat Hanh. *Peace is Every Step. The Path of Mindfulness in Everyday Life.* New York: Bantam Books, 1991.

Weiss, Avraham. *Spiritual Activism: A Jewish Guide to Leadership and Repairing the World.* Woodstock, VT: Jewish Lights, 2008.

Zahalka, Iyad. *Shari'a in the Modern Era: Muslim Minorities Jurisprudence.* Cambridge: Cambridge University Press, 2016.

Index